PRACTICAL SOCIAL WORK

Series Editor: Jo Campling

BASW

Editorial Advisory Board:
Robert Adams, Terry Bamford, Charles Barker, Lena Dominelli,
Malcolm Payne, Michael Preston-Shoot, Daphne Statham and
Jane Tunstill

Social work is at an important stage in its development. All professions
must be responsive to changing social and economic conditions if they
are to meet the needs of those they serve. This series focuses on sound
practice and the specific contributions which social workers can make
to the well-being of our society.

The British Association of Social Workers has always been conscious of
its role in setting guidelines for practice and in seeking to raise
professional standards. The concept of the Practical Social Work series
arose from a survey of BASW members to discover where they, the
practitioners in social work, felt there was the most need for new
literature. The response was overwhelming and enthusiastic, and the
result is a carefully planned, coherent series of books. The emphasis is
firmly on practice set in a theoretical framework. The books will
inform, stimulate and promote discussion, thus adding to the further
development of skills and high professional standards. All the authors
are practitioners and teachers of social work, representing a wide
variety of experience.

JO CAMPLING
A list of published titles in this series follows overleaf

Practical Social Work
Series Standing Order ISBN 0–333–69347–7
(*outside North America only*)

You can receive future titles in this series as they are published by placing a standing
order. Please contact your bookseller or, in the case of difficulty, write to us at the address
below with your name and address, the title of the series and the ISBN quoted above.

Customer Services Department, Palgrave Ltd
Houndmills, Basingstoke, Hampshire RG21 6XS, England

PRACTICAL SOCIAL WORK

Robert Adams *Social Work and Empowerment*

Sarah Banks *Ethics and Values in Social Work (2nd edn)*

James G. Barber *Beyond Casework*

James G. Barber *Social Work with Addictions*

Peter Beresford and Suzy Croft *Citizen Involvement*

Suzy Braye and Michael Preston-Shoot *Practising Social Work Law (2nd edn)*

Helen Cosis Brown *Social Work and Sexuality*

Alan Butler and Colin Pritchard *Social Work and Mental Illness*

Crescy Cannan, Lynne Berry and Karen Lyons *Social Work and Europe*

Roger Clough *Residential Work*

David M. Cooper and David Ball *Social Work and Child Abuse*

Veronica Coulshed and Audrey Mullender *Management in Social Work (2nd edn)*

Veronica Coulshed and Joan Orme *Social Work Practice: An Introduction (3rd edn)*

Paul Daniel and John Wheeler *Social Work and Local Politics*

Peter R. Day *Sociology in Social Work Practice*

Lena Dominelli *Anti-Racist Social Work (2nd edn)*

Celia Doyle *Working with Abused Children (2nd edn)*

Angela Everitt and Pauline Hardiker *Evaluating for Good Practice*

Angela Everitt, Pauline Hardiker, Jane Littlewood and Audrey Mullender *Applied Research for Better Practice*

Kathy Ford and Alan Jones *Student Supervision*

David Francis and Paul Henderson *Working with Rural Communities*

Alison Froggatt *Family Work with Elderly People*

Danya Glaser and Stephen Frosh *Child Sexual Abuse (2nd edn)*

Gill Gorell Barnes *Working with Families*

Cordelia Grimwood and Ruth Popplestone *Women, Management and Care*

Jalna Hanmer and Daphne Statham *Women and Social Work (2nd edn)*

Tony Jeffs and Mark Smith (eds) *Youth Work*

Michael Kerfoot and Alan Butler *Problems of Childhood and Adolescence*

Joyce Lishman *Communication in Social Work*

Carol Lupton and Terry Gillespie (eds) *Working with Violence*

Mary Marshall and Mary Dixon *Social Work with Older People (3rd edn)*

Paula Nicolson and Rowan Bayne *Applied Psychology for Social Workers (2nd edn)*

Kieran O'Hagan *Crisis Intervention in Social Services*

Michael Oliver and Bob Sapey *Social Work with Disabled People (2nd edn)*

Joan Orme and Bryan Glastonbury *Care Management*

John Pitts *Working with Young Offenders (2nd edn)*

Michael Preston-Shoot *Effective Groupwork*

Peter Raynor, David Smith and Maurice Vanstone *Effective Probation Practice*

Steven Shardlow and Mark Doel *Practice Learning and Teaching*

Carole R. Smith *Social Work with the Dying and Bereaved*

David Smith *Criminology for Social Work*

Christine Stones *Focus on Families*

Neil Thompson *Anti-Discriminatory Practice (3rd edn)*

Neil Thompson, Michael Murphy and Steve Stradling *Dealing with Stress*

Derek Tilbury *Working with Mental Illness*

Alan Twelvetrees *Community Work (3rd edn)*

Hilary Walker and Bill Beaumount (eds) *Working with Offenders*

Management

Veronica Co...   **...der**

First edition 1990
Reprinted six times
Second edition 2001

Published by
PALGRAVE
Houndmills, Basingstoke, Hampshire RG21 6XS and
175 Fifth Avenue, New York, N. Y. 10010
Companies and representatives throughout the world

PALGRAVE is the new global academic imprint of
St. Martin's Press LLC Scholarly and Reference Division and
Palgrave Publishers Ltd (formerly Macmillan Press Ltd).

ISBN 0-333-72413-5

This book is printed on paper suitable for recycling and
made from fully managed and sustained forest sources.

A catalogue record for this book is available
from the British Library.

10   9   8   7   6   5   4
10   09   08   07   06   05   04   03

Printed in China

Contents

List of Figures

Acknowledgement

The authors and publishers acknowledge with thanks permission from the President and Fellows of Harvard College to reproduce Figure 4.2, from R. Tannenbaum and W. H. Schmidt, 'How to choose a leadership pattern', *Harvard Business Review* (May–June 1973). © 1973 by the President and Fellows of Harvard College. All rights reserved.

In memory of Veronica Coulshed

Introduction

Since it was first published in 1990, this book has made an immeasurable contribution to the understanding and practice of management in social work. I have approached the task of producing a revised, second edition with the same commitment to improving standards as I detected in Veronica Coulshed's original text, and sharing, too, her belief that good management plays a crucial role in that process.

Aims of the book

In writing this text, only shortly before her untimely death, Veronica Coulshed drew upon her whole career as a social worker, a team leader in a hospital and in social services, and a manager in social work education. This range of experiences had exposed her to the turmoil of cutbacks, uncertain futures and increasing demands. She was conscious of writing at a time when everyone in the human services – teaching, nursing and social work, for example – was being faced with the expectation that what they offered should become more efficient and effective. Living up to these requirements, she said, had underlined the need for everyone to manage and organise their work within adminstrative processes and managerial *diktats* which were sometimes made to feel more important than the people who operated them. Then, as now, social workers often tended to feel powerless at work. Some even scoffed at her notion that part of their role might be to learn how to question procedures, to shape policy or to improve services.

Veronica Coulshed was concerned by this alienation of staff. She wrote her book in the hope of lessening disillusionment with organisation and management, believing that to study these concepts would be to gain power through information. She further

1

considered that learning about the influence of the context in which practice takes place would help social workers analyse their own performance at work.

Her central idea here, developed in Chapter 1 of the book, was that all social workers are managers. Their circles of activity ripple outwards from managing themselves, at the core, to managing others, and onwards again to managing systems. This concentration on managing oneself and other people is underpinned by theories about the nature of organisations and how they are structured. Working from the premise that front line practitioners and managers can benefit from understanding these ideas, her book sought to translate a complex literature into workable, everyday knowledge. It also wrestled with making that literature more relevant to management in social work and to a human, as opposed to an abstract mechanistic context. The hope was that, rather than feeling propelled by their agencies, readers might then be equipped to help change them.

Veronica Coulshed was concerned, too, that typical career pathways led many social workers out of direct practice and 'in at the deep end' of supervising others or managing teams. She recognised that too many employers failed to offer appropriate preparation or training for this change of role and wanted, through her writing, to assist those who were moving into first line management positions by outlining the duties confronting them and exploring some of the skills and values which would help them become good managers. This second edition of her book again seeks to address those newly appointed and aspiring managers who wish to use their power responsibly and ethically, within a broader anti-oppressive agenda, for the promotion of social welfare and social justice.

Finally, but not least importantly among her aims, Veronica Coulshed hoped that the material she offered would be useful to students on qualifying programmes. The competence requirements for the Diploma in Social Work include the ability to understand and work within an organisation (Central Council for Education and Training in Social Work, 1989, 1996) and she wanted everyone engaged in social work teaching and learning, as much as in social work practice and management, to acquire a critical stance towards their own endeavours. The workbased learning approach of the Post Qualifying and Advanced Awards in Social Work shares these objectives (Central Council for Education and Training in Social Work, 1997).

In working on this second edition, and from my more than twenty years' experience of social work education, I, too, share this commitment to broadening educational concerns to encompass organisational issues, believing that social workers can empower others only if they feel as empowered as possible themselves within their employing agencies.

The managerial context of social work

Despite (or perhaps as a result of) living in an age of 'admin' and managerialism, social workers tend to hold negative attitudes towards the administrative and managerial aspects of their organisations and of their own workloads. Yet the time-consuming requirement to record assessments and care plans on computer, to attend meetings, to balance budgets and so on, brings administration into the heart of social work. The possibility has long gone of fieldworkers immersing themselves in their own self-contained activities and leaving adminstration to 'them' at County Hall, the Town Hall or at headquarters (if they happen to work for a voluntary organisation). In truth, the administrative process seems almost to have become an end in itself. The amount of office paperwork has grown until it gives the impression of being the top priority.

Although this puts social workers in closer touch with what might be the creative potential of informing and even influencing the translation of management information into policy development, it is actually being experienced as work that is routinised, rule-bound and controlled by management. At one time it was possible for social workers, as 'street-level bureaucrats' (Lipsky, 1980) to function with a fair degree of discretion. Ironically, as the responsibilities of social workers have mushroomed, their autonomy has correspondingly shrunk. Those who frame the policies designed to ration inadequate resources in the face of growing demand are anxious to avoid legal challenge or official wrist-slapping by maintaining a firm hold on all levels of decision-making.

A central problem with this faith in managerial competence, backed by administrative good order and rationality, is that it is incapable of sorting out the untidiness of human difficulties or the uncertainties of direct practice in social work or social care. Neither management courses nor the mainstream management literature make adequate allowance for this. They tend to imply that the activities being managed are straightforward (deriving from the handling of inanimate objects and processes in manufacturing industry) and that organisations and the people in them operate like Mr Spock in the early *Star Trek* series: all reason and no emotion. Unluckily for those who try to operate by these rules, social work organisations exist to serve messy, untidy, infinitely varied human beings and, indeed, all organisations are (at least up to now) staffed by them. Even were this not the case, so much is expected of managers today that it would probably be impossible to live up to the promises held out to the public by the issuing of neat lists of eligibility thresholds, service priorities or performance indicators, let alone the prescriptions of some of the early thinkers on management technique.

The 1980s saw an emphasis on the need for everyone in what America baptised the 'human service industry' to be efficient, effective and economical (the 'three Es'). No one would want to dispute the requirement to provide 'Best Value' when dispersing restricted public funds to a public with rising expectations but, when market values and business criteria entered social work, some agencies did appear to be trading high standards of caring and safety for cost-effectiveness. Nor was this only an in-house phenomenon in the statutory sector. Services were increasingly contracted out to private sector, that is profit-making, ventures, while the voluntary sector employed marketing consultants both to compete and to raise funds from other sources. These moves towards a business ethos may well have deepened the already growing rift between social work professionals and their managers, with the two cultures now apparently pursuing different ends.

Though economic considerations are now unavoidable, they are not absolute. The notion of 'virtuous management' may sound like a contradiction in terms but it means that a discontinuity of values on becoming a manager, whether in the statutory, voluntary or private sector, is not preordained. For example, it is not essential to abandon an interest in service users on assuming supervisory control. One of this book's fundamental aims is to explore the possibilities for hanging on to social work values on entering the management arena; that is, for combining the 'three Es' with compassion, integrity, and determination to uphold the humane purposes of social welfare organisations.

This may all sound somewhat obvious to those managers who are naturally good at steering a course through conflicting philosophies. But a reading of management literature will quickly illustrate that, until recently, some rather devious and even brutal qualities of leadership have been not only admired but recommended. This book will re-examine such thinking from the perspective of those who reject the image of the ruthless, single-minded manager who is wily about office politics and who can get the better of subordinates, competitors and superiors alike – the manager who thinks that all problems can be solved by the mechanical use of rational–technical tools such as flow charts, procedural manuals and decision-making models.

It is a pleasure to report that management theory has itself been moving away from such games*man* ship towards what is known as the 'feminisation' of management styles. Both male and female managers are being encouraged to value networking and co-operative decision-making over lone, competitive point-scoring because the organisation stands to gain most when all its best minds are on board and when all are free to contribute their own ideas, however greatly these diverge from the traditional 'norm'.

Veronica Coulshed was characteristically ahead of her time in writing about women colleagues in social work trying to persuade their managers to see that concern for people at work and honest relationships were signs of strength, not weakness. She appreciated the full irony of business and industry catching onto these ideas – the traditional territory of social work practice, one might have thought – just at the time when social work managers were belatedly adopting the traditional 'masculine' approaches of leading from the centre in leaner and fitter organisations that devalue and discard those who fail to toe the line or those squeezed out by re-organisation and 'downsizing'. While financial corporations were valuing the contribution of women by starting to provide crèche facilities and flexible working arrangements, while design firms were sharing power in 'flat' hierarchies where everyone sat round one large table and pooled creative ideas, while industry was introducing 'quality circles' where workers at all levels shared the input into management ideas, and while businesses of all kinds advertised for leaders with good communication and interpersonal skills, an open style and accessible manner, social work management was abandoning the profession's roots in just these individual and group-based skills. Company directors were being urged to 'become obsessed with listening', to 'defer to the front line', and to 'practise visible management' (Peters, 1988) at a time when social service and probation managers were centralising control away from area or district teams and imposing ever more rigid ordering and controlling on the work of staff they rarely met.

It is not difficult to understand why this might be. Social work operates under the pressure of legislation, political control, policy imperatives, media attention, and numerous other influences beyond the strictly professional. New Labour, for example, is responding to revelations of sexual abuse in residential settings and to poor management in some authorities with aggressive talk of regulating and controlling social work activity, training and entry to the profession beyond anything we have yet seen. At the same time, the world of social work contains ambiguities and contradictions, even about its purposes and goals, which is leading to a political search for 'core functions' and for unequivocal statements about the need to base practice on clear evidence of 'what works'.

This may not be the ideal moment to return to Veronica Coulshed's advice that the existence of so few 'certainties' on becoming a manager might mean that the occupation of social work would be best served by admitting to service users and the wider public that it does not have all the answers and that there are limitations to its resources, human and otherwise. But some teams have found it helpful, for example, to explain to local communities why services are restricted and why understaffing means that they cannot do all they would wish. Whatever management technologies may have to offer – and they are certainly an improvement on autocratic whim – there remains a need to stress to all social work's stakeholders that many aspects of the work rest on uncertainty and unpredictability, and that, despite published procedures, risk assessments, computerisation and workload review systems, some mistakes will continue be made. There may be firm high ground where we can make ready use of management theory and skills, but those familiar with Schön's (1983) ideas on 'reflective practice' will recognise the 'swampy lowlands' of human distress where professional decision-making is far more complex than the current obsession with occupational standards and competences would suggest (Ixer, 1999). This book will aim to face up to daily life as it really is for social workers and to look at management theory from their vantage point, in the belief that it does contain much material that is quite – and some that is very – useful to the busy practitioner or team leader.

A note on terminology and language

A note about terms which might be confusing or misunderstood may be helpful at this point.

First, whilst being fully aware of subtle differences between them, Veronica Coulshed elected to use the terms 'manager', 'administrator' and 'leader' interchangeably in order to avoid repetition. She also did so to emphasise her view that all social workers are managers, in the sense that 'management' can be defined as the process of organising resources to get work done. At the same time, she recognised that the management of people is a far more varied business than dealing with policies on paper and she pointed to Warham's (1975) analysis of administration as a generic process in which direction, management and supervision are key elements. In this formulation, if 'administration' refers to the overall process, then the component elements correspond to three general levels in the hierarchy: at the top, the directing function involves long-term planning and objectives; in the middle, the management function sustains the system as a going concern; while, at the bottom, the supervisory function at the team leader level oversees the use of the resources and policy instructions provided by management to ensure that work performance is up to standard. In a small private or voluntary agency, the directing, managing and supervising functions may be vested in one person, but more usually they are divided up.

Next, the term 'bureaucracy' is used here as a neutral concept which denotes a particular facet of organisational structure, not in the disparaging usage common in social work. As will be shown in Chapter 2, the concept did not have any pejorative connotation originally, but can be used as a yardstick of formality and impersonality in any organisation. Similarly, 'professionalism' is used in the positive sense of implying proficiency, an appropriate maintenance of personal and professional boundaries, and a commitment to high standards; while 'professionalisation' signifies only a process of developing towards an 'ideal' type of model for the organisation of a particular form of work (with registration with a General Social Care Council perhaps marking another step along the way), and does not carry any connotation of being preoccupied with power or status.

Although the profession has seen a fragmentation into new agency configurations, such as those of purchasers and providers, and new roles, such as that of the care manager – as well as the regrettable loss of probation from social work education – I shall continue to use the term 'social work' as a generic one. It remains the designation that is globally understood to encompass both the profession and the academic discipline with which we are here concerned and I, for one, retain my pride in it as encompassing a shared concern for social welfare, social justice and social action.

I have the usual annoying English habit of writing about 'social services' and 'local authorities' as if these terms covered the organisation of social work and social care in the statutory sector throughout the UK. I am well aware that Scotland has social work services and that Northern Ireland's equivalent provision is run by Trusts, but I confess I find it difficult to maintain a flow while also naming all these alternatives. I must beg colleagues in the other countries of the UK to forgive me.

Other aspects of language may have changed since this book first appeared. The talk in many settings now is of 'service users' or 'customers' rather than of 'clients', for example, and new coinages appear all the time, such as 'benchmarking' and 'hot desking'. Throughout the text, I have attempted to use expressions which are currently the most widely used or recognisable, rather than necessarily closest to Veronica Coulshed's original.

Producing this edition

In one other, critically important way, revising this book has not presented any problem of language whatsoever. When I first met Veronica Coulshed, we felt as if we already knew each other from reading each other's work. We felt an affinity, particularly, in the fact that each of us had seen in the other's work an effort always to write in plain English, no matter how complicated the idea being discussed. We felt this was something we had in common and that it was likely to mean we would get on. We were right, though sadly we had little time to get to know one another.

This commitment in all that Veronica wrote to communicate clearly – her drive to reach the widest possible audience with the fewest possible obstacles – has made it a positive pleasure to work on this text. There has never been the slightest doubt what Veronica was driving at or what personal and professional commitment lay behind her commentary on the issue in question. Veronica was a natural communicator and teacher, someone about whom generations of students continue to say that she helps them understand things they have really struggled with until coming across her work. Veronica's ability to summarise without oversimplifying, her choice of only the most useful references, and her knack with helpful illustrations, all add to the 'readability' of her book and have all been retained in essence in this edition. That is not to say that the revised text stays especially close to the original. So much has moved on, and so quickly, that it has felt truer to what Veronica herself would have done to grasp the nettle of major change in the hope of ensuring that no reader's interest or understanding is lost along the way. As a result, though both our names appear on the spine, I must accept the lion's share of blame for any infelicities or inaccuracies in this revised edition.

That said, I want to pay tribute to Veronica for being so far ahead of her time in spotting many of the 'coming' trends. The purchaser–provider split, the introduction of a new mangerialist ethos throughout social work, and the countervailing trend elsewhere towards a broadening of what counts as good management were all, for example, firmly located in her text a decade ago and they remain equally important now. But no one, not even she, could have foreseen the pace of change in social work throughout the 1990s.

Structure of the book

The book begins by proposing in Chapter 1 that we are all managers and emphasising, therefore, why it is useful for social work staff at whatever level to study management ideas. Chapter 2 sketches in the background of thinking about organisational structures and theories about management and people at work. The rise in the requirement to demonstrate that users are receiving the best possible services is reflected in a new focus for Chapter 3 around models of quality standards and the management of change, with a role envisaged for all staff in helping to move things forward. In Chapter 4, the focus shifts to the designated leaders of social work organisations and to their key contribution in terms of managerial vision and strategic planning. Chapters 5 and 6 consider the human resource side of management; that is, the recognition that a welfare organisation's biggest investment is in its staff. This means that it cannot hope to operate effectively unless it puts in place good policies and practices on all staffing matters, starting from recruitment and selection and progressing through integrated systems for staff appraisal, staff development and staff care. Since there can be no quality without equality, diversity is the focus of Chapter 7.

Having laid out all the responsibilities that managers carry in today's social work agencies, we turn finally, in Chapter 8, to examine what scope there may be for individual managers to find their own styles and to empower others to give of their best, as opposed to abusing the power inherent in organisational leadership under the guise of 'running a tight ship'. Management (though not managerialism) could, it is argued, actually liberate social work to pursue not only its early values of respect for persons, but also new principles of equality, social justice, and the highest achievable standards of service for hitherto marginalised and devalued groups within society.

AUDREY MULLENDER

1

Why Study Management?

This chapter outlines why it is useful for social workers at every level to know something of the discipline called 'management'. It asserts that all social workers are managers of a kind and debates whether, to look at this the other way round, all managers in social work organisations should have a background in social work practice. Regardless of one's views on this question, it does have to be accepted that today's managers employ not only many skills which are transferable from practice but also others peculiar to the management world, in scope if not always in detail.

The relevance of management theory to social work

As social work organisations move through an era of fragmentation, discontinuity, contracting out and delayering, each staff member is finding a need to understand how organisational systems work. This is essential both to survival and to finding one's own place in the scheme of things. It also makes sense amongst ever increasing managerial demands for detailed information and budgetary accountability. Every social worker is having to learn to think on a much broader canvas than has ever been the case before. This involves looking outwards to service users and resource providers – as well as to politicians who increasingly expect to set the agenda – looking back over work that needs to be monitored and reviewed, and forwards in order to plan and to set aims and objectives. This breadth of vision is something that managers have always needed and the management literature has useful things to say on the subject.

Thinking like a manager also enables social workers to bring a critical eye to bear on their own organisations, the services they provide and the standards they set. When people are busy, they

sometimes forget to stand back and reflect on how they are perceived, especially by users. Developing a dispassionate approach to
what is going on is beneficial; a detached concern helps to maintain a questioning, analytical stance regarding how services are
delivered and received. Each time we approach the reception desk
of an area office, or visit a group care establishment, it is salutary
to ponder on how we would feel if we were a service user or a resident there. There is nothing sadder than to visit an elderly relative
or a former neighbour in a home and to find that, despite good standards of physical care, their individuality is being eroded because
a major goal of the enterprise appears to be one of profit and the
staff are not encouraged to question what they are aiming for or
what the organisation's objectives are.

Through studying management, too, we can try to prevent ourselves becoming mere instruments of managerialism or its scape-
goat if something goes wrong. Some employers, for instance, have
not been beyond disowning the judgements of their staff, even
when their own position in the hierarchy made them ultimately
responsible for training and supporting those individuals. The relevance of management studies to social work might lie in helping
us to see when it is the system, not ourselves, which is at fault and
when standards are not good enough and need changing.

Why all social workers are managers

The suggestion that all social workers are managers is probably, at
first glance, not a welcome one. Similarly, those who are about to
become managers may be facing the transition with mixed feelings
– while keen to learn the techniques and gain the rewards of the
competent leader, they may also fear losing touch with direct practice and perhaps becoming deskilled. The stereotype of a manager
is of a person (disproportionately likely to be male) who has
sacrificed social work values to the importance of filling in forms
or gathering data on computer and who gives priority to what his
manager in turn expects rather than to what users and practitioners demand. Yet, in fact, many practitioner skills in social work
are also managerial ones, and all social workers increasingly work
to managerialist agendas, so the difference may be one of degree
rather than of kind. It has been exaggerated by practitioners not

knowing what their managers really do and by a failure on both sides to appreciate that working to change an organisation is not so very far removed from working for any of the other kinds of planned change that are the mainstay of social work itself.

The most obvious overlap concerns the management of people. Whether these be service users, carers, the general public or those who regulate service provision, management, just like practice, involves the ability to write and speak clearly, and to engage in purposeful interpersonal relationships. So perhaps social workers who become managers have a head start here? On the other hand, believing that they 'should' have a flair for 'people skills' could embarrass those who are newly promoted, impeding spontaneity and making them self-conscious for a time. It may help them to remember that managing people is at the heart both of providing services to users, families and wider communities through social work methods, and of organising and working towards the effective delivery of those services by others.

The principles and skills involved in managing personnel are common to all organisations – private, public and voluntary. The objectives may be different from one agency to another, and at each level within a department, but the means used in attempting to reach them remain constant. Engaging with and relating to people, helping others to achieve their goals, supervising their efforts, maintaining morale, consulting a wide range of sources prior to making decisions, problem solving, and introducing and managing the crisis of change are just some of the tasks common to the practitioner and the manager.

There are also transferable skills from particular methods and modes of social work intervention. The systemic thinking which underlies the techniques of family therapy, for example, is just as relevant when trying to sort out the patterns of relationships which exist in larger systems such as organisations as it is in families. Equally, when leading a team, many of the ideas gleaned from groupwork also stand one in good stead. Just as Allan Brown (1992) proposes that those who have experienced mutually trusting, collaborative and creative teams make good groupworkers, so those with experience of groupwork are likely to contribute to positive team spirit and to constructive co-working as facilitative team members or team leaders. Knowledge of group cohesion, openness, risk-taking and interdependence in groups can be transferred directly to the role of team manager, though the context and aims naturally differ from those experienced in groupwork intervention.

A further good preparation for management is the role of the care manager. Undertaking assessments and co-ordinating packages of care within tight budgets has become the *sine qua non* of many front line practitioners. Valuable skills developed include those of bargaining, mediating, negotiating, liaising and advocacy in order to make the best use of resources. And one could certainly argue that social workers who have become more financially aware, even without holding the purse strings of a fully devolved budget, will make better managers later on. There will be less of a divide to cross than in the days before unit costs of service were known (that is, before the purchaser–provider split), when social workers were largely unaware of the direct impact of resource restraints and when decisions to refuse services were taken much higher up the hierarchy than may be the case now.

For those social workers who are budget holders, there may be some worrying issues to be resolved. For instance, there may be inherent contradictions in orchestrating community care packages within resource limitations while also acting as an advocate for better client services overall, or in balancing a user's needs while also shopping around for the least costly forms of care. While we may not argue with the need to keep the taxpayer in mind, there is the problem that, when professionals are given too much economic responsibility, especially for budgeting, they become distracted from their fundamental aims. As Priestley (1998) demonstrates in respect of care assessments of disabled people, these frequently appear to be budget-led rather than truly needs-led, and the discourse of 'need' is in any case contentious since it covers only personal and domestic tasks, not assistance in having a social life, for example. It remains to be seen whether direct payment schemes will give service users more access to real choice and whether social workers will learn from disabled people that they do not have a monopoly on defining need.

Though these narrowly financial concerns may be recent, the management of resources has, in fact, always dominated the social worker's tasks if we count within this the management of time and of the self. Front line workers devote many hours to travelling, attending meetings, negotiating, doing 'admin' and referring on. It is startling how many social workers and their managers are unable to ration themselves across a working day or week or to delegate effectively. While the theme of the 1980s was to assume that managers should be available at all times and respect was reserved for the 'workaholics' (the 'lunch is for wimps' ethos), the managers of the future (and ideally all workers) should be noted for their capacity to reflect on what they are doing and to draw boundaries around the energies available for their career and those available for personal and family commitments. (Lunch is back in fashion, as is building exercise and 'quality time' into the day.) Self-management of this nature is one way of preventing stress-related illness.

As well as managing resources, social workers and social care staff at all levels participate in meeting required standards. In child care policy and practice, for example, the 'Quality Protects' programme (Department of Health, 1998b) sets very specific objectives for social services departments to meet. Individual social workers are told very clearly what information they need to gather about looked after children, in the shape of the Assessment and Action Records, and in national codes and guidelines for both foster care and the residential care of children. Standards for adult services, too, are enforced by independent scrutiny. The move of inspection services from the local authority to regional commissions for care standards (Department of Health, 1998a) and the registration of qualified and residential child care staff by the General Social Care Council are key aspects of the Government's 'modernising' agenda which, at the same time as centralising control, arguably gives every worker a stake in understanding and meeting performance targets.

Standards and procedures are equally a part of a new ethos in the voluntary and private sectors. Most voluntary organisations have to comply with Charity Commission requirements, and all independent providers operate within a contract culture which means that staff have to be constantly aware of quality standards and required managerial practices. Nor do freelancers escape from procedures, guidelines and form-filling. Trainers, consultants, mentors, guardians *ad litem* and other self-employed people who use their social work qualifications and experience to work from home are increasingly expected to operate their own quality controls to nationally recognised standards and the contracts they obtain for their services typically require this to be the case.

A final reason why we would argue that all social workers are managers is that each person in a department can be an instigator or a contributor to change and innovation. These do not always have to come from outside; changing the agency from within occurs quite frequently and one need not be in a position of power to influence agency practice. If we view organisations as psycho–socio–political systems and study people's behaviour within them, we are then in a good position to change our working practices, especially if, in their current form, they are adding to the burdens of users, carers and others. Undertaking projects for Post Qualifying and Advanced Award programmes in social work, or for an MBA (Master in Business Administration) is one opportunity that increasing numbers of people have, for example, for standing back and thinking about a focused area of work where they can be particularly influential.

What is special about managers?

It may be that some readers will disagree with the assertion that social workers are practitioner–managers. It could fairly be pointed out that being a manager consists of more than undertaking managerially dictated duties; there are specific tasks involved, not least enabling others to get work done and carrying forward the overall aims of the organisation. So let us consider a few of the distinct functions of the manager.

First, while managers and social workers both control resources and exercise authority, the extent to which they do so differs. Second, the social worker is a specialist in delivering the services from her/his particular domain, whereas a manager's tasks relate to the organisation as a whole or at least one section of it. Thus, those who control group care services would take into account additional factors when deciding to allocate a place in an establishment to an older person, including the overall policy of the agency and the total number of people competing for the resource. Managers have to make decisions and be concerned for clients whom they have never met. Third, though practitioners keep an eye to the future when planning their work on a particular case, top managers have a macro-interest in the future of the whole organisation, ensuring that it will remain a going concern to meet future needs while also dealing with ever-changing current circumstances. Fourth, social work and management processes share a concern for problem-solving and enabling, but the degree of authority in organising people to get work done is greater for line managers. In addition, styles of leadership and the performance of managerial tasks, such as the exercise of authority through decision-making, have an effect on other people's performance, not simply one's own; thus, the size of a worker's caseload, the allocation of work and the supervision of it are usually part of the duties of team leaders and senior members of staff. The selection and orientation of new staff, finally, although involving the team, is normally a specific task for people in management positions.

Before we move on to explore another side of this coin, by questioning if all managers should be social workers, let us recap the position so far:

1. Managerial administration is the process of *organising resources to get work done* and, at this level of generality, all social workers are involved in it.
2. Although certain roles carry the title of manager, team leader or senior, in every organisation each person is part of the administrative structure and is thus administratively, as well as professionally, *accountable for the work they do.*
3. At the same time, managers who have this title have specific functions which are *essential ingredients of their role as administrators*; some of these are different in degree rather than kind from that of social workers, but others are related to the authority which is exercised.

Should all managers be social workers?

Is it necessary for those who develop and maintain social welfare organisations to be qualified in social work? When the social services departments were first created, it was thought that those heading them should, if possible, be qualified in social work and, ideally, be experienced and/or trained in administration (Seebohm Report, 1968). At that time, many top managers graduated through the practitioner ranks and only a few were from other professions, such as medicine and law. More recently, not only have social work-qualified managers started to disappear but the social services as a separate entity have too. In a growing number of authorities, there is no longer a single dedicated social services department. Rather, two or more services are merged, such as housing and social services, or all council services are provided through a corporate approach. This is in line with governmental policy on 'joined up thinking' since it makes it easier to remember that a young person who needs to be looked after by the local authority, for example, also needs to be well taught, protected or controlled by community safety policies, and so on. Under corporate governance, non-social work services such as personnel and IT (information technology) may be provided by other business units within the authority, as opposed to having specialist staff employed in social services. This makes savings in staffing, cuts down on the tiers of management and improves communication between what were formerly separate 'empires'.

In the voluntary sector, there are equally major changes. Charitable organisations have had to become more businesslike, more competitive in an age of contracting out, are held to account for their performance, and are reliant on marketing their image and their work in order to sustain an income; their managers face new challenges accordingly (Jackson and Donovan, 1999). Of course, there is enormous diversity among voluntary bodies in the UK and only a fraction have a social work identity or even employ qualified social workers. The question of who their 'managers' should be is therefore complex.

All these developments radically change contemporary thinking about what is needed in a manager. When even well established charities are having to look for figureheads who are good at 'fronting' their organisations, the idea of being professionally qualified in social work may seem almost irrelevant. And the emphasis on commercial 'success' may dictate a different set of priorities from those traditionally held by organisations which see themselves as preventing human distress and working in partnership with users – for whom there may be little public sympathy or support.

Moreover, just as good teachers or good nurses do not necessarily make good managers, experienced social workers may not make an automatic transition, either. The specific tasks of management administration which were outlined above, and the broader perspective which is required of social work leaders, are not part of everyone's equipment. If we look back to the Introduction, it was suggested that administration combines the three elements of *directing* (long-term planning), *management* (sustaining the system as a going concern) and *supervision*. If, as was said there, these correspond with three general levels in the hierarchy, then we might be able to answer the question by proposing that, in large organisations, the two top tiers primarily call for sound management (and are precisely the levels at which staff are increasingly studying for MBAs), while the supervisory roles are best carried by those who have competence in the professional activity they are supervising. Interesting backing for this view comes from a study which shows that third tier social service managers mainly do have professionally qualifications, but that their thinking may well turn to obtaining management training once they begin to move up the career ladder (Lawler and Hearn, 1997); they begin to identify as managers rather than as social workers. Nevertheless, it is only in the most senior roles that professional managers are starting to be seen – that is, those who have trained in generic management skills and who have chosen to use them in the public sector, as opposed to those who have risen through the ranks to a top-level management post.

A personal view would be that people with social work qualifications and backgrounds have a great deal to offer at all levels and that it would be a shame if more did not aim for the top, including women, black staff and others who have been traditionally under-represented at that level. Adding management training and skills on the way up can only help.

Whatever the position held in a social work organisation, there are certain commitments which all managers have to make and particular dilemmas to address, as listed below:

1. Despite the breadth of issues tackled in the personal social services, this is nevertheless a highly *specialised field*.
2. Social workers have their own *skills, knowledge and values*. As professionals, their expertise in planning and decision-making within their own field has to be acknowledged and mirrored in the way the agency involves them in administrative processes.
3. Any plans for developing services or for rethinking the agency's mission (that is, its purpose) need to reflect the *equal*

opportunities goals which have become part of social work's traditions; a commitment to anti-oppressive practice would be among these.

4. If the manager comes from a different occupational background, credibility might more readily be established by showing a genuine willingness to learn about social work's *current professional concerns and practices*.

5. The importance of *relationships* will be highlighted: between service users and workers; among team members; with other disciplines; and also with numerous local, regional and national bodies.

6. What distinguishes human service management from that in non-service sectors is the fact that many agencies are dependent upon other organisations; planning has to take into account the *restraints* imposed by legislation and policy imposed from outside, as well as those inherent in relying on others to purchase or provide services.

7. Management approaches in social work cannot always be the *rational and tidy* ones suggested in the management literature. Service goals may contradict one another (for example, caring versus controlling anti-social behaviour) and there are additional demands in making services holistic and appropriate rather than fragmented or impersonal, as well as in matching them wherever possible to the felt needs of a particular community (for instance, in providing home care services which are acceptable to people of varying ethnic backgrounds).

8. Human services operate in very *turbulent environments*, frequently subject to political whims and media-led changes; long-term plans have therefore to be flexible.

9. While coping with all this uncertainty, the manager of a service organisation also has to recognise that staff work from imperfect theories and conflicting ideologies about the 'causes' of human behaviour, that they are called upon to tackle unpredictable and unknowable events, and that they increasingly focus largely on the 'heavy end' of human distress and need, as in child protection and mental health services. This makes *staff care and staff development* particularly important in social work, but also means that any requests from management are likely to be experienced as yet one

more demand from those who are not actually involved in doing the front line job.

10. Perhaps most importantly, the commitment of social work managers must not be to the organisation as an end in itself or to their own personal ambitions, as can be the case in business. The *raison d'être* of social work is its *service users and the general public more widely*; consequently, the focus has to be on high quality services and on the work of the professionals who implement them.

The challenge to management outlined in this book is for the harnessing of management theories and styles in social work which are best suited to the developments of a new millennium. The time is overdue to flush out those managerial approaches which may have sounded impressive or 'macho' in their day but which have proven unable to balance the requirements of a principled and intelligent workforce, a vulnerable but potentially self-determining body of users and their carers, and a general public which, while committed to the maintence of high quality welfare services, also cares about community safety, good stewardship of public (or charitable) money and the public mandating of trends in social policy. If this makes management sound as if it is all about listening to, and working with, an infinite variety of people while undertaking a taxing job, then social workers ought to be extremely good at it! And, of course, many of them are.

2

Management Theory and Organisational Structures

In this chapter, we shall examine some of the best known approaches to the science or art of management, to the structure of organisations, and to the thinking that both shapes people's behaviour and is shaped by it. Starting from the classical theories of management, we will look at: scientific managerialism, which tends to treat employees like cogs in a machine; the human relations school of management theory which added the people into the equation, and at the study of organisational structures, particularly bureaucratic hierarchies and organisations as systems, because these models will be most familiar to social workers. (Later chapters will consider the culture of excellence with its emphasis on quality and others of the current trends, including reward management).

Within each approach will be explored the key contributions of some of the main pioneers associated with that school of thought. This is, after all, the world of management gurus and top business executives who sometimes become better known than the ideas they promote or the products they sell. A key source for the whole chapter will be Clutterbuck and Crainer (1990), who provide a fascinating account of the lives of these formative thinkers and doers (though their book is not geared towards the public sector).

The social workers of today will recognise throughout this chapter the competing trend towards maximising efficiency, on the one hand, and, on the other, recognising the contribution of people – the human resource – to the organisations in which they work. They will also find a number of ideas and terms they recognise but the origins of which may be less familiar.

It may seem odd in a book which focuses on management in social work to look at ideas which were developed chiefly in the worlds of manufacturing and commerce. Nevertheless, just like workers on the factory floor or shop assistants, social workers are part of complex organisations – which can help or hinder them in delivering the service they believe people need and deserve. And, equally, the individual practitioner, or the area or district team, can be perceived by management as a help or a hindrance to achieving organisational goals. People's experiences of being in social work will be influenced, then, not only by their own efforts and abilities, but also by many other factors. These include: the shape of the organisation; the way the job is organised within it (including the degree of devolved control over decision-making and resource allocation); and the whole culture of the workplace. Increasingly, the demands on social work agencies are intensifying, not only to improve their own internal functioning but also to turn outwards to work in partnership with other agencies and to be responsive to the expectations of the general public and of particular user groups. No agency can just muddle through on acquired wisdom or good intentions. This is why social work managers increasingly gain MBA qualifications and why social workers themselves need to have some understanding of how their agencies work at the organisational level. This chapter may provide a useful starting point.

Classical/traditional models

The study of management

PRINCIPLES OF MANAGEMENT: HENRI FAYOL

Organisations do not manage themselves. If policy is to be uniformly followed and resources fairly allocated, communication and co-ordination have to be deliberately facilitated. The first rational approach to organising an enterprise was taken by Fayol, a French mining engineer who rose to become the managing director of the company that employed him. It was Fayol who *defined* management, in writings up to 1916, both in terms of its elements (what managers do) and its principles (how they can do it most effectively).

The means Fayol used to pull his company round from the brink of collapse are still familiar to us today in the form of: annual and

10-year business plans; organisational charts in which every post has its definite place; recruitment and training to ensure that the right person holds each post; top-down command and direction of the organisation; control of the whole enterprise on the basis of clear and rapidly prepared accounting data (which we would now broaden to 'management information'); and meetings of divisional and of departmental heads, presided over by one manager who co-ordinates all their work. Fayol is probably best remembered for his 14 principles of management, among the most important of which for our purposes are the following items:

1. *Those at the top are responsible for identifying key objectives.* (We shall return to this, Fayol's 'unity of direction', under the fashionable label of 'mission statement', in Chapter 4.)
2. *Specialisation is achieved by dividing groups to undertake similar functions.* (In social work, this can be by user group, problem type, method of working, setting or context, population group, practice role, specific tasks, or stage in the allocation and progress of the work.)
3. *Each worker should report to only one senior.* (This, again, is a principle still followed today, although there can be complications with it, as we shall see below.)
4. *Each person should have a job description.* (Ever more important – see Chapter 5.)
5. *The ideal 'span of control'* – that is, the number of people doing similar work supervised by one person – *should be six to eight.* (Senior social workers may end up supervising more than this, especially when covering vacant posts.)

CRITIQUE AND LEGACY OF FAYOL'S IDEAS

Critiques of Fayol's work (see, for example, Drucker, 1977) point out that he based much of his theory, his 'functional principle', on a relatively small-scale company, employing one kind of worker to do one kind of job, with a single product (coal) which needed very little done to it before it could be sold, and serving only a few markets in which it had a virtual monopoly. He rested too much upon this one example. His design principle is not well adapted to complexity, size, innovation or externally imposed change – all of which feature heavily in social work. He also assumed top-down management – forecasting and planning being, in Fayol's view, the main task of the organisational head – rather than the participation, partnership and teamwork of which there is so much talk today – or the answerability to outside interests, like the government and the local community, that pertain in social work.

The key limitation in Fayol's thinking lay in trying to pre-scribe one set of principles to cover all eventualities. Yet, for some time, others continued in this line. Luther Gulick, for example, believed that any organisation could be as efficient as a piece of machinery if sound management practices were introduced, with both work and power divided according to an overall plan. As a result of analysing the executive tasks carried out by the US government in the 1930s, he coined the acronym PODSCORB, or: Planning, Organising, Directing, Staffing, Co-ordinating, Reporting, Budgeting. These functional elements of administration certainly have to be covered by any management structure, and Gulick's work still has influence, but it fell at the end of the period when management thinkers tried to devise simple, generalisable recipes for success.

Eventually, empirical research led by Joan Woodward in the 1950s revealed that there are, in fact, no optimum structural char-acteristics (such as number of levels of hierarchy or ideal span of control) or principles of administration that apply to all organisa-tions. What affects success is the fit between structure, task, tech-nology, management, employees and environment. These therefore came to be studied in a more holistic way in later work (see 'human relations' and 'systems' approaches, below).

Managerialism

'SCIENTIFIC MANAGEMENT': FREDERICK W. TAYLOR

Taylor (who lived from 1856 to 1917) was the originator of the movement known as 'scientific management' and gave his name to 'Taylorism': 'perhaps the first true management movement' (Clutterbuck and Crainer, 1990, p.24). Just as Fayol tried to make management rational, Taylor tried to make specific tasks rational, drawing on his lifelong interests in engineering and inventing. He set about systematically studying work, breaking each physical task down into its component movements to discover the most efficient way of performing each job – and then considered how management techniques could control the workers to work consistently at maximum efficiency.

Everyone is familiar with his methods – the stop-watch, the 'time and motion' study – and with their outcomes in the form of piece-rate working and incentive schemes. He looked at people as if they were machines, except that humans make errors and, in his view, work only to earn money. Taylor's interest in management lay in not allowing people to make machines less efficient than they ultimately could be.

The worst excesses of this approach may have been tempered in the UK by the trade union movement, and more recently by a better understanding of what makes people tick (see next section), but its legacy lives on. Whenever we hear talk of output measures, functional analysis of occupations, performance indicators, maximum specialisation, and so on, we are in the world of Taylorism and of scientific managerialism. Care managers may also be interested to hear that, as a management consultant, Taylor introduced systematic purchasing and supply procedures, while his rigorous inspections of quality (with even the quality inspectors being audited) also has a familiar ring.

CRITIQUE AND LEGACY OF TAYLORISM

On the plus side, Taylor wanted to take the unnecessary toil out of work and believed that increased productivity would lead to a living wage. But he studied the bottom end of the hierarchy without being 'bottom-up' in his attitudes towards management control, putting the onus on the workers to make an organisation profitable without according them any status beyond the mechanistic. His methods gave no scope to imagination or innovation. Workers were treated as less than human and would not have been seen as able to innovate or change their own working patterns for the better. Nevertheless, Taylor is remembered as the first person to study work as a subject in its own right.

HENRY FORD (1863–1947)

Some of the early, top-down managers certainly got things done. Ford, for example, was a genius at marketing. He paid his workers twice the going rate in order to turn them into a market for his own cars, and introduced mass production methods to keep up with the sales of an affordable, reliable and practical product that everybody wanted. Other modern touches we can recognise included special offers (a $20 refund promised, and delivered, to every purchaser in the country if sales hit a certain target) and international marketing efforts. By 1920, the Ford Motor Company was producing a car a minute and was the largest and most profitable manufacturing enterprise in the world. Ford never trusted managers, hung onto control himself and sacked anyone else who tried to make decisions; he saw no reason why one department in his business empire should know what another was doing and eventually lost a great deal of money. There are no real parallels in social work, although a few directors of social services have been good at marketing either their departments or themselves.

Of more relevance to us is the recognition that, now we are postmodern, we are also post-Fordist. The assembly line in industry has been replaced by fragmented work groups, in fragmented locations, with fragmented careers. The advent of the telecottage, where the analyst or accountant works from home, is the epitome of this development. Though the trend is less evident in social work than in many other sectors, there are growing numbers of freelance trainers, consultants, mentors, guardians *ad litem* and other self-employed people using their social work qualifications and experience to work from home. Interestingly, post-Fordist home-based working and 'hot desking' are also beginning to affect the organisation of social services, with a number of authorities deciding they can save money on unnecessary office space if social workers work from home as much as possible, using laptops and teleworking, and access workstations in the nearest office rather than each having a separate desk in a fixed location and travelling miles back to base from each visit. All employers are seeking to improve record keeping and budgetary control through computerisation, with electronic case files allowing managers to access information at any time and to look for trends across cases. There are implications for user confidentiality as well as for the health and safety of workers (eye and muscle strain from using computers, risk of violent theft of the laptop, stress induced by reduced clerical support and by the lack of colleague contact and teamwork). 'Post-Fordism' is now a reality in social work and is bringing new challenges with it. Certainly, procedural efficiency, based on performance indicators and monitored outcomes, appears to have taken the place of building relationships.

SUMMARY OF CLASSICAL THEORIES OF MANAGEMENT

To sum up, the study of management is rooted in the classical tendency to see organisations as machines and their employees as cogs, each carrying out one specialised task. Associated particularly with continuous processing and mass production, this model regards managers as holding top-down responsibility for planning, monitoring and motivating the work of others within their span of control. These ideas are now regarded by theorists as too rigid and predictable to reflect the contemporary world of work, yet there are certain echoes of them in the government's managerialist agendas for social services of standardised performance targets, league tables based on numerical measurements, and efficiency gains.

Organisational structures

MAX WEBER: THE EFFICIENCY OF BUREAUCRACY

The name of Max Weber (1864–1920), a German sociologist, has become synonymous with the concept of bureaucracy, though he did not invent it. Rather, he formulated a typology of organisational forms, based on the exercise of power and authority (that is, the behaviour *within* organisations and not just their outward shape), from which the bureaucracy emerged as the most technically efficient. This does not mean that Weber found it attractive; indeed, he found it a rather terrifying vision of the future.

Weber's interest was in what makes people follow instructions. A leader, he concluded, may exercise *charismatic* authority through a combination of personal qualities and vision (unfortunately true of some abusive residential regimes, as well as religious and political movements), or may hold *traditional* power on account of hereditary position. Weber's third type, authority with a *rational–legal* basis, is that exercised within bureaucratic organisations and is the form which dominates in social work. In this model, the arbitrary power and influence of the founder of a business or political dynasty is missing. Rather, the conformity comes from following formalised rules and procedures, and working within clear-cut structures.

Notably, Weber defined the bureaucratic organisational structure as a hierarchy of *offices*, or posts, rather than of individuals. Each office carries specific responsibilities for which the person occupying it should have the relevant skills. This we would recognise as a job description (see Chapter 5). It means that the fundamental structure of a bureaucracy may be illustrated as a set of roles; each individual occupies a box within the structure, located in relation to the rest of the hierarchy. The design of this structure would look like that shown in Figure 2.1, which is basically a pyramid with the head of the organisation at the top, middle managers in between, and front line workers and their assistants at the base.

Typically, the bigger an organisation gets, the taller this pyramid becomes. This is one reason why 'downsizing' usually involves cutting out whole layers of deputy or middle managers.

Shorn of its emotional connotations (of over-rigid, mechanistic rule by paperwork), we can see that there are elements of bureaucracy in all formal organisations. According to Weber (1947), the five main characteristics of a 'pure' bureaucracy are:

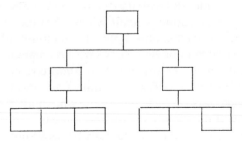

Figure 2.1 *Hierarchical structure*

1. A *clear-cut division of labour*, with activities rationally dis-
    tributed as official duties (you work within your job descrip-
    tion and on work as allocated, not what you feel like doing that
    day).
2. The distribution of duties through a *formal administrative hier-
    archy* in which each office is supervised by the one above it and
    in which communication is required to pass up and down
    through this supervisory chain. (A social worker does not just
    ring up the Director to ask for more resources or for advice on
    a difficult case, nor do people conduct their work through those
    they happen to get on with.)
3. A prescribed system of *rules and procedures* (which, if not fol-
    lowed, can lead to disciplinary action and which, conversely,
    should safeguard the worker if the rules *are* followed but a case
    does not turn out well).
4. The exclusion of *personal considerations* from the conduct of
    official business (both by the employee and by the organisa-
    tion – here, thinking has moved on, as we shall see below,
    but it is still absolutely the case that social workers must be
    able to distinguish between their personal and professional
    boundaries).
5. Salaried employment based on *technical qualifications* and
    constituting a career within the hierarchy (recruitment and
    selection against job descriptions and person specifications,
    staff development, and promotion prospects all relate to this
    element of a bureaucratic organisation).

CRITIQUE OF THE BUREAUCRATIC MODEL IN SOCIAL WORK

This formalised, hierarchical model is still commonly found in
social welfare organisations (albeit with elaborations – see below)
and it does offer some benefits. There are undoubtedly advantages
to a large workforce in having clear lines of command, coherence,
and predictable rules. The organisation is more readily answerable
to those who use its services – in allocating resources fairly, for
example – and also to staff members who may feel aggrieved.
Workers know if they apply for promotion what abilities they will
be expected to have, and can usually expect staff development
opportunities to assist them if they want to move on in their career

because this is also to the advantage of the organisation. Some security is offered inasmuch as staff know who does what and that there is stability in the system.

There are also limitations for social work in this organisational form:

1. It is best suited to *routine, stable, unchanging tasks.* Consequently, there have always been doubts about its appropriateness for social work practice. Not only is social work forever in a state of flux at the wider level, as thinking about social welfare changes along with the political climate but, at the front line, it also has to deal with the messiness and unpredictability of people's lives. This makes it hard to give anything but the most general indication of how each person should be treated – or, at the other extreme, risks turning people into categories and losing the social work skill of working with each as a unique individual in a specific set of circumstances. This is what some social workers fear is happening, for example, as they complete Assessment and Action Records on looked after young people – as if a checklist of apparently objective judgements could adequately encompass the professional and ethical dilemmas involved in working with human diversity and agency (Garrett, 1999).

2. Another complication in fitting social work into a rigid organisational structure is the vexed question of *professional autonomy* (Aldridge, 1996). Social workers are not expected to have to be told in detail how to do their jobs. They bring with them the ability to make specialised and complex judgements about people and their lives which is the hallmark of the qualified professional. Consequently, a hybrid term of 'bureau-professionalism' is sometimes used to apply to the social work context. There is a debate as to how far managerialism has superseded this model by imposing centralised control, or whether professional autonomy is retained at the point at which social workers and care managers continue to make individual judgements in complex cases and perhaps to find other space in which to manœuvre (Harris, 1998).

3. There are many, *potentially competing stakeholders* in social work beyond the immediate employing organisation. First, social workers retain more autonomy than factory-floor

workers because they draw their professional skills, knowledge and values from outside points of reference (Mintzberg, 1989), particularly those of a university-based academic discipline and a professional association with its own ethical code (in the UK this is the British Association of Social Workers). Both of these are linked into global groupings of practitioners, teachers and researchers who are in continual debate about what social work is, what it can achieve, and the standards by which it should operate. Second, the organisations that actually pay social workers' wages, are themselves loosely grouped into an 'employers' lobby' consisting of many disparate organisations across the public, voluntary and private sectors. There are also many other relevant groupings that are bigger and more influential than a single agency, from representative bodies such as the Association of Directors of Social Service to the 'benchmarking club' involving 20 councils in London (*Community Care*, 14–20 January 1999, p.6) through which managers are pooling information on performance and establishing baseline charges and standards. Third, there is increasing pressure on social work, and rightly so, to be responsive to users and carers (and to their more organised voices in user-run groupings), as well as to the general public who feed their views into local community care plans, for example, as well as paying the taxes that fund public services and withholding donations if they do not like what charities are doing. All these different stakeholders are called on to work in partnership, for example at the national level on the General Social Care Council and the Training Organisation for the Personal Social Services, plus their equivalents in Scotland, Wales and Northern Ireland, as well as locally in Diploma in Social Work and post qualifying partnerships. There are inevitably tensions in this process.

4. The more diverse an organisation's activities and the more types of people it serves, the *greater the complexity required in the shape that holds everything together*. Thus a social services department, for example, tends to sprout side shoots in the form of specialist teams or, increasingly, workers are outposted into multidisciplinary teams where hospital consultants or those running youth offending teams will be as influential as the social workers' own departmental managers. Also, there is an increasing need for non-social work, technical specialists to

manage or advise on whole parts of the organisation or department's activities, such as computing, legal or equalities issues. Their policy priorities and links with staff may cut across operational line management – that is, across the overseeing of the basic business of that department or agency. Similar complications exist in large voluntary organisations where the management of fundraising and policy development is as important as running the direct services provided. It is increasingly difficult for the manager in a complex public sector organisation to encompass this degree of diversity either in organisational structure or technical expertise. There have been, for example, some enormously expensive mistakes made in computer purchasing (notably in health settings), when managers have not known that they were being given bad advice.

Despite these complications, on paper at least, the up-and-down chain of accountability and delegation remains clear however many strata there are, though the level of responsibility and the boundaries around the roles at each level clearly differ. There are, however, both formal and informal variations on the bureaucratic organisational form in and around social work:

1. Informally, as we shall see in a later section, *organisations are living entities*, imbued with the characteristics and inter-relationships of the staff who people them. Weber's mechanistic charting of organisational structure does not display the way people 'bend the rules', circumvent their line managers, or find themselves acting outside their role (for example, domestic staff in group homes who are sought out for a personal chat by the children living there). People also 'act up' in their posts, either with or without official sanction, from the care organiser who is trusted beyond her actual responsibilities to the temporary senior covering leave or secondment. Interestingly, acting up has been found to be an important way in which women gain the confidence, experience and credibility to apply for management jobs (Allan *et al.*, 1992; see Chapter 7). But it can also be a way in which some individuals and not others are groomed for promotion, and a means of exploiting the good-will or insecurity of someone whose career development is not advanced accordingly.

2. There are some jobs, such as staff development officer, that
    always present difficulties in deciding where to *locate the
    postholders*. Are they in the senior management team or
    middle managers? Is their work part of strategic planning, or
    can only the operational managers know how the changing
    nature of the work on the ground throws up new training
    needs? Ideally, they should be bringing together operational
    and strategic considerations, but this tends to put a strain on
    over-simple ideas about structure.
3. Overall, the hierarchical chart conveys no sense of *where an
    organisation is going* or of what it is becoming over time – that
    is, of its 'organic' elements. With such a rapid pace of change in
    social work, restructuring has become the norm and organisa-
    tional thinking has to be dynamic, not static.
4. There are a few clear exceptions to the hierarchical model of
    the pure bureaucracy that social workers may come across. It
    is important to recognise and value their difference:

(a) Collectives

In a women's refuge, for example, there may be a collective of
workers, though less often than formerly (see Chapter 7). They
share tasks, are accountable to a wider grouping of women, often
including service user representatives, rather than through a hierarchy and make the rules jointly with them. They value what
workers who may themselves be survivors of men's violence can
bring in personal as well as professional terms to their work, and
they do not work their way up through a career structure. Where
there *are* women designated as managers, this often tends to have
been imposed as a condition of outside funding by people who
assume that good management means managers. Similarly, staff in
bureaucratic organisations who telephone a collective often ask to
be put through to someone in charge; they do not understand that
authority may not reside in any one person.

(b) Parallel hierarchies

Other organisational variants that social work students may wish
to consider can be found in hospitals and in universities where

senior doctors and senior academics work in parallel hierarchies alongside senior administrators who are not equipped to question their medical or subject-based specialist knowledge in conducting an open-heart operation or marking an exam in Ancient Greek. Many pre-1992 universities also have elected heads of department, on a rotating basis, who may be junior (in promotion terms) to some of those for whom they hold many line management responsibilities. Increasingly, in both hospital and university settings, though, the central management is becoming more powerful and there are also external moves to find ways of imposing verifiable standards, such as updating for doctors on evidence-based medicine or measures of graduateness amongst students.

Human relations theorists

To Weber and Fayol, people were roles in a hierarchy of responsibilities; to Taylor, they were cogs in a machine; to Ford, the consumers of his products and the workers on his assembly lines. A reaction against these mechanistic concerns with structures, tasks and markets came in the form of the human relations movement. The key thinkers behind this approach recognised that people not only work for an organisation, they *are* the organisation. Of equal importance as the manifest formal structure is the informal structure created by the behaviour of people, as individuals and in groups, as they live out the unpredictabilities and emotional vagaries that social workers know so well.

Human problems and working them out together:
Mary Parker Follett

Mary Parker Follett (1868–1933) was instrumental in shifting the emphasis in management from a concern with organisational control to one of sensitivity to human factors. Active in social work in turn-of-the-century Boston, it was through establishing evening classes and youth employment bureaux that Follett came to study industry and management as a political scientist. She saw management as a dynamic concept where power must go with responsibility. Authority should be vested in knowledge and experience, wherever these were located in the organisation, not in mere position on a hierarchy. It required *consent*. Just like most social workers, she considered that management should be based on the ethical principle of respect for human worth and dignity, not the emotionally sterile pursuit of efficiency at any cost.

Through her interest in people, Follett recognised that workers and managers often do not have a common aim and that, within teams and other work groups, there may be a good deal of conflict. In what we would now recognise as turning every threat into an opportunity (see p.91), Follett believed that a group working together could air each person's viewpoint and build the best from each into an idea that no one would have been able to see on their own. Not only might this lead to a better overall solution, but it would not depend on one side winning over the other or on an untidy compromise.

Follett drew her thinking about the worth of all people and the dynamic integration of organisations into four fundamental principles which are still relevant today:

1. To achieve co-ordination, it is important that people, regardless of their position, should have *direct contact with one another*. Horizontal communication is as important as vertical.
2. Everyone concerned with a policy or decision should be involved *right from the early stages*. They should not be brought in afterwards as this denies the benefits of participation, increased motivation and raised morale.
3. Co-ordination depends on seeing all factors in a situation as *inter-related*.
4. Co-ordination and executive decisions are *continuing processes*; nothing is final. And, because so many people contribute to a decision, it is an illusion to suggest that, ultimately, the person in the hierarchy who carries the authority is the one and only person on whom responsibility can be placed.

Though Follett believed in the essentials of leadership – the ability to see and understand the organisation and its context in their entirety and to have a vision of the future – she did not accept either the cult of the leader or the right of leaders to assume they know best or to set themselves above the rest. Rather, for her, the managerial vision should flow from the common purpose and from the shared work and aspirations of the whole group.

MOTIVATING PEOPLE: ELTON MAYO

Just as people can affect the working of a system, so too can they be *affected* by it; that is, by the general climate in the workplace and by the way they are treated there. Elton Mayo's research revealed that every organisation has an informal structure which affects how people behave, how the system functions, and which management methods need to be adopted to raise morale and assist people to be mentally healthy at work. His importance lay in drawing attention to all the other aspects of motivation and productivity beyond the purely financial, which was all that Taylor believed made people work to their full capacity.

Mayo saw that business methods that take no account of wider human issues, such as emotional reactions and the social climate of the workplace, can lead first to subtle sabotage and then to formalised industrial conflict. He was ahead of his time, too, in seeing the need to adapt to rapid changes both in technology and in society. He believed in explaining change to the workforce and in taking their attitudes into account when introducing it (see the section in Chapter 3 on the management of change).

Mayo is best known for his work on the Hawthorne experiments. Through observing the behaviour of small working groups in an electric company over more than a decade from 1924, he explored the informal social systems which grow up amongst employees and which, because they underlie both co-operation and resistance to change, must play a part in the effective organisation of work. People have a natural propensity to associate with one another and they care what 'their' group thinks about them. To be motivated, they need a management style which maintains and builds upon this spontaneous co-operation in groups, which takes a genuine interest in both the individual and the group, provides new interest from time to time (the 'Hawthorne effect' was a surprising finding that all workers, both the experimental and the control group, improved their performance just because there was an experiment going on and people were taking notice of them), and also recognises that workers, employed in an enterprise which has been artificially created to achieve certain ends, do think about what good their work is to the wider society. All of this makes perfect sense in social work.

CHRIS ARGYRIS

In his 1957 book, *Personality and Organization*, Argyris, of the Harvard Business School, suggested that workers do not grow or become self-actualised in structures which offer them little control over their work. Rather, people who do not experience autonomy and involvement adapt their behaviour in ways that are immature, passive and dependent. Initiative is lacking, people 'clock watch' and take longer and longer breaks, they cling to habitual routines, resist change and impede progress, and show minimal commitment to the agency or its work. Management responds with repressive control, staff grow yet more infantilised and resistant, and a downward spiral is created that, unforunately, is not unknown in social work settings. If it were possible to encourage ways of working that did not put individual and organisational needs in opposition, then Argyris considered that worker satisfaction and productivity might both improve.

His model of management takes a multidimensional view of a worker as not just a strong arm or a good mind but a *whole person*. Organisations are made up of people, and managers need to think about the way they conceptualise, and hence treat, the people they employ – the extent to which workers' personal and social needs are met. This model is, then, a more 'organic' one than those in the classical tradition. It emphasises the unplanned aspects of the organisation, such as: employee morale and motivation (seen as naturally present and therefore needing only channelling), informal social groups, an individual's need for job enrichment as well as good pay, and the way teams might control, collaborate and participate in task achievement. Information gathered through routine monitoring and evaluation would be used, not to check up on people, but to help people in their activities. Managers at the top would increase their interpersonal competence by being honest and showing their real feelings.

Argyris is also known to social workers as the author, with Donald Schön, of a 1978 book setting out a theory of learning which bases diagnosis and action on human reasoning, not just routinely learned behaviour. This will be returned to in Chapter 6.

DOUGLAS MCGREGOR

Another psychologist, McGregor, built on Abraham Maslow's (1954) motivation theory of basic human needs, with which many social workers will be familiar. Once basic physiological and safety needs have been met, he argued that people at work become interested in *self-fulfilment and responsibility*. So work is not just a source of money but of self-respect, risk-taking and creativity. (Contrast the way that Taylor thought about his workers.) If this is so, then positions have to be designed and fitted to people in the hierarchy, rather than the other way round.

McGregor coined the terms 'Theory X' and 'Theory Y' to describe the authoritarian and participative approaches to management. An organisation based on Theory X would assume that people are naturally lazy, irresponsible and resistant, rather than being made that way by the organisation they work in. Managers would have to assign tasks and, like Taylor, be job-centred rather than person-centred; supervisors would ensure that their subordinates were kept busy. The design of the organisation would be one of clear lines of authority, narrow spans of control and centralised decision-making.

On the other hand, the organisational implications of Theory Y, where people are naturally striving, taking pride in their accomplishments and seeking new experiences, would indicate a structure which delegates responsibility and control, encouraging workers to *participate* in decision-making. Some social services departments and some voluntary sector agencies still manage to operate in this style and consider that it is easier to meet quality standards when staff are committed to their work and when the organisation is not dogged by uncontrolled sick leave, high staff turnover or low morale (see Chapter 6).

RENSIS LIKERT

Likert was always interested in leadership styles. He actually asked employees in US companies how they were treated (it was from his attitude research that he gave his name to the 'Likert scale' which grades responses to survey questions) and, in a 1961 book based on this research, categorised four systems of organisational management along a continuum from exploitative and authoritarian, through benevolent authoritative, to consultative, and finally participative. Though he found the benevolent authoritative management system to be the most common at the time, he favoured the *participative style* as most successful in the longer term. A close-knit work group (see Figure 2.2) which supports management's aims can, he thought, induce its members to be more efficient, just as a resistant one can pull performance down.

On the other hand, a team which forgets that it is still part of its employing organisation, and which uses its collaborative strength to deviate from organisational norms or purposes, is likely to find itself pulled back into line.

To avoid this, the leaders of effective work groups not only get to know people as individuals and allow maximum participation in decision-making, but also ensure that the group's contributions are linked to the overall performance of the organisation. These managers need to function as 'linking pins' between the group they manage and the management group. In other words, they need to think of themselves as members of both groups because they consitute the primary communications chain within the organisation. When drawn on an organisation chart, the manager is a linking pin at the top of a triangle, the base of which is formed by his/her team (see Figure 2.3).

The downside of this is, of course, that middle managers may feel like the meat in the sandwich – hemmed in from both sides as they

Figure 2.2   *Teamwork collaboration*

Figure 2.3 *Link-pin structure*

try to respond to ever-increasing team and management pressure (each of which may in turn be operating under wider-ranging influence such as government regulation, user and carer demands or trade union views). The senior social worker will know exactly how that feels!

CRITIQUE OF THE HUMAN RELATIONS SCHOOL

The great strength of the human relations theorists is to have demonstrated the major impact that social factors have on work behaviour. This impact is so strong, whether for good or ill, that organisations need to build on the motivation of the personnel they employ both by valuing each individual and by building co-operation in teams. The efforts of the later human relations theorists, such as Argyris, McGregor and Likert, naturally became increasingly sophisticated and demonstrated that the relationships between intrinsic job satisfaction, group morale and output were more complicated than simply being happy at work and being part of a co-operative work group. There were key elements of management style and structure, as these related to the workforce, that could have a profound effect. Even so, critics felt that some of the research led to unrealistic conclusions, such as the idea of handing over all problem-solving to work groups lower down the organisation.

An overall criticism of this body of work is that, although these theorists have drawn on psychology, sociology, philosophy and anthropology, they remain located within business studies and centrally concerned with the productivity needs of organisations. At the end of the day, this is still about controlling work, not about personal issues or interpersonal relations for their own sake; it is almost as if aspects of people's humanity are being understood only to be used against them so as to turn them into more compliant workers. And, since people are seen as being there to serve the needs of industry rather than the other way round, the approach cannot be good at asking the big questions. Does our society have the right organisations, undertaking the right work, or might some of people's resistance within their employment settings be the result of dissatisfaction at this wider level? This can certainly be the case in social welfare where social workers and others are involved in major debates about the overall nature and aims of the welfare state, well beyond the details of practice. Thus, while the recognition of the need for good human relations might be a more congenial approach than the authoritarian concepts of scientific managerialism, the intention behind it is still to make worker satisfaction and increased productivity complement each other through collaboration. And 'collaboration' can be a dirty word where principles are at stake, as wartime history recalls.

Nevertheless, it is all to the good that, as rationality and bureaucracy have proved inadequate concepts to meet the efficiency imperative in organisations, greater interest has begun to be shown in 'softer' concepts such as culture, emotions and gender (Hearn and Parkin, 1995). The human messiness that the Weberian legacy viewed as 'inimical to rational, efficient capitalism', has now become an essential part of theorising about organisations (Clegg, 1990, p.150). Social workers are on home ground with such thinking, of course.

The organisation becoming more complex: the systems model

As we saw in the last section, more sophisticated thinkers have increasingly come to see that organisations are made up of people and that this greatly affects what happens in them. Systems thinking had a similar genesis.

In the period before and after the Second World War, a number of academic disciplines became interested in how inanimate as well as animate organisms work as systems – moving from consideration of the brain to newly developing computers and thence to business organisations and other large institutions. The key ideas were that each organisation is both a system itself and is made up of other systems, that all systems tend towards an internal equilibrium, and that organisations are 'open' systems in that they interact with their environment.

Origins of the organisational model: Eric Trist

At the Tavistock Insitute of Human Relations in London, Eric Trist and his colleagues developed a theory of 'open systems' which recognises the dynamic movement in and out of organisations as well as inside them. Classical models had been constructed from observing virtually closed business systems, usually pursuing specific, economic goals, and had left out the external context as well as the 'people factors'. Organisations, though, employ and serve human beings and they also operate in turbulent, ever-changing fields where the outside world can be as influential as policy made internally (in social work, think of media scandals over child deaths, or government changes in welfare legislation).

When Trist and his colleagues studied the effects of mechanisation on the Durham coalmines, what is interesting to social workers is that they realised they had to put the people into the equation. They found that, if an organisation was to operate effectively, its *technical systems had to mesh with its social systems*. Technology had disturbed miners' small and semi-autonomous shift groupings. As a result, social stress occurred, with resultant absenteeism, scapegoating and defensiveness. (It is interesting that both high rates of sick leave and a 'culture of blame' are currently in the news in social work, just at the time when 'managerialism' seems to have forgotten once again that employees are people.)

Trist showed that the organisation of work has social and psychological properties of its own – that is, that social and technical systems interact. In particular, he demonstrated the role of motivation in productivity and team-building. Unlike robots, people find satisfaction in finishing a whole task, controlling their own behaviour, setting their own targets and in working together as a team. These insights may be ripe to be rediscovered, with care managers complaining that they are merely inputting information into computers with no chance to use their wider social work skills.

Key concepts in thinking about organisations as systems

The systems approach does not prescribe any particular organisational design. Rather, it is a way of understanding the structure an organisation already happens to have, the processes that go on within that structure, and the way that changing particular interactions might help it work better towards its desired outcomes.

Systems theory offers us a number of concepts which may be of relevance in thinking about organisations. Each social or health care organisation can itself be conceptualised as a system, by analogy with a biological system such as the human body. This means that:

- it has *boundaries* around it
- it is composed of *sub-systems* (in the body's case these include the circulatory and respiratory systems and in social services they include information and financial systems)
- it interacts with other discrete systems in *super-systems* (people interact with each other in societies; organisations interact with each other, for example, in a wider system of welfare encompassing health, social care, housing, financial support, and so on).

Confusingly, we tend to utilise the word 'system' in professional speech for a sub-system ('finance system') or for a super-system ('system of welfare') more readily than for the discrete system itself, the organisation. This is probably because in the first two cases we have to make an effort to conceptualise all the financial arrangements or all the welfare agencies working together, whereas we always think of the organisation as one defined entity. In this section we will describe all three types just as 'systems' but we need to remember that they overlap and co-exist in a range of ways.

The boundaries around a system may be to various extents open or permeable, or they may be closed. A body's respiratory system is open to the air being sucked in and pushed out; the circulatory system of the blood is permeable to the oxygen extracted while the air is in the body. These two sub-systems working together help the body to maintain its energy levels and thereby its total functioning. In an organisation, we may speak of an information system being open to those who record material in it or look up that material; it may become open to a new set of people, such as service users, if they are given rights to see their files, or if details about the agency's decisions begin to be published. The information itself is part of what the organisation needs to carry out its work, like oxygen in the body.

WHAT HAPPENS INSIDE SYSTEMS

The analogy between breathing and using information can also be used to understand the terms applied to energy use by systems:

- *input*   is energy being *fed into the system across the boundary* (breathing in air; gathering information)
- *throughput* is the use made of the energy *inside the system* (oxygen extracted in the lungs, passed into the blood, and circulated round the body to help create heat and movement; information recorded and used to decide what type of assessment or individual care plan is needed)
- *output*   is the energy passing *back out of the system into the environment* (breathing out carbon dioxide; publishing statistics on the services devoted to individual care plans over a 12-month period).

There is a further process whereby output loops back on itself to affect input and throughput. 'Healthy open systems must devote part of their resources to monitoring the impact of their outputs on their environment' (Chetkow-Yanoov, 1992, p.25) and, certainly, social work organisations would aim to use monitoring information to improve their work. Current thinking about 'Best Value' (Department of the Environment, Transport and the Regions, 1998) is aimed at ensuring that this information includes service users' views about the services they receive:

● *feedback loop* A health check-up might test exhalation to judge the state of the lungs; a care agency, looking back over reviews of care plans and people's responses to them, may in turn alter what care managers do in constructing future plans.

A simple diagram of this input, throughput, output – happening in the operation of a welfare agency – can be shown as in Figure 2.4

Interestingly, in recent years, there have been several ways in which previously closed systems, particularly of decision-making, have been opened up:

● *new input*   Planning has been opened up to the wider public through new consultation procedures which draw in new ideas, for example into the local authority's community care plan.

● *new throughput*   Boundaries between service organisations are becoming more permeable both to each other, as they collaborate in new ways, and to service users and carers who may be more involved in decision-making.

● *new output*   Joint planning agreements made by social services and health bodies have practical results – for example, in new discharge arrangements for people leaving hospital.

Consumers/
community

Organisational

processes

Change

(inputs)

(throughput)

(outputs)

Boundary management

Figure 2.4 *An open systems model*

Systems thinking in social work and care management

The manager's key role in the systems approach is to focus on how the sub-system(s) he or she manages relate(s) at all the points of 'interface' with the larger, total system and the outside world – known as 'boundary management'. (This is very different from earlier thinking, which saw managers as being there to solve internal conflicts.) The systems approach relates well to care management, for example, because the latter emphasises the crucial links between commissioners and a range of external and in-house providers, as well as the important interlinking between all the different parts of the organisation that deal with quality standards, complaints, contracting, budgets, and so on, and other external bodies such as housing and health authorities.

Perhaps the missing element for care managers, as the role has developed in many authorities, is the freedom really to be managers of these interfaces – to construct imaginative care packages drawing upon a wide range of informal carers and formal care providers (including writing their own skills into contracts), rather than the somewhat uniform responses that often apply, and to handle all the complex communications involved. If all social workers are managers, as was suggested in Chapter 4, then these tasks are certainly encompassed by social work skills, and groups of care managers working together in teams could get more involved in juggling budgets and in thinking about the standards needed in contracts for services.

CRITIQUE OF THE SYSTEMS MODEL

Though systems approaches are an improvement on the over-simplistic classical models, they are still only artificial attempts to capture the complexities of the real world and, despite the use of 'organic' language, the approach is somewhat pseudoscientific, with no allowance for human emotions. The model is also artificially politically neutral, functionalist and normative, taking little or no account of the *interplay of power dynamics* within the organisation, including where there may be racist, sexist or other oppressive elements built into the systems or the aims of the organisation, as well as inherent in the attitudes of particular staff.

Like any theoretical model, systems theory is only an attempt to look at something essentially familiar in fresh ways. It does not exist in reality, so it can mislead us, and it can get in the way of other ideas. For example, the analogy with biological bodies is not at all exact. Two organisations could decide to share a sub-system (a post-adoption or out-of-hours service, for example; health and social services undertaking joint commissioning) without losing their distinctive identity. If we worked too closely to the agency/human body parallel we could overlook some important possibilities for working in partnership.

Most worryingly, systems analysis may be a force for unhealthy conservatism. It does not cope well with the 'big questions'. For example, a system such as a corrupt or bankrupt organisation may actually need to lose some of its parts or to dissolve altogether. The model contains no clear place for political questions such as how the system came to be the way it is, who holds the most power within or over it, why some systems suck in more energy (resources, personal information) than they can put to good use, who decides what constitutes 'good use' – or how fundamental inequities, such as poverty and racism, can ever be radically opposed by systems which have been created in their image and which typically operate to sustain them. In using a systems analysis to look at organisations, we need to take care not to ignore these bigger questions of power and powerlessness.

To sum up, as organisations have become bigger and more complex, the systems model has attempted to offer a manageable way of thinking about them, as if they were giant bodies, with all their activities interacting. Everything connects to everything else and it is in the interactions, and at the boundaries where they take place (internally and externally), that change can happen. Social workers are traditionally attracted by the ideas of openness, team-work and interdependence in systems thinking. They also like the fact that a theory they may have learnt for social work practice or for systemic family therapy (Coulshed and Orme, 1998) can double up for use in understanding organisations.

The model has served us well in encouraging managers to think about what inputs will produce the desired outputs and, with a dynamic sense, about processes of development and change. It is being outdone now, however, by the sheer complexity of the scope and inner workings of many organisations. The loosely coupled system (Leigh, 1988) refers to the various sub-systems as now virtually independent, each needing to be understood on its own terms in order to understand the whole. Across a social services department, for example, children's provider services, children's commissioning, adult provider services and care management all operate separately. Some elements of the work are 'outsourced' to contractors and private tenderers, the standard of whose work must also be overseen, thus adding a further layer of complication.

Where are we now? New managerialism and the freelance fringe

So fast has the rate of change become in organisations and so complex their structure, that none of the above models is now considered adequate to understand or manage them. A whole new set of models of organisational structure that attempts to grapple with this layer of complexity will be outlined in Chapter 4.

It becomes critically important for the relevant director to hold everything together – enthusing all the organisation's staff with an overall vision and with a shared culture and values, imbuing the organisation with a corporate image and managing the changes necessary to cope with new challenges and demands. Chapters 3 and 4 will look at these issues of culture and change, vision and mission, as key aspects of management thinking and will explore whether they are one way of putting the professional initiative and innovatory flair back into increasingly standardised welfare preoccupations.

3
Cultural Change and Quality Standards

As we saw in Chapter 2, management and organisational theory moved from abstract model-building to understanding the workforce as human beings rather than as cogs in a machine. Paradoxically, organisations can become more efficient if, instead of trying to tidy the people in them into neat little pigeonholes and control their every action, human needs are responded to and human strengths – creativity, enthusiasm, engagement – are fostered. In social work as elsewhere, this has to happen in a context of constant change which can create enormous uncertainty and even hostility. This means there is quite a challenge facing the managers who must provide the leadership to motivate staff under difficult circumstances and manage the process of change.

In the business world, meanwhile, another body of people has also come to the fore: that is, the customers who have to be attracted to consume goods and services through careful product design and marketing. In social work, too, quality services and value for money are seen as essential ways of meeting the needs of the consumer. Such matters can be looked at only within a broader approach to the whole culture of the organisation and its overall mission, so consequently we will start with a consideration of these before moving on to quality and the management of change.

Culture

Organisations, like national and ethnic groupings, have a pervasive culture (and can also have sub-cultures within them that resist the dominant way of thinking). This culture – 'the way things are done here' – can be very positive, as in a 'culture of excellence', or essentially negative, as in the tendency in social work towards a 'culture of blame'. Here, hostile media coverage, lack of political and public support, and scapegoating when something goes wrong lead employees to fear failure and to care more about 'covering their backs' than about giving a good service (see also Chapter 6).

McKenna and Beech (1995, p.51, drawing on Hofstede, 1980) list some of the variations in national cultures that can also be seen in organisations. They express these in terms of low or high degrees of the following:

- *Power distance*: how autocratic the leaders are and the extent to which subordinates are trusted.
- *Uncertainty avoidance*: how willing people are to take risks, bend the rules, change jobs.
- *Individualism–collectivism*: Western individualism as against loyalty to family and community, the supportive workplace and the corporation.
- *Masculinity–femininity*: competitive ambition as against networking, caring, bringing out the best in others (see Chapter 7).

Handy (1993), a very influential management thinker, offered a different but overlapping listing of four types of organisational culture: *power culture* (strong leadership from a small group at the top), *role culture* (clinging to bureaucratic roles, rules and regulations), *task culture* (emphasising technical know-how, project teams) and *person culture* (matching tasks to people). Different cultures suit different types and sizes of organisation. They may also vary from one part of an organisation to another, although it is considered part of the management role to get the whole organisation pulling together.

The current trend is to try and change the organisational culture to one that is more likely to lead to success, with greater emphasis on trust and participation, managed risk, corporate loyalty, teamwork and good staff care. The aim is to make an organisation's structure and culture serve its overall strategy – what it is trying to achieve over time. Too much attention to structure or culture alone can result in an inward-looking enterprise in which nobody actually has a clear idea where they are going or how to get there, so strategy from the top is also important.

The interest in corporate culture arose initially from wondering why some nations' businesses were doing particularly well – first Japan in the 1980s and then the 'Tiger economies' of the Far East, until the near collapse of the financial markets affected them all adversely in the late 1990s. Among the factors thought to explain the earlier success were corporate loyalty and a commitment to quality shared by all, which we shall explore below, and investment in the selection and training of a stable workforce, which will feature in Chapters 5 and 6. Although only some aspects of the approach could be transplanted to the West where social norms are very different, there began to be seen greater interest in people, more emphasis on the group and on teamworking, and more understanding that trust and participation can lead to better results not to loss of control.

An American response to the search for successful management practices able to create the right organisational culture was Peters and Waterman's *In Search of Excellence* (1982). They considered what was special about some of the USA's most successful companies where the best was brought out in staff and an unparalleled service given to customers. Their book was very influential in the UK, shifting attention to the importance of leadership and of human resource management (HRM). Peters and Waterman were timely and enthusiastic rather than rigorous in their approach, but some of the key principles they arrived at do make sense in advocating:

- *action and decisiveness* from management, not endless reports and committees
- *staying close to the customer*: listening to them so as to know and respond to their need for quality, service and reliability
- *autonomy and entrepreneurship*, with smaller companies competing against each other, instead of one vast corporation, and taking risks in new directions
- *productivity through people*, which means that everyone's efforts count and everyone shares the rewards
- *hands-on managers*, in touch with the staff, who are driven by clearly defined values
- sticking to what the company *knows best and can do well*
- *simple, lean structures* with fewer layers and fewer managers

- tight adherence to *fundamental organisational values*, controlled from the centre, with greater autonomy for staff in other regards, that is through operational decentralisation.

Social work perhaps shows the structural changes, unfortunately the most arguable of the principles, most strongly – seeking improvements in services through a competitive welfare market in which SSDs have shed many of their provider functions or organised them separately from commissioning (Walsh, 1995) and reorganisations in which layers of managers are made redundant. There is also a much increased emphasis on the service user, with needs-led assessments rather than service-led ones, for example, though this may not equate, even then, with meeting customer preferences. Not every staff group will feel that it enjoys greater autonomy or a management that is in touch and giving a clear lead through value-driven action, though most staff groups might feel this would be a good idea. Nevertheless, the proliferation of Investors in People (IIP) awards in SSD settings (including whole departments, e.g. in Kingston upon Hull) does show some awareness that everyone's efforts count towards overall success. Nearly half the voluntary sector agencies with an annual income of £1 million or more either hold or are working towards the IIP award, but none of those with an income under £100 000; the Voluntary Sector National Training Organisation is encouraging more to seek the award (*Community Care*, 25 November–1 December 1999, p.36).

Peters and Waterman began the shift away from managers seeing all the answers in abstract organisational structures, towards the 'new managerialist' or 'new wave management' focus on the people factors of staff and customers. At the same time, they did consider that organisational culture and success could be measured, in factors ranging from absenteeism to reputation (for customer care or equal opportunities, for example), and translated into performance indicators. This latter approach has arguably taken over in UK social work and social care, expressed by government in the language of quality but frequently emphasising top-down regulation over bottom-up autonomy and initiative. This may actually mean that key elements of the excellence findings are lost sight of. The impetus towards the development of occupational standards and professional competences, and government commitment to monitoring against performance indicators and national frameworks of standards does not equate with the centre keeping hold of key values while decentralised operations are free to innovate and take risks.

And, though the belief that excellence lies in the characteristics of managers as much as in those of the overall organisation could be seen to be reflected in a range of programmes and schemes introduced by the Local Government Association, the Social Services Inspectorate and others to develop social services managers, so too could the key role government sees them as playing in carrying through its imposed agendas.

Quality

Overall approaches: quality control and quality assurance

The quest for high quality services can give rise to two contrasting images: either management checking up on the workforce or a collective effort to give the best possible service. These two approaches can be summed up as *quality control* and *quality assurance*.

Quality control, at its narrowest, implies looking at standards after the event and taking measures to rectify mistakes and stop them happening again. A somewhat broader version, which is becoming the norm in local government, involves *continually checking services against agreed standards*. It is a top-down model and is certainly in tune with managerialist approaches. Every organisation needs an element of quality control (though it is not enough on its own, as we shall consider below). No single social work practitioner or manager can achieve significant improvements alone. Even if they attempt to raise the standards of their practice, they cannot judge whether they have succeeded unless they are part of wider-scale monitoring and feedback procedures with an agreed baseline of standards (Darvill, 1998b).

Quality assurance has more of an air of putting measures into effect in advance which will ensure that a *better, and constantly improving job of work* is done. It is a more proactive approach, taken in the belief that 'You cannot inspect quality into a service' (Dunnachie, 1992, p.19). Quality assurance is a bottom-up concept and tends to start from making the staff feel more involved so that they will pass this on in a better service to the consumers. This does tend to require a culture change in many organisations, not least in respect of involving care staff who have traditionally been accorded low pay and low status. If domestic and residential care workers are regarded as unskilled manual workers, doing 'women's work' that is not real work at all (see p.183), they are less likely to be effectively drawn into the process of assuring quality.

Adams (1998) suggests a wider range of models: *quality rectification, quality maintenance, quality enhancement* and *quality maximisation*. (The first pair are effectively sub-divisions of quality control and the second pair of quality assurance.) As the names suggest, quality rectification is error-driven; it implies responding only to complaints, adverse audits, investigations and inquiries, and whistleblowing (Hunt, G., 1998). Quality maintenance is standards-driven; it involves a more systematic approach to quality control but is based on achieving minimum standards, not on envisioning the ideal approach to service delivery, and it imposes standards largely set by 'experts', either in the form of the organisation's own managers or an external body.

Quality enhancement and quality maximisation are forms of quality assurance. Quality enhancement goes beyond minimum standards into setting goals that lead to continual improvement; it embraces quality management systems such as TQM (see below) which do involve a culture change (see p.188) because people need to start listening to each other, but it does not question the overall approach to service delivery or the existing power relations within or beyond the organisation. Quality maximisation is, for Adams, an *empowerment model* that changes organisational culture more fundamentally, to embrace listening equally to all the stakeholders including the collective voice of users. This could mean recognising, for example, that no standards, however high, will ever make professionally determined care packages as acceptable to many disabled people as services they can select and purchase for themselves, with the right to a social life perhaps featuring as importantly as personal care (Priestley, 1998).

An error-driven model may look the cheapest because it involves the least change but it is not. There are always costs involved in *making mistakes and then rectifying them*. These include the costs of dealing with complaints and, in extreme cases, being taken to court or to the Local Government Ombudsman, perhaps paying compensation or having to hold an inquiry. Added to this are the intangible costs of developing a poor reputation, so that future work becomes more difficult on many fronts, and the long-term costs of not providing preventive services so that problems intensify and replicate themselves over time. It is generally more cost effective to get things right, even allowing for the costs of offering the improved service and of monitoring its quality. Over and above all of this, in social work and social care, we must never underestimate the human costs involved in failing to provide a good enough service, though that may be seen as a moral rather than a management question.

Quality standards

Before quality can be measured, there needs to be a general understanding of what it is. In everyday language, 'quality' goods and services often mean luxury ones, for which people who can afford to do so are prepared to pay more. In social work, however, quality services are neither the most expensive nor those that service users would necessarily choose – after all, many families would prefer not to have child care social workers involved at all and people in receipt of care packages might well want more than can equitably be provided. Rather, they are services that are fit for their purpose and reasonable in cost, with a degree of informed choice available wherever possible.

Thinking about cost has moved on. Under the Conservatives, the move towards compulsory competitive tendering (CCT) implied going for the cheapest option. Under New Labour, however, a move towards 'Best Value' (Department of the Environment, Transport and the Regions, 1998) means achieving the most advantageous combination of cost and quality. In determining 'quality', a duty is placed on local authorities to consult local people on service aims and standards. This includes those who use services and also local taxpayers, who ultimately pay for them. Performance indicators are thus able to reflect local needs as well as national standards, for example providing appropriate services for diverse communities. The general legislative framework for Best Value requires: an overall statement of what a local authority

intends to achieve; an agreed programme of fundamental performance reviews over a 4 to 5–year budgetary cycle, beginning with the weakest areas; targets for improved performance
and efficiency, published with annual reports on progress in Local
Performance Plans; independent audit; and intervention by the
appropriate Secretary of State in the case of serious or persistent
failure.

There are, in fact, a number of 'customers' and 'stakeholders'
(other parties with an interest) who may need to be involved in
setting quality standards. In addition to users and their families,
these include the general public, elected members on social
services' committees and boards of trustees or management
committees in the independent sector, other disciplinary groupings
in social and health care and in criminal justice, and central
government. Each has a different, if overlapping, set of interests
and each must be borne in mind by those responsible for writing
quality standards.

A statement of standards must be approved by some of these
groups and broadly acceptable to others. It must also be couched
in specifics, outlining precisely what is to be achieved, to what level
of performance, and how this will be measured. The last aspect is
particularly important. A standard is insufficiently precise if we are
not going to know when we have achieved it.

Anyone who has studied research methods will realise the complexity that this implies. In the social sciences, it is all too easy to
slip into measuring only the *quantitative* elements of a service (e.g.
how many meals are provided, of what nutritional value, at what
cost) because this information is relatively easy to collate and
compare. The national standards for mental health services in
England and Wales and their performance indicators, for example,
have gone for what is measurable and evidence-based, leaving the
less tangible, more qualitative issues out of account and thereby
discounting much of what social work does best (*Professional
Social Work,* February 1999, p.3). Most social work and social care
services, in fact, need to ask subjective and process-related questions such as the extent to which users feel in control of their lives,
able to influence the services they receive and treated as a person
by the organisation's staff (Qureshi, 1998). There is an additional
complication in terms of all the people whose views may be relevant in assessing outcomes, just as they are in setting standards –

not only users and carers, but also a range of agencies at different levels, those funding the service, and so on.

Just because it is complicated does not mean that no effort should be made to measure less tangible standards, however. This might be done in two stages. An initial questionnaire survey of all users, or a series of meetings with residents, or of focus groups with representative users, might reveal what factors people consider most important in the services they receive. These might then be usable as specific measures of quality. For example, consumers of meals-on-wheels might want not only a hot, nutritious meal, delivered on time and with a varied menu (all easy to measure), but also the opportunity to exchange a few words with the person delivering the meal. This could be built into the timing of delivery rotas and measured by sampling user feedback. It is important not to confine users to a limited set of options at this first stage because those options would come from our thinking, not theirs. A user group of adults with learning difficulties, for example, gave feedback that they did not consider professionals being smartly dressed to be a standard that was important to them; indeed, they associated people in suits with those who had deprived them of liberty and choices in earlier life. The way people treated one another was far more important than how they looked.

MEASURING OUTCOMES

Once it has been decided what to measure, there are as many ways of doing so as there are of conducting research. In addition to the gathering and use of all possible forms of quantitative data, methods of measuring qualitative outcomes include an audit of records, a questionnaire survey, in-depth interviews with a sample of users, focus groups, or non-participant observation of the service while it is being delivered (Ellis and Whittington, 1998). There can also be routine user feedback built into the way the work is actually conducted – for example, user comments in reviewing care plans and in residents' reviews, or simple surveys administered by those delivering the services. Levels of unmet demand in the community might be ascertained through community access points, freephone telephone lines, reply-paid cards, councillors' surgeries, or commissioned public opinion research. Levels of response, of frankness in replies and of breadth of coverage will vary according to the method used.

Possible outcomes to measure include: user satisfaction, user knowledge of services, achievement of intended changes in users'attitudes, behaviour or quality of life, and users' ability to cope without further services. Clearly, the desirable outcome is dependent on the setting and user group. In some contexts (e.g. mental health), it might be a sign of failure, for example, if some people did not feel able to return for further help when they needed it whereas, in others, such as adopting children or leaving care, it is hoped that people will be launched on a path of living life unaided.

Though far from easy to arrive at, outcome standards are too general by themselves and need further work to express them in the form of indicator statements. Ellis and Whittington (1998) emphasise that these must be SMART: *Specific, Measurable, Achievable, Relevant* and *Targeted*. An example they give of a generally desirable outcome is that of enabling the tenants of a supported housing scheme to make decisions about their own lives to the full extent of their abilities. Specific performance indicators might include holding monthly tenants' meetings, sending invitations to all, levels of attendance achieved, individual involvement in drawing up and reviewing each care plan, and so on. Most of these are easily measurable although, of course, there are degrees of individual involvement and it would be easy for consideration of this to become tokenistic. Indicators might therefore need to be quite robust in what they measure and how they measure it. Again as in research, 'triangulation' of the data (gathering it in several different forms and cross-checking them) may be useful. At the extreme, it may also provide checks and balances against the continuation of malpractice which one form of monitoring alone has failed to detect.

The above example of tenant participation is fairly straightforward in terms of who is involved in giving and receiving the service. Were the quality of a whole care package to be monitored, however, this might involve several different service providers and some services with a chain of people involved, from suppliers of each foodstuff used in meals-on-wheels, for example, through the company that prepares the meals, the SSD as purchaser, and the delivery process. There will be contractual arrangements at each stage which can each have standards written in; for example, the nutritional content and portion sizes of the completed meals. The outcome of the care provided to the user will depend on all these people getting it right first time, every time. It is important to think quite broadly about this when considering what service people get in your setting. In social services offices, for example, the impression people receive can be as influenced by the reception staff as by the duty officer they see. This means not only that users should be given the opportunity to comment on reception services, but also that receptionists should be involved in the discussions that set quality standards.

User and carer views

The ultimate test of quality will always be what users and their families think of the services we provide. They are the equivalent of 'customers' in the business world and they have a right to be involved both in setting standards and in reviewing the outcomes of care. It does take special efforts to obtain the views of social work's consumers. There is evidence, for example, that few children in the care system know about complaints procedures, let alone use them (Wallis and Frost, 1998; and see below).

We need to think both about what users are asked to comment on and how this can best be done. Most publications on quality offer broad criteria by which quality can be measured in terms of user response. Maxwell (1984), for example, lists:

- *Appropriateness*. Individuals get the right response to their needs.
- *Equity*. Individuals and groups get a fair share of the resources available.
- *Acceptability*. Services satisfy users' expectations.
- *Accessibility*. Services satisfy requirements such as convenience, opennness, information, physical layout, and so on.
- *Efficiency*. Resources are used to generate the maximum benefit for those in need.
- *Effectiveness*. Services achieve the intended outcomes.

Given that many users have to contribute towards the cost of services, one might add to this list:

● Value for money.

Furthermore, if services are going to be user-friendly, Pfeffer and Coote (1991) add that they should be:

● participative, involving service users in decisions and choices
● integrated across agencies and sectors of care and
● responsive to individual needs through flexibility.

Although it is not easy to set standards with users or to build these into contracts, increasingly, useful work is being done on this which can be drawn upon. There are, for example, standards for domiciliary services developed through consultation with users. They are: reliability, continuity, kindness and understanding shown to users, cheerfulness and competence, flexibility, and knowledge of the needs and wishes of users (Nuffield Institute for Health and United Kingdom Homecare Association, 1997). Although this work can be transferred from the private to the public sector, it is always going to be more difficult to extend it to informal carers such as neighbours or volunteers, upon whom many users rely. So there will be limits to what can be achieved.

In statutory social work, the standards to be met will need to reflect wider expectations, not just what a service user or their family might want. Even then, Casson and Manning (1997) show how parents' views can be incorporated into child protection standards in, for example, consistency of worker, being kept informed at all stages of an investigation, and having an opportunity to comment on the accuracy of reports. Children and young people have also asked for some say over whether and how they are medically examined and over the way an investigation of their abuse is investigated.

Formal standard-setting

Perhaps because there is some difficulty in measuring quality standards in interpersonal fields such as social work, imported frameworks are increasingly preferred. In the early days of concerns with quality, some social work services sought a British Standards award, BS 5750 Part 2, which set a standard, not for a particular product, but for a quality assurance system and its component procedures. This, in turn, was used as the basis of the ISO 9000 series, first established in 1994, which operates international standards in systems of quality management. The components (see Casson and Manning, 1997) cover:

(1) the need to have in place: a published commitment to an overall quality culture; specifically designed standards for each element of the service; up-to-date procedural guidelines; systematic staff training in their application; and regular checks that standards are being met and guidelines followed

(2) adequate record-keeping that tracks what has been done, by whom, that it met the standards and has been completed satisfactorily

(3) clear and effective communication with users and with other stakeholders (e.g. other professional colleagues involved in the service) about the service and the standards aimed for; regular reviews of outcomes for users; and designated responsibility for identifying and dealing with any problems that may arise.

The BS/ISO approach is essentially a maintenance model and arguably has been largely superseded. A more developed quality management system would go beyond this into taking action, based on the appraisal of actual achievement, for continual improvement. The same processes of consultation, and of staff and user involvement, would go into determining action plans and their review as went into setting the initial quality standards.

The Charter Mark scheme for the public sector, operated by central government, includes these elements in asking for evidence of acting on users' ideas and making improvements to services. Charter Marks are awarded by a panel of judges on the basis of a 10-page application and a visit by an independent assessor. The criteria are: setting standards and telling users what they are, publicising all services to users, asking users about services needed and their ideas on improvement, making good use of their ideas, giving users choice wherever possible, providing a polite and helpful service, providing an effective and 'user-friendly' complaints procedure, ensuring value for money, being able to give evidence of improvements and evidence that users agree a good service is being provided. Their popularity is growing, with nearly 300 holders in local government and a further 488 applications by 1998 (based on Cabinet Office News Release CAB 197/98, 22 September 1998).

While, increasingly, organisations are volunteering to measure up to one set of standards or another, many in social work and social care prefer to see systems of standards employed which are specific to their own employment sector. Hence the National Occupational Standards (NOS) for social care are being adapted by some social services organisations as a wider measure of quality, while the Business Excellence Model (BEM), developed by the European Foundation for Quality Management (EFQM), has updated for the public sector its aim of assessing areas of strength across the organisation as a whole and developing annual improvement plans so as to make the strive for excellence a continuous process (see summary in Darvill, 1998b). A survey of the sector has shown that most SSDs have chosen to apply one formalised set of standards or another, and sometimes more than one (Darvill, 1998b).

At the same time, external checks over which there is no choice have proliferated. The Department of Health sets great store by regulation and quality control. Joint reviews by the Audit Commission (which polices local government performance across the board) and the Social Services Inspectorate, operating to yet another set of standards, have sharpened up what they are looking for and become more critical (Department of Health Social Services Inspectorate and The Audit Commission, 1998). Negative reports have led to directors retiring early and government threats to take over – particularly where authorities are perceived as failing to safeguard children – with the intention of creating what has been called a 'no excuses' culture (Hirst, 1998). A clearer national agenda is emerging as to what is 'good enough'. This underpins both the Best Value criteria applied by local authorities in operating their own services and the national standards for the inspection and registration function of the eight regional Commissions on Care Standards (which inspect community services as well as care homes). For the first time, this has given users and carers the ability to challenge any authority that falls short of a nationally agreed benchmark. The General Social Care Council also has a role in maintaining standards through the registration of staff.

A local authority remains responsible for judging its own performance but, increasingly, this too is required to take place against national standards such as the Quality Protects performance assessment in child care. Over and above this, the local authority is free to measure its services against its own published eligibility criteria for assessment and receipt of services, including degrees of priority; its community care, children's services and community safety plans, including the broad objectives these set for future work; the current pattern of available services as against user preferences; the implementation of service contracts and other joint working arrangements with other agencies; and complaints from users.

In the voluntary sector, a 'compact' aims to deliver certain pledges from government on respecting the sector's independence and right to longer-term funding in return for an undertaking by voluntary organisations themselves. They are expected to promote best practice and equality of opportunity, and to consult and involve users wherever possible, including in the development and management of activities and services (Hunter, 1999). This is the nearest government can get to imposing standards on a sector over which it has no direct control beyond the broadest considerations of financial rectitude and non-political activity. It is a recognition that the 'third sector' plays an increasing role in the direct delivery of social care services, that it is a major player in the economy of the UK with over 6 per cent of national employment and almost as many again engaged in volunteer activities (Kendall with Almond, 1998), and that government cannot deliver its policies on combating social exclusion without a high quality contribution from this source.

Quality systems

Quality management requires a 'disciplined and systematic approach' (Warr and Kelly, 1992, p.2). The most basic measure to improve quality – measuring outcomes, taking feedback and using these in future planning – returns us to the input/output/ throughput systems feedback loop we saw in Chapter 2.

It is not always necessary for the impetus to come from senior management. It is perfectly possible to introduce a quality assurance system at team or establishment level and models for doing so can even be bought off the peg. Grover (1992) describes how a multidisciplinary mental health project brought in a consultant to help them review their systems of staffing and finance, linking with external agencies, team functioning and service delivery. A constantly repeating quality cycle of action, monitoring and change was introduced, with detailed action points. The staff jointly owned the process of change although service users' views were not fully integrated. Though not perfect, this is a good example of a small group of practitioners in a community care setting taking a systems approach to change without waiting for their parent agencies at the macro level to do it all for them.

QUALITY CIRCLES

One particular technique imported to the West from Japan which emphasised the involvement of staff lower down the hierarchy was quality circles. The idea was to move away from rigid management hierarchies and compartmentalisation of task performance (the conveyor belt representing the most extreme form of the latter) and to encourage groups of employees (originally from the shopfloor, later in groups spanning the hierarchy) to meet with a facilitator to solve problems affecting everyone in relation to the product or working conditions. Members of quality circles would be offered training in problem definition and analysis, teamwork and communication. Their involvement, personal growth and increased job satisfaction was said to be good for corporate success. In the UK, employees were mainly indifferent or hostile to quality circles and there has also been scepticism as to what kinds of problems they were ever really engaged in solving and how useful an approach can be if it is a technical 'bolt-on' to an otherwise unchanged organisation (McKenna and Beech, 1995).

TOTAL QUALITY MANAGEMENT (TQM)

TQM (Piggott and Piggott, 1992; see also Morgan and Murgatroyd, 1994 for a public sector application) attempts to go beyond quality systems into a culture of quality for the whole organisation. Consequently, it combines both quality control and quality assurance. It emphasises top-down vision and planning, including commitment to quality at the most senior level, and bottom-up involvement and motivation of all the staff. It is strategically driven, in terms of 'hard' factors such as performance standards and the monitoring of quantitative management information (numbers of users, cost of services, outcomes of interventions), and particularly because it operates within corporate objectives, but it also emphasises 'soft', people-oriented factors such as customer care and staff skills and teamwork. The hallmarks of the approach are *getting things right first time every time*, ending up with customers who are delighted rather than merely satisfied, and continually improving performance (see Chapter 6 on ways of building this in through appraisal and staff development). Casson and Manning (1997) point out that it implies implementing a system robust enough to meet all the agreed standards even when people go on leave or there are temporary staff employed. This includes guidelines detailed enough to remind the child protection social worker to check that the room is at a comfortable temperature and that there are tissues handy before every case conference. It is the implementation that counts, however: 'Every specification of quality must have clearly thought out ways of consistently delivering it' (Casson and Manning, 1997, p.28).

As its name suggests, TQM cannot be envisaged as an add-on, but typically requires a *pervasive culture change* towards a management approach that values every member of the organisation. Quality is the key to success and quality is the responsibility of every employee. As a result, both staff development and staff care become very important (see Chapter 6). TQM also needs all parts of the organisation to be working well together and it needs action rather than rhetoric.

Often, the strategy is seen as needing to start by making staff feel involved and motivated, 'winning their hearts and minds', before working outwards to service users and carers. Staff's views and efforts become as important as management-led or external regulation, monitoring and inspection. Importantly, this means the whole staff group being involved, not devolving all the responsibility for quality to individual staff (though there will, of course, be designated staff to operate the quality system). Similarly, if Ellis and Whittington's (1998) idea of a quality assurance group is taken up, those who have been interested in joining the group will have to make special efforts to ensure that everyone else remains committed. It might be easier to involve a whole team or staff group in taking quality on board, even if particular tasks are delegated and reported back on as the work progresses. It is empowering for staff to be accorded this kind of dignity and respect, and to be thought capable of innovative ideas, not just of carrying out tasks in a routine way to meet targets they had no part in setting. This has to have constant support from the very top so that everyone sees quality as part of the job they are expected to do. Staff also have to feel trusted before they will, in turn, feel committed.

TQM is closely linked with human resource management (McKenna and Beech, 1995) because it brings to the fore all the staffing issues of recruitment and selection, staff development and staff care (see Chapters 5 and 6). Indeed, staff development becomes doubly important because it not only improves performance but may become the major channel for communicating and working on quality issues. One would also expect to see flexibility in working practices, autonomy in decision-making and a supportive environment for staff in any organisation committed to TQM.

How far this is possible when corporate objectives remain the guiding force (in other words, what would really happen if a team stepped out of line or had a totally off-beam idea) is questionable. But, in some social work agencies, even a degree of change in this direction might be very much valued by staff.

In social work, a good example of a local authority introducing a thorough-going TQM approach into one whole area of service is Newham's work on child protection (Casson and Manning, 1997). This has now resulted in the publication of an easy-to-follow guide for any manager seeking to emulate the approach. There is also a quality assurance workbook available for social care settings (Ellis and Whittington, 1998). Both publications are set out with learning objectives, exercises, activities and practice examples. They could be used by individuals studying for a vocational or professional award, by whole teams seeking to discuss quality issues, or by a social work agency proposing to implement change along quality-inspired lines.

The practitioner as quality manager

As we discussed in Chapter 1, there is scope to regard every practitioner as a manager. In so far as the individual care manager has the responsibility for the 'total quality of care as it is experienced by the user' (Department of Health Social Services Inspectorate and the Scottish Office Social Work Services Group, 1991, para. 6.13), this is certainly true of quality standards. In monitoring the effective working of the individual care plan, a care manager may be responsible not only for his or her own work but for enforcing the standards specified in contracts with contributors to the plan and overseeing any agreements with carers or volunteers, for example. The concept of 'service congruence' covers the broader question of whether the care plan as a whole is achieving what it set out to. The care manager will need to create his or her own systems for feedback as well as identifying measures of success. The satisfaction of the user will, of course, be of primary importance. For some complex plans where the user, for example, is confused and cannot give direct feedback, a similar range of views may need to be sought as were involved in the original assessment of need. In such a case, the carer's views are likely to assume a major role.

Critique of quality in social care

Various criticisms have been levelled against ideas of quality management as they operate in social work. These include allegations as to its general unsuitability for interpersonal care services, the politicisation of certain issues within it, its creation of additional bureaucracy, and its failure to grapple with social work agendas concerning user empowerment and anti-oppressive practice. We will look briefly at each of these in turn.

UNSUITABILITY

The pursuit of quality was brought into social work and social care from the industrial and commercial world and there is both an up and a down side to this. On the one hand, it makes even greater sense to aim for high standards when you are working directly with people rather than manufacturing washing machine parts or selling clothes, because improvements in quality will lead to an improved quality of life at the most basic level. On the other hand, it makes results harder to judge since you cannot physically measure a product or count sales or profits when your job is caring for people in a residential home. Of course, the occupancy rate of the home and the balancing of the budget (with an element of profit if the establishment is in the private sector) are important but they are not the whole story. Standards and performance indicators can be set, as we have seen, but they will always be imprecise, involving value-based and sometimes essentially political judgements as to what constitutes an improvement.

POLITICAL ISSUES

A local authority's own recording of unmet need, while raising legal complexities (because there are limitations on the extent to which an authority's lack of resources can be taken into account when deciding whether or not to provide services; see Paterson, 1999, pp.153–4), could potentially act as one of the most important mechanisms for feeding into future planning, leading to improved or better targeted services. Most quality systems work by checking standards against a predetermined norm. It is particularly difficult to take issue with this and to argue that the norm itself is wrong, either in principle (top-down services, for example) or in operation (e.g. over-narrow eligibility criteria).

PROLIFERATING BUREAUCRACY

We are moving into an era where there is a risk of duplication in monitoring quality. Money that might otherwise have gone into providing direct services is being channelled into more and more bureaucracy surrounding checking up on that provision.

This is a managerialist agenda and, in addition to the cost to users and carers in reduced spending on services, it risks making staff feel that they are under surveillance rather than involved in a quality culture.

USER EMPOWERMENT AND ANTI-OPPRESSIVE PRACTICE

The extent to which anti-oppressive objectives are integrated into thinking about quality, or the voice of service users and carers built into monitoring and other quality systems, varies greatly. Quality models are no exception to the fact that most management literature comes from the conservative ethos of business administration. Social work thinking about anti-oppressive practice and user empowerment gives us our own ways of approaching many of the issues in question but, up to now, social work managers (many of whom take MBAs with little public sector, let alone social work content) have often failed to respond to this more radical challenge. As we saw above, Adams' (1998) quality maximisation model represents one attempt to do so.

Since quality can be judged from a number of viewpoints, it is important to be clear about who is the most important arbiter of quality and who owns the quality measures and outcomes being used. Black groups, for example, have long argued that there can be no quality without equality. Power differentials between the parties – as, for example, between a Black woman carer and a white male care manager – should not be ignored when seeking and evaluating feedback on services. This is no doubt one reason why children do not use complaints procedures (Wallis and Frost, 1998), though they place unmanageable demand on the anonymous and child-centred services of ChildLine. Most writing and talk about quality betrays its origins in white, male managerialist thinking and leaves us still with a long road to travel on equal opportunities. There are also links with staff care policies (see Chapter 6), since these should underpin total quality, but they rarely extend to full-scale counselling services for employees, or funded day care schemes for those with young children or adequate responsibility leave for parents and those caring for other relatives. It is hard to give the best service to users when you are ill at ease, harassed or under unreasonable stress yourself in your own working environment.

Concluding thoughts on quality

However it is pursued, quality should give a sense of a continuous process of organisational development, both through building on current good practice and through making improvements where these are needed. Quality control and quality assurance need not be in conflict – and, indeed, many social care agencies are pursuing a mixture of these measures, some at government behest and others of their own volition within an overall ethos of 'customer care'. This is marked by maximising opportunities to obtain user feedback, whether through consultation procedures such as focus groups and local meetings that feed into community care and children's services plans, or through more bureaucratic measures such as complaints procedures and monitoring the extent to which quality specifications have been met in service contracts. Staff's voices, too, should be heard so that they have the chance to raise concerns and make complaints rather than 'blowing the whistle' externally.

Whatever kind of organisation you work for, whether it is a local authority or health and social services trust, or a voluntary or private agency, it would be interesting to look back over what changes have been adopted in the pursuit of quality. Where has the impetus for change come from? Has it been new legislation or government policy, senior managers going on courses, the fact that others were doing it, a desire to raise public profile or improve the corporate image, or a dissatisfaction with past performance? Whichever of these has played the greatest role, it is also worth asking yourself to what extent quality thinking has also meant equality thinking, or whether wider social work concerns with the empowerment of disadvantaged user groups and employees have been swept aside in the pursuit of a glossy new corporate image.

Whatever the motivation, however, and whatever the eventual outcome, pursuing quality standards inevitably involves processes of change. Rather than wait for change to overtake us, organisational thinking urges us to plan for and manage change so that we can maximise its benefits and minimise its risks.

Managing change

Stable and static organisations concentrate on efficiency and they tend to be centralised and bureaucratic as a result (Mintzberg, 1989), along the lines we saw in Chapter 2. As organisations become more complex, however, and as the prevailing conditions within which they operate combine increased expectations with less support, there is a tendency to decentralise and to become more organic – developing and adapting as needed in order to manage fragmenting demand within a turbulent environment. Throughout the 1960s and 1970s, as the personal social services grew, they continued to operate as centralised bureaucracies. More recently, social and political pressures have necessitated the appearance of new organisational forms (to encompass the purchaser–provider split in community care, for example), and restructuring has become the hallmark of the age. Staff are also expected to be multiskilled and adaptable, moving about within the organisation or perhaps having serial careers. How do organisations manage these processes of change?

Resistance to change

As early as 1541, Machiavelli (see 1961 edn) noted that anyone attempting innovation had a hard time of it. Those who had done well out of the old ways of working would oppose change on principle, while even those who could see they might do better would be cautious about trying anything new and untested. Consequently, there would be fierce opposition from some and only lukewarm support from others, the latter's support being further dampened by other people's anger or indifference. Machiavelli went on to distinguish between those who could force through changes on their own and those who required the support of others. Although we have all come across new directors acting like new brooms sweeping clean and pushing through their favoured reorganisations within a year or two of arriving (albeit without using the physical force that Machiavelli had in mind), it is usually the case in social work that we do need to work out who our allies are, and to win over at least some of the opposition, before attempting to steer any major change through a meeting or committee.

Some four centuries later, this need for clarity about who (or what) favours change and who stands in its way was portrayed by Kurt Lewin (1951) in his idea of a *force field analysis*. This is a practical approach which assists in the diagnosis of change possibilities. A diagram is constructed which depicts 'driving forces' (those which work for change) and 'restraining forces' (those against change). The method can be used either purely analytically, to decide which kind of change is going to be advisable or possible, or as an action tool for carrying through a change which some support and others oppose.

Armed with a full-scale force field analysis, the manager can make the necessary decisions about how to cope with innovation and the kinds of conflict it may reveal – for example, where there are clashes of values or power bases. Taking as an example the situation facing the manager of a children's home that is due to be turned into an intensive treatment unit, some of the factors faced are outlined in Figure 3.1.

Glancing at this diagram of forces for and against change, it would seem that the fact that accepting change is the only way to stay in a job is going to be a strong motivating factor. So similar numbers of driving and restraining forces do not necessarily represent equally balanced situations. This can be represented diagrammatically by making some of the arrows thicker than others. The nature of the trade union objections will need to be explored and a process of negotiation begun. It may well be that the proposal can be implemented in a way which is as fair as possible to staff whilst also meeting the new service need that the organisation has identified. Those employees who do not want to learn new skills or weather changes to working conditions may perhaps be given every assistance to find jobs elsewhere. Overall, the diagram makes very clear that the old equilibrium, the old status quo, will go and that a new one will be established in a different place.

Figure 3.1 *Force field analysis – changing a children's establishment*

Above all, the analysis reveals that there are two ways to make the change happen: strengthening the support and reducing the opposition. Interestingly, we can have a tendency in debate to concentrate on arguing against those who speak out against us and to forget about winning over and working with the potential allies. It is actually a good idea never to go into a meeting to raise a tricky problem or propose a change without having done a rough calculation in advance, on the basis of sounding people out, as to where your support is going to lie and what objections you are going to have to answer. Missing aspects in this model include silent opposition and genuine indifference. Only the protracted debate that real change is likely to involve can bring these into the equation and it should not be supposed from the force field analogy that change is ever a 'one off' event. It is always a process over time.

Resistance to change is not intrinsically bad. It can hold up ill-advised plans until they have been subjected to more detailed consideration and it can offer some stability where organisations opt for change for its own sake. Employees' natural caution also reminds us that they have a right to know where they stand in terms of job security, terms and conditions of employment and working relationships they may have been building up over a period of years. But there is a *feelings level* as well as a rational level to people's reactions to change. People feel comfortable with familiar ideas, values and working methods; any process of change, according to Lewin (1951) requires them to unfreeze, then change, then refreeze into the new arrangements. Good human resource management involves giving people enough time to make this adaptation and keeping them well informed, while it is happening, as to why change is necessary and what its implications will be, both for them and for the organisation.

Change techniques

Although we have commenced this exploration of change with a consideration of resistance to it, the management literature is equally full of positive accounts of how people can be innovatory, and how they can carry through their ideas for change. Kanter (1991) is one of the 'gurus' who is most associated with the notion of change as creative. Her writing combines descriptions of how particular individuals are especially good at seeing things in new ways and communicating their visions (requiring, also, the personal qualities of leadership and persistence to see change through), with an awareness that change in modern organisations requires the building of coalitions and teams so that shared effort is rewarded by shared credit.

Thus interest has moved to the process of change and how this can be managed. It is not about 'top down' ideas that are imposed by managerial will. Kotter and Schlesinger (1979) identify the following six styles of change management (which are actually ways of overcoming resistance):

- education and communication
- participation and involvement
- facilitation and support
- negotation and agreement
- manipulation and co-optation
- explicit and implicit coercion.

Different approaches suit different situations. Legislative or policy change, for example, is usually interpreted as a need for new information and is therefore managed through education and communication. An example in social work might be an authority-wide memo on a new European Health and Safety Directive, followed by one-day training events geared to different levels of staff. Managers recognising that an organisation is facing imminent bankruptcy will feel that stronger measures are needed, and may accompany the inevitable memos and meetings with varying degrees of manipulation, co-optation or coercion to impose cost-cutting measures such as voluntary or compulsory redundancies. It is likely that these change techniques will lead to later problems within the organisation, as anger and resentment lead to resistance and lowered morale, but there may appear no other choice at the time.

Negotiation and agreement are generally required when codes and conditions of employment are affected. Participation and involvement are helpful when those with responsibility for implementing change lack the knowledge, power or expertise to do so alone – for example, when new computerised systems are introduced. They may also be the favoured style of change within some teams or agencies. Facilitation and support will assist staff to adjust to change, and should be routinely available whatever other measures are employed. Change, and the uncertainty it engenders, can be very unsettling for staff and a good staff care policy (see Chapter 6) should allow for this in providing a range of services including financial and pre-retirement planning for example, as well as counselling. Staff may also wish to seek confidential career planning advice if they think their present job may be at risk.

Unless we are able to change ourselves, we will have difficulties in effecting change in organisations (Pugh, 1993). The process of implementing change is dynamic; a rigid or unreflexive approach (i.e. one where we are unable to see our own part in what is happening) creates fresh resistances in others and new obstacles in operating systems.

Whilst it is true that public sector organisations have faced widescale change in recent years, change is not a constant feature in any single dimension – be it through time, for example, or in one particular task or job. Closer examination reveals wholly new priorities co-existing with attributes, practices, cultures and systems which have shown a remarkable capacity for endurance. An instance of this is that, frequently, the personal services that are delivered to service users remain the same over long periods, even while the arrangements for their allocation vary. This has certainly been true of community care, where the fundamental organisational change required to implement the division of service purchasing from service provision has often not been accompanied by the intended shift into greater diversity in the services themselves – in the types and timing of meals delivered to people's homes, for example, or in the supports available to assist carers. Sometimes this is due to a sheer lack of innovation, and sometimes to conscious opposition – for example in the form of political attempts to safeguard the public provision of labour-intensive services.

The degree to which change percolates from the top down or the bottom up varies between organisations, according to the distribution of power and the management style adopted. There are examples of change which have arisen from the demands or influence of 'front line' staff. The development of equal opportunities policies, units and projects in some organisations are examples of this. Eventually, new developments become part of the organisational structures and systems but, at first, there is a struggle to gain support from an unequal power base. Work in a London Borough to promote equality of opportunity for women, for example, explicitly used the organisational processes and politics which can at times constitute the barriers to change to achieve the desired results. Notably, a broader women's agenda was recast in terms of the representation of women in senior positions, which brought on board a number of key departments (Itzin, 1995).

Because he recognised that change is threatening and can make people go rigid and then turn hostile, Pugh (1993) devised a number of 'rules' for the successful implementation of change in organisations:

- Work hard at establishing the *need for change.*
- Don't only think out the change, *think through it.*
- Initiate change through *informal discussion* to get feedback and participation.
- Positively encourage those concerned to give their *objections.*
- Be prepared to *change yourself* (including by recognising that improvements are possible to any idea and by being open to 'bottom up' suggestions).
- Monitor the change and *reinforce* it (including telling everyone about the ways in which improvements are being demonstrated) (based on Pugh, 1993, pp.110–12).

Change in organisations is likely to happen rapidly only in a situation of crisis. Most changes occur over a long period, and usually over a much longer timescale than the change agents had hoped. Given the need to engage others in the process (middle managers often being particularly important to win over) – and to manage opposition in constructive and helpful ways if the change is to be successfully achieved – considerable time will need to be allowed for the process. Change itself can be debilitating to the individual. Performance and self-esteem can plummet and will not return to normal until those undergoing the change have adapted to it. This may occur in a 'cycle of coping' (Carnall, 1995) which includes the stages of denial, defence, discarding (when it is realised that change is inevitable), adaptation and finally internalisation. Change agents can anticipate this cycle, learning from the early stages about issues that may need to be tackled before the change will work and giving staff every support to move through to the point where they can incorporate the changes into their ways of working.

Involving staff in change

A project which has been devised by those affected will often produce less resistance. Where staff see that the change reduces rather than increases their burdens they are more likely to welcome it and, if autonomy and professional values are not threatened, acceptance will probably be gained. It is critical, therefore, that a team is involved and consulted, and that a consensus on the decision is attempted. A plan which has built-in revision and reconsideration, moreover, conveys empathy to opponents who need to have their objections taken seriously. Where there is defensiveness, frequently there is underlying fear; again, the manager who listens, gives clear information and can be trusted is more likely to negotiate needed changes successfully.

Of course, not all ideas for change come from the top. Indeed it could be argued that the most novel ones emerge away from those in power who may well see innovation as a disturbance. Team leaders, for example, can cash in on times of change and organisational crisis to push forward their own plans which may be more likely to be adopted at moments when solutions are actively being sought. There are also certain environments that favour the involvement of staff in change. Factors which can help include: decentralised structures with open channels of communication; well resourced teams with time to discuss ideas; clear procedures from which to start; a risk-taking ethos; and staff who enjoy their work and are committed to getting it right.

Nonetheless, initiating change in social welfare is especially difficult because of the interdependent nature of organisations with other systems. For example, say a voluntary body decided to implement a team approach to resource allocation. It might emerge that others, such as the purchasers of services, other funders, or the Charity Commission required one nominated individual to hold responsibility.

In such a circumstance, management tactics might be to foster 'facilitative interdependence' (Weiner, 1982, p.115) by (a) identifying interagency needs and issues and ensuring that the planned change would contribute to service improvement; (b) promoting the visibility of the change and reinforcing its positive ramifications for all the services; and (c) forging links with other bodies, explaining the reasons for change while lobbying for support from other systems in the task environment and other networks so that there would be a greater chance of collaboration and coordination. Whatever the dynamics of change, if the results of introducing new ideas are counterintuitive – that is, less than the desired effect (Luciano, 1979) – this can be traced back to improper or incomplete planning. The systems view of organisations, as presented in Chapter 2, saw them as having their own internal sub-systems and being part of a super-system. If there are planned changes, a proper outcome could result from estimating the implications for the sub-systems and external systems with which the organisation interrelates. The growing interdependency of the personal social services and the health services, especially, will encourage jointly planned and executed projects which will need to manage the complexities as well as the possibilities for change across organisational boundaries.

One management technique which can prove very useful when change becomes necessary is MBWA or 'management by walking [or wandering] about'. Peters and Waterman (1982), though not the originators of this idea, did draw attention to its value. The most senior manager, in particular, will gain trust and respect by becoming a recognisable face to employees and by asking their opinions. Equally importantly, he or she will have a sense of what is happening at the 'front line', will be able to forestall many problems, and will be much better able to anticipate the need for change and win agreement to it.

The only way to be genuinely well informed is to meet all levels of employees at their workplace. This is also an excellent way of raising morale and of demonstrating a shared commitment to improving the quality of service the organisation offers. The manager becomes more visible and can also more effectively lead by example if he or she is not permanently shut in an executive office behind a large desk. MBWA is not just about asking the royal walkabout question: 'And what do you do?' It can be targeted on getting to know who are the key trouble shooters in the different locations and forging links with them, checking that people are committed to the overall aims and values of the organisation, finding out how work is organised on the ground, looking for ways to make links and minimise conflicts across the organisation (because the manager has this oversight better than anybody), and finding out what will motivate or free people up to do a better job (based on Leigh, 1988, p.187). More precisely, the visit can be made to discuss the organisation's mission statement or to talk through a particular process of change. It is important to ensure that MBWA does not make people feel they are being inspected or give line managers any reason to think their authority is being undermined. The overall aim is to create a climate of openness and it may be particularly positive if teams, establishments or projects feel able to invite managers in when they have something new or positive to share. In social work, managers may be required to make rota visits to establishments for which they are responsible. Although these do have a more formal, managerial function, it may still be possible to inject them with some of the positives of MBWA by adopting an open manner and focusing on some of the same issues.

Though MBWA can help to change an organisation, it focuses only on what the people at the top do. In order to change a whole organisational culture, something more thoroughgoing will be needed. Total quality management (TQM), which was discussed earlier, is one such approach. McKenna and Beech (1995, citing Schein, 1985) point to a number of ways in which human resource management (HRM) issues pervading a whole organisation can combine with leadership style to change the culture. Leaders are important *role models* – they can set an example through the issues they focus on, the way they react to crises and through enabling others to develop as future managers in a supportive environment. The whole organisation, however, also sends important messages through what it values in selecting, rewarding and promoting staff, what it emphasises in policy-making (in everything from staff development to restructuring), through its physical environment (pleasant reception areas, multilingual signboards) and corporate imagery (coat of arms, logo), its formal mission and customer care statements and the informal mythology to which it gives rise. Most of these can be manipulated and it is not impossible to inaugurate a new era with a new message.

Unfortunately, cultures – of stress, of blame, of managerialism and competition – are not usually chosen but come about through a combination of wider welfare changes, public image and pressure of work. Changing such an ethos is not easy but it may well be very necessary if staff are not only to survive but to give a high-quality service. Neil Thompson (1996, p.662) urges 'an explicit strategy of culture change' in the face of evidence that organisations themselves can both engender and allay stress.

Change in social work

Rather than focusing always on staff as the cause of problems, cutting edge thinking in social work now sees the whole agency as needing to become a 'learning organisation' (originally Argyris and Schön, 1978, now in wider use) and a 'competent workplace' (Pottage and Evans, 1994), a term which implies harnessing the practice wisdom and skills of the workforce within the overall mission of the agency to give the most effective response to users. It is the culture of the workplace that brings out the best in staff and even the best of workers and teams will become demoralised in a poorly managed organisation. The National Institute for Social Work offers workshops on undertaking organisational audits and team self-audits to identify what structures, systems, procedures and management activities impede the ability of staff to deliver high-quality services built on what users want and value and what frameworks of standards and outcome measures could structure these in.

There is a literature specifically aimed at social work professionals and managers who seek planned change within their own organisations (Smale, 1996, 1997; National Institute for Social Work, 1995; and Gann, 1996 for the voluntary sector; see also Rosen, 1999). Indeed, social work has its own model of managing change available in the form of a workbook (Smale, 1996). Its message involves breaking down the process into clearly defined components. It also places considerable stress on the 'people' aspects of change. Before action even begins, it is considered important: to plan it with all the people involved, to share the problem with them so that they become part of finding the solution and making it work, to identify the significant people and connections for the particular changes that will then be needed, to see managing the process of change as one of working with the people involved, and to recognise that all new ways of working, new technology and new policies have change implications of some magnitude for staff. Smale (1996) puts the emphasis on the people involved and, within this, he encompasses such skills as: enabling, persuading, reassuring, bargaining, forming alliances and partnerships, on the one hand, and, where necessary, avoiding, by-passing, or seeing one's own ideas carry the day on the other. Smale also personalises the forces for and against change by asking questions such as who wants change and why, who finds the status quo to be a problem, how people's circumstances could be improved by implementing change, and what can stay the same so that people do not suffer unnecessary loss or unintended consequences. He also asks what behaviours and relationships will need to alter as a result of the innovation, and recognises that it is easier to adapt to new tasks than to changes in the way we relate to other people. He looks for what the proposed change means to people, including in terms of clashes of values and symbolic meanings. He looks for the enthusiasts and those who will be motivated by the change, and he breaks down the key players into a number of roles, from 'innovators' who introduce the idea and 'product champions' who spread the word, through 'change agents', with their 'process consultants' on the outside and 'minders' in the senior management, to active 'opponents' and 'laggards' who prefer to live in the past. Nor is this picture individualised, as the list also includes 'opinion leaders' and 'network entrepreneurs', for example.

The Smale model is an action-oriented one, with steps through the process and questions to ask oneself at each point. Again, there is both a 'people' feel and a sense of the force field analysis throughout, with tips on which types and groups of people to bring together or support to make the change happen, which to regard as crucial in terms of consent or resources, and which to keep out of the way because they could block the change or take counter action. There are other ways, too, in which the social work roots of the model are clear – for example, recognising that people need to mourn what they experience as losses, that people know their own jobs and consequently what deadlines are realistic for them, that there will be staff development dimensions of any change and a need for managers to exchange information, and that there may need to be new team building opportunities or attention to interdisciplinary working. Finally, he follows through into feedback after the change and continues to show the force field influence by suggesting that working with allies at this stage may give a better return than concentrating on overcoming resistance. It may also be more effective to look at what underlies the resistance and whether this indicates that modifications are needed to the process or nature of the change. Smale also gives the very good advice that subsequent evaluation needs to look, not solely at how smoothly the process went, but also at whether the original problem has been solved and whether any new ones have been created which may require further problem-solving and change efforts.

Following a people-oriented model like Smale's should help to prevent there being too many casualties of change. In social work, after all, people are often not being entirely self-interested in opposing change. They may have the interests of users and carers at heart and they may sincerely believe that a poorer service will result. Perhaps the move towards greater consultation with users and local communities, under the Best Value initiative for example, will help to avoid confrontation between opposing groups within organisations who all think they know best.

Organisational contexts

The organisational context is also important. While some organisations are actively empowering, most show some resistance to change:

> Some agencies are hospitable to empowerment as a goal. Others are not. Some don't know because they have never faced a situation which challenged their values to any serious degree. Agency culture grows over time, often starting with a very positive philosophy about human dignity and meeting needs. Then, under the accretions of paper work, over-worked staff, ill-tempers, rigid conformity to rules – to say nothing of difficult clientele and intractable problems, policies begin to change – both formal and informal ones – and the clients begin to receive a disservice . . . For many reasons, clients can find themselves feeling utterly frustrated and helpless in dealing with an agency whose mission is ostensibly to serve them. (Pernell, 1986, p.112)

Many, for example, are skilled at absorbing and diluting new ideas in accord with their own norms (Cohen, 1975, p.92), demanding compromises and spinning out decisions until momentum is lost. As Stock Whitaker points out (1975, p.426), 'covert resistance' – verbal assurances without active support – can be far harder to deal with than out-and-out opposition because it may emerge only gradually and be quite subtle in its manifestations. She gives the example of an agency where key powerful personnel absented themselves from staff meetings thus rendering an external facilitator impotent to effect change. A mental health self-advocacy group found that a similar thing happened in early joint meetings with hospital administrators. These opportunities for patients' representives to meet with senior managers were sabotaged by more junior colleagues being sent along or by a complete failure to attend, sometimes without apology. This issue had to be taken up urgently with management before users lost faith in the whole initiative.

It is certainly well worth putting together a good case to persuade management of what your ideas have to offer and how they can be used in a particular instance. To second guess the response with the untested plea, 'management would *never* let us try that here', is certainly never justified since there is frequently more space in which to operate than is assumed and, even where there is not, it is morally more acceptable to look, and if necessary campaign, for more freedom of activity than to collude with its absence. As Pernell (1986, p.112), drawing on work on black empowerment, has said of any agency's service delivery system:

The importance and potential that it might be changed from obstacle course to opportunity system requires of workers who identify the need for change a search for their own powers of persuasiveness, of diplomatic skill, of assessment of accessibility and leverage points for inducing modification of current practices.

Other agencies beyond one's own employer, such as funders and contractors, can also present obstacles. Similar skills are needed for working with them.

An organisation that copes well with change can be thought of as a 'learning organisation' (Argyris and Schön, 1978). This is an organisation that helps people to learn by constantly questioning itself. If people continually have to adjust their behaviour to fit the pre-existing norms of the organisation when they take decisions in its name, whatever the outside evidence of a need for the organisation itself to change, there is no real learning. (And no amount of quality control or quality audit will challenge this because the monitoring assumes that the standards and procedures are all correct.) Only when the organisation as a whole questions its norms, in the face of a conflict of values, does it restructure its strategies and assumptions (which also govern its employees' behaviour) in a healthy new way. When it does this, it not only learns, but learns to learn again in the future. When it fails to learn new lessons, it perpetuates conflict and encourages entrenched positions. (Aryris and Schön call the two reactions 'single-loop' and 'double-loop' learning, double-loop being the one that feeds back in to create change for the future.)

As will be familiar to social workers from Schön's other work on 'reflective practice', he and Argyris believe that it is only as managers (and professionals) examine their own reasoning processes that they will understand how they respond to the errors, mismatches and conflicts that present the prime opportunities for new learning – and, crucially (for practice teachers as much as managers), how they help others to do this. There are similar concepts in groupwork practice and in crisis intervention theory which suggest that it is at times of difficulty that groups and individuals have the greatest energy and opportunity to move forward in new ways. We will also see in Chapters 5 and 6 how encouraging people to talk about such key points can be used in selection and appraisal interviews.

Examples of social work organisations altering their norms in recent years in the face of new values from outside have been the adoption (partially at least) of a social model of disability and of hugely altered attitudes towards the rights of people with learning difficulties to live an independent and fulfilling life. Previously, the talk was all of disabled people 'adjusting' to their limitations, not of society (including social work) adjusting the way it treated them.

Concluding comments on change

Change is possible, then, but to manage it rather than be bowled over by it requires vision, persistence and strong alliances. The most effective of these are undoubtedly where staff and local people can pursue shared objectives. This is certainly the intention of the Best Value initiative, for example, which requires consultation on service aims and standards, and for some years now has been a theme of the move towards community involvement in drawing up Community Care Plans, Children's Services Plans and Community Safety Plans.

Conclusion

This chapter has been bound together by a sense of forward movement – towards the pursuit both of the highest quality and of managed change to attain that goal. Nothing in the organisational world stays still nowadays and there is a very real feeling of needing to take hold of what is happening before it takes hold of us. Considerations of quality standards and of managed change demonstrate that there is a role for staff at every level in thinking through and working towards the delivery of the best outcomes for service users and their carers. From this sense of a shared endeavour throughout the organisation, we will now move on to look at the role of top managers in offering leadership and a management vision. Far from cutting across the views of others, effective leadership should help everyone else to feel that they are playing a vital part in crewing a ship that is being competently steered through ever choppier waters.

4

Management as Vision, Strategy and Leadership

Although providing leadership is only one aspect of what the top manager does, it is the most visible – particularly when it is lacking. In the view of the project director for the joint Audit Commission/Social Services Inspectorate SSD reviews: 'Where authorities are failing, it's usually down to a lack of a clear steer and grip on the organisation by management and a lack of accountability' (Hirst, 1998, p.8). He also relates this to the overall culture of an organisation, as we did in Chapter 3. Consequently, leadership is often seen as synonymous with management. To show how it relates to the whole organisation we will link it to vision and strategy, and will go on to comment on leadership roles and styles.

Vision and mission: the link with strategic planning

When we are going about our day-to-day work, we have little time to stop and think about the wider purposes we are serving or whether all our efforts are being expended to good effect. For the senior manager, this is an essential part of the job. Like driving a car, managing an organisation is more than operating technical controls – you have to know where you want to go and steer the whole vehicle accordingly, even in the face of traffic that is trying to cut right across your path.

In social change work, it can be very rewarding to pause and ask the big questions. What is the vision of the world we are trying to create? What style of organisation would be best at achieving this? The best motivators and innovators have a very clear image of where they are trying to get, and are extremely good at taking other people with them.

A vision must always be positive. There is a very good example of 'visioning' in a book on opposing homophobia (Pharr, 1988). There, the example is of imagining a world without sex role stereotypes, revealing the extent to which violence, the expression of affection, life ambitions, the placing of love and trust in other people, the choice of careers and of personal appearance, and many other fundamental aspects of human life revolve around narrow ideas of sexual identity. There are unquestioned assumptions of equivalent magnitude operating in organisations, often serving to oppose change and maintain the status quo, which it takes vision to open up to scrutiny. The feminisation of management thinking is one example of questioning the old order, as we shall see in Chapter 7.

In social work and social care, it takes managers with vision to bring the customer care and staff care agendas to the centre of attention. It also takes vision to shift managerial concerns beyond narrow conceptions of balanced budgets and procedural conformity onto quality standards that reflect the aspirations of all the interested parties, including service users and their familes, for whom the best outcomes of care may not always be those that look the tidiest on paper.

Visionary leadership (Westley and Mintzberg, 1991) can therefore be linked with strategic management because, as well as pursuing operational management that gets the job done, an organisation needs an overall strategy or direction. Westley and Mintzberg suggest that visionary leadership is far more than a process of having an idea, conveying it to staff and seeing that it is carried through.

First, they see the whole process as needing to be *dynamic and interactive*, not purely 'top down'. We saw in Chapter 3 how important involvement and two-way communication were to motivating staff. In visionary management, the emphasis is on language that fires people up, on an active, not a passive audience who are ready to be engaged and to take the new ideas into their day-to-day work, on repeating the message in different ways and helping people to take it on board, and on building mutual trust and empowerment through shared enthusiasm. Westley and Mintzberg use the analogy of a theatrical performance that sweeps its audience up into the drama. All good managers, like good teachers, have something of the performer about them and they certainly need charisma, though they also need integrity – a genuine belief in what they are saying. Interestingly to social workers, the theatrical metaphor makes it clear that there is a strong emotional content as well as a task focus in the conveying of a leadership message to an organisation. And the organisation has to be 'in the mood' to hear it; where staff are undervalued, badly treated and disgruntled they are unlikely to be swept up into anything except discontent and opposition to change.

Second, both *content and context* are important: the leader must have the right idea at the right time or no one will listen. Third, as with everything we have looked at in this book, there must be *flexibility* in visionary style. Some ideas start with instant inspiration, others are carefully evolved according to the changing needs of the organisation. Either way, an intense and durable vision will find its way through committee procedures, project development groups, translation into operational functioning on the ground and other organisational paraphernalia so as to make a difference to the way the organisation works and the service it gives to the public.

A strategy becomes more, then, than the single first idea. In Mintzberg's work (see Moore, 1992) he has shown that, whether the strategy emerges inspirationally or is deliberated upon in an incremental way, it has to be translated into a *plan* – a consciously intended course of action – and into a pattern of *consistent behaviours* that carry through the plan. For Mintzberg, strategy is also a position that is taken up (between a product and a market, for example, or between any organisation and its environment) and it is a shared perspective by means of which the collective mind of the organisation decides where to go (like the brain deciding it wants the body to turn and walk to the left) so that the operational managers can then make the body carry out all the actions involved in making that set of movements and send messages back to the brain to say that it has been done and that overall balance has been maintained. In this sense, a strategy is an abstraction but it becomes real when it is translated into action. So every plan requires an *implementation strategy* or nothing will actually happen. And every plan also requires *monitoring and evaluation* to find out whether it was indeed implemented and whether it had the desired effect.

Strategy

All thinking about strategy builds on the work of Drucker (Clutterbuck and Crainer, 1990), an Austrian emigré to the USA in the late 1930s and a considerable influence on the management gurus who came after him. He was the first to emphasise the role of the top manager in articulating a vision and fostering a corporate culture, and the first to show that organisational structure should follow strategy, not the other way round (one reason for all the reorganisations in times of rapid change). He was also a visionary himself in seeing the importance of putting the customer first, using quality as a measure of productivity, and decentralising to cope with these new demands and with the knowledge revolution. He also developed the idea of management by objectives (see Chapter 6) which is very much about conveying a strategy from the top which the whole organisation then translates into action. Drucker's (1954) listing of the seven tasks of the manager of tomorrow starts from managing by objectives and adds: taking risks further ahead and lower down the organisation, making strategic decisions, building an integrated and self-monitoring team, communicating rapidly and clearly to motivate others and engage their participation, taking an organisational overview including his or her own part in it, and informing decisions and actions from an international and sociopolitical perspective.

Strategic planning at its most basic is simply about setting *organisational objectives* and then *mobilising available resources* (what can be afforded) and the *integrated activity of staff* to achieve those objectives. In social welfare this means shaping services in the light of law and policy, and managing the practice that delivers the policy. Strategy can be broken down into steps (McKenna and Beech, 1995), albeit that these make the process sound more orderly than it can probably be in practice where ideas and responses to situations tend to emerge over time:

● defining *corporate philosophy and mission statement*, setting out the overall values of the organisation and what purpose it exists to serve
● systematically analysing the *current social context* and the *political and economic climate* in which the organisation's welfare services are currently being delivered (including demographic

trends, changes in welfare policy and advances in communication technology, the 'going rate' for costs and charges nationally, the current best practice in making services more acceptable and accessible to minority groups of services users)
● evaluating any *advantages* or *limitations* the organisation itself may have.

These last two steps add up to a SWOT analysis, with the organisational Strengths and Weaknesses being set against environmental Threats and Opportunities (see Figure 4.1).

On the basis of all this information and clear thinking about overall purpose, the next steps are:

● developing *objectives and goals* for the organisation which will fulfil its mission (this is the stage at which performance

STRENGTHS | WEAKNESSES

OPPORTUNITIES | THREATS

Figure 4.1 *SWOT analysis*

standards, budgetary targets and staff development goals are all set, against achievable deadlines – it moves the strategic planning on into business planning and also takes account of the organisation's legally constituted role and the partnerships it has built with other organisations)

• developing *detailed strategies designed to meet the targets over time*, sometimes jointly with other organisations, including through any planned change of direction, changes in operating systems or processes, or human resource policies

• building in *contingency plans* to cope with any unforeseen events or emergencies

• thinking about the *overall profile and the long-term effectiveness* of the organisation

• *implementing* the strategy and constantly *evaluating* it against the stated aims and targets.

The trend in business is towards assuming that top managers are the key human resource and that appointing, rewarding and developing what they have to offer will most effectively steer a company. This is a controversial idea since, in social work for example, the skills and knowledge of all the staff are vital. *Reward management* (Armstrong and Murlis, 1994) is a fashionable term for using pay and perks ('financial and non-financial rewards') to offer incentives as a motivation to staff. It tends to be opposed in strongly unionised sectors of employment, including the public sector, where collective bargaining has traditionally obtained advantageous terms and conditions for staff and where parity and teamwork highly prized. Reward management can and should have its own forms of equity and transparency built in, but there is no doubt that it undermines nationally agreed pay rates and employment conditions. Nor do all individuals respond equally well to it. A particulary conscientious worker, for example, may be offended at the idea that a bonus is considered necessary to motivate him or her to do a good job.

From strategy to structure

Following on from the examination of organisational structure in Chapter 2, we can now revisit this concept, building the idea of strategy into organisational flexibility in place of the more traditional forms. Mintzberg (1979) has written about five ideal types:

- the *simple structure* (a small family firm where the manager can respond rapidly in person and does not need much delegation or hierarchy)
- the *machine bureaucracy* (e.g. a conveyor belt operation with a strict hierarchy)
- the *professional bureaucracy* (social work traditionally followed this model, as we saw in Chapter 2, with social workers owing as much professional as organisational allegiance and enjoying considerable autonomy).

The two newer forms are:

- the *divisionalised form* (a large company with many divisions, each with budgetary targets but autonomy in meeting them; since the purchaser–provider split, SSDs may look more like this)
- what Mintzberg calls the '*adhocracy*' because it is an organisation that has no standard product or service but consists of project teams that come together to respond to new opportunities; some groupings of freelance trainers and consultants operate like this in social work, picking up contract work, sometimes with a central core of employed staff.

Handy (1995) has referred to these organisations with *ad hoc* task forces as 'shamrock organisations' because there tend to be three groups of professional, contractual and occasional staff allowing the organisation to enlarge as it wins new contracts and then to disband teams that are no longer needed. Some voluntary organisations providing services under contract to SSDs operate like this, as do the research activities of social work staff groups in some universities, where research assistants may come and go with the flow of work. Indeed, voluntary organisations have a long history of operating with a threefold structure consisting of a core of paid directors, professionals and administrators, contract staff running projects or fund-raising, and a flexible fringe of part-time volunteers.

Over time, these looser structures can lose their innovative edge or organisational clarity. They may need reorganising around the edges – for example, to regularise the way various projects relate to purchasing organisations while also maximising autonomy in developing new forms of service that are responsive to the expressed needs of users. Overall, though, Handy (1995) considers that the pace and unpredictability of change will demand managers who can think unconventionally and organisational forms in which they have freedom of movement. As well as shamrocks, he highlights the rise of 'federal' structures. Again there are charities that have run along these lines for many years, for example Women's Aid and Age Concern which have autonomous local groups or branches, together with an umbrella organisation nationally (a 'federation') that provides advice, support and an element of co-ordination, as well as undertaking national lobbying and campaigning. Local authorities have increasingly decentralised and sub-divided their functions but they have not federated because they are legally obliged to retain central financial and operating control.

The current trend in local government is towards 'joined up services' with one corporate grouping drawing all key policy-making back into the centre. This might lend itself to some of the newer organisational forms in future, better able to adjust to the identification of wholly new ways of meeting need and the falling from favour of old-style ones. Handy also identified a 'triple I' organisation based on *information, intelligence* and *ideas*, with executives, professionals and specialists all committed to constant learning and working in more egalitarian design or project teams, not as managers and subordinates. This feels a long way removed from new managerialism in social services but, again, there are voluntary bodies that work more along these lines – for example, those that come together to allocate new forms of funding or to develop new services.

In social work, we need clear strategy and structure but we also have to look beyond them. As we saw in Chapter 3, top down management has serious limitations. In the 'caring services', people are everything. The need to listen to staff and make them feel valued and involved – indeed, to regard them as the organisation's greatest asset – will come about only if responses to change and the means adopted to meet the objective of delivering high quality services also have well developed 'bottom up' components. This involves remembering that staff are individual people not depersonalised 'posts', that they have a variety of skills and strengths and that they need motivating in different ways to give of their best. As we shall see in Chapter 6, however, no one feels motivated unless there is a supportive environment which is free of harassment and bullying and is committed to tackling racism and sexism, as well as to staff care and development needs. The principles of natural justice are also important in ensuring that staff's concerns are seen to be dealt with promptly and always given a fair hearing.

Operational planning

Logically, operational plans should be based on strategic ones; they should be short-range (about one year) and spell out specific goals. Aims and objectives should be positive, motivating, and written in terms that each member of staff can identify with and apply directly to his or her own work. They should also give a sense of constant improvement through being prioritised and including a progression from the more immediately achievable to those which, though realistic, will require effort. There should be measurable outcomes set against defined timescales.

The fact that Britain's human service provision is still largely funded by national and local taxes and by charitable giving, even though charging for services is a growing trend, has meant that there has not traditionally been the same imperative for staff lower down the organisation to be involved in explicit budgetary planning and cost controls as in a commercial organisation that must compete in the market place. All this has changed, of course, with the separation of purchasing and providing functions and the increasing move to a mixed economy of welfare.

Operational planning now forces us to focus on these key resource issues, as well as on levels of demand for each service, its quality standards and the consideration of alternative ways of providing care. For instance, home care organisers might be asked to check current and short-term plans by asking questions related to specific topics, as shown below.

1. *Care management*: What are your guidelines for undertaking needs assessment – that is, what do you assess and how is this done? When do you review user needs? What are your plans for the construction, monitoring and review of care packages?

2. *Organising your section*: Are you integrated with others in the department? Have you decided on the sizes of workload for your home care managers? Have you delegated sufficient authority to ensure flexible use of the home care workforce?
3. *Resources*: Do you have a financial plan which includes the development of the service over the next year? Have you decided how you will allocate resources across your catchment area and communicated this to your budget holders?

Checklists such as this demonstrate that operational planning is concerned with continuous monitoring and evaluation of service provision. It is obvious, too, that it is based on costing. Because planning and finance are so inextricably linked, a brief outline of how budgets are formed and controlled follows. In fact, although there has been much talk of 'devolved budgets', it is still generally the case that senior managers agree and monitor resource allocation and expenditure. There has not been the devolving downwards of responsibility that was heralded. Nevertheless, spending does have to be checked and accountability for it demonstrated by front line staff and first line managers in a way that previous generations of social workers simply would not have recognised.

Budgets

The process of drawing up a budget, for a department or a field of work within it, starts by examining the cost of maintaining existing provision and meeting new demands, whether these result from demographic changes (e.g. increasing numbers of older citizens) or new initiatives planned in previous years (such as a new day centre which opens in the financial year under review). Managers have to contain spending within overall financial targets which, in turn, are balanced against all the other commitments of the organisation. Budgets for each service are sub-divided under various 'heads'; thus the cost of residential care, for example, has heads for everything from staff wages to postage costs. Within this, some costs will be 'fixed' and inescapable, others will be 'variable' because volumes of service can be decided according to what can be afforded. 'Marginal' costs relate to one-off and special activities which are less relevant when planning the core budget.

The traditional form of budgeting is known as the 'incremental approach', so called because it builds up, year upon year, by considering the difference between the current and the proposed budget. Another name for it is 'historic budgeting' because it uses what has been spent in the past as the basis for what will be allocated in the future. With this model, the annual submission of a budget to a governing body uses the current year's budget as the building block on which the analysis of the next year's needs are based. Each line item can be accepted or reduced by chief officers or members of the committee who decide the overall resources likely to be available. Senior managers seeking adequate levels of resources to commission the services they need may tend to submit proposals beyond what they require if they know that in recent years amounts have been routinely cut.

When expenditure is running ahead of target, middle-rank managers may decide either to reduce the amount of service provided or to transfer resources from another area which is underspent. This is known as *virement*. To some extent, managers may be allowed to do this without going back to consult the committee that fixed the budget, providing the sums involved are not large, the virement is broadly within the same area of service, and monies are not transferred from the resources allocated for staffing costs.

Budgets are kept track of by means of computer print-out or by directly accessing a central finance system on screen. A major drawback is that the weekly or monthly totals will omit costs already committed (for instance, furniture on order) but not shown as incurred, making it easy unwittingly to overspend. The solution is to run a parallel system of *commitment accounting*, if necessary manually, to include these additional items of expenditure as soon as they are known about.

Another problem with the annual add-on, line-item budget is the fact that the focus is always on *specific costs* rather than on the value of service goals, the quality of particular projects and so on; goals are always in money terms with this approach. An alternative method is what is known as 'zero-based budgeting'. The idea here is that every subdivision of the service would start from zero each year and would have to rejustify its existence before the commitment of resources was allowed. Such a budget proposal would have to: describe the particular objectives of every separate service package, explain the benefits to be derived if funded, outline the consequences of not funding; give details of projected costs; and comment on the alternative ways in which the service could be provided and the 'value for money' represented by each (including what would happen if no service was provided at all). In theory, this would allow decisions to take priorities into account and would preserve any particularly effective projects; a rational approach such as this might also leave space for developing new programmes of care, although they would be in competition with other budget proposals.

More and more, the new role of social worker or care manager as answerable for budgetary expenditure demands a knowledge of accounting and operational planning. It certainly involves understanding both resource obligations and resource constraints and being able to appreciate, argue – and, where possible, reconcile – a range of divergent views, while balancing budgetary control against operational flexibility (Pettinger, 1997). Also, front line managers may find themselves in the role of decision-makers regarding the allocation of funds to commission services. Alternatively, they themselves may be working for an organisation whose survival depends on obtaining funds from local authority and other bodies through contracts or grants. There are separate skills involved in writing tenders for contracts and applications for grants which include being able to itemise a budget, outline service standards and highlight the benefits that the commissioner of the service would obtain by engaging this particular contractor.

Leadership role and style

What make a 'good leader?' If people are asked to list the qualities of the best and worst leaders they have known, they produce a list something like that given below. An effective leader:

• is *considerate*, friendly, supportive, fair and objective
• is *enthusiastic*, builds confidence and inspires others
• gives *credit* where it is due, and appreciates suggestions and ideas
• encourages *participation in decision-making*
• lets the staff know *what is expected of them*

- sets *specific goals*, measures progress and gives concrete feedback
- is aware of *training and development needs*, across the whole team or organisation
- keeps everyone informed about *decisions and developments*
- acts decisively in sorting out *work-related problems*
- *delegates* authority and responsibility appropriately
- emphasises the importance of each person working at *his or her best*
- devises *plans in advance*, including for contingencies
- makes sure that the team *co-ordinates its activities*
- enables the team to *get on with its work*
- establishes *contacts with outsiders* to promote liaison
- represents the team's needs to senior managers and is persuasive in *negotiations* with them for resources, staffing allocations and so on
- helps to settle *conflicts and disagreements* amongst the team members
- *takes action* if people do not pull their weight or if they violate the rules
- does all the above for the *administrative* as much as the *professional* staff
- ensures the team occasionally *has some fun together*, as part of wider team-building.

The items in this list clearly combine personal qualities with organisational knowledge, participative values, and task and process skills (note the conjunction of knowledge, values and skills, as in all good social work). The recurring aspects of a good leader, in any work setting, include particularly well developed 'people skills', problem-solving abilities, and the capacity to think systemically within accepted organisational structures and channels. There are theories about leadership that define these ingredients for success in terms of: *traits* or characteristics; *styles*; the ability to work within a particular *situation and environment* ('contingency theories'); and skill in carrying out the necessary *functions*, which span coping with the tasks, the team and the individuals the leader is called upon to manage (Pettinger, 1997).

Mintzberg (1973) has described the work of managers in relation to 10 roles, of which 'leader' is only one. He lists: three interpersonal roles – figurehead, leader, and liaison person with the outside world; three roles in gathering and passing on information internally and externally which he calls monitor, disseminator and spokesperson; and four roles relating to decision-making – those of entrepreneur, disturbance-handler (again internal or external, dealing with conflict or unexpected change), resource allocator and negotiator. The effective manager will combine all of these roles into an integrated whole, resolving any 'role ambiguity' or 'role conflict' and emerging with 'role confidence', whereby the individual takes pride in the role held and feels his or her self-worth to be confirmed by it (Pettinger, 1997).

Theories of leadership effectiveness also attempt to engage with the best 'style' to adopt under particular circumstances. They are concerned with discovering what natural leadership style we have and then learning to adapt it, as the occasion demands, so as to deal effectively with the *task* (the job to be done) as well as the *people* dimensions (satisfying the needs of the team members and of the individuals within the team), bearing in mind the *situation* which faces us. And, these days, we want to keep the 'customer', or service user, to the fore. As we have already seen with organisational structures and management principles, it is impossible to dictate what works best overall or to give one magic set of answers. Everything nowadays is down to flexibility.

Leadership variables include *trait* (any personal qualities we may have, such as persistence), *style* (for example, person-oriented or task-oriented, laissez-faire, authoritarian or democratic) and *situation* (the set of circumstances facing the leader or manager at the time). Leadership style can be conceptualised according to characteristics such as the degree of emphasis on each of the following:

- *compliance* with rules and procedures (though, increasingly, there is an expectation that these will be internalised – i.e. that the manager will believe in them, not just carry them out)
- *delegation* of responsibility to others
- *standards* set and monitored in all aspects of the work
- *rewards* for excellence rather than criticism and blaming, or rewarding on grounds of seniority, favouritism or cronyism
- *distance* maintained through managerial aloofness or reduced over time by building warm and trusting relationships with team members.

Managers can work out their own managerial style by asking themselves whether (in accordance with the above list) they have arrived at a point where:

- procedures are sufficiently well organised that people can be left to get on with their jobs but not so constraining as to hinder initiative
- staff are encouraged to take responsibility and 'own' their own decisions and initiatives without too much risk of mistakes; what are the manageable and comfortable limits on delegated power?
- standards are set too high or too low (or not set at all)
- everyone is regularly praised, and rewarded and criticised fairly
- there is a friendly and comfortable working atmosphere in which people can ask for support or advice when they need it.

Clearly, these aspects of style interact. In a high-risk job like social work, people are not comfortable if there is too little monitoring of standards or too few checks and balances on procedures, but they also resent being treated like technicians rather than professionals. Above all, the manager has to try and understand how each team member (for a senior manager, this will be the management team) perceives their level of involvement with the organisation and the work in hand. The ideal is to maintain a balanced focus on both task and people aspects of the work (see Chapter 7 for more comment on masculine and feminine styles of communicating and working with others), with the ability to move along the autocratic–democratic axis as occasion demands. To exemplify this idea, Figure 4.2 displays a spectrum of seven behaviours or leadership styles. Moving from left to right, the area of freedom for the team increases.

Leadership behaviour, then, is not just a question of a fixed personal style. With practice, it should emerge from the balance of role, style, task, relationship with the team and the situation being faced. If you are a well established team leader, trusted by the group, you will be able to adopt a democratic stance, encouraging the team to be highly participative, and be able to delegate with confidence. On the other hand, if you are a new leader or one with a poor relationship with the team and if you have no real influence, then your position will be a difficult one, even more so if the task is unclear

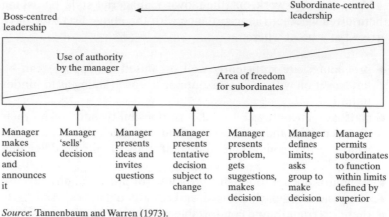

Boss-centred
leadership

Subordinate-centred
leadership

Use of authority
by the manager

Area of freedom
for subordinates

| Manager makes decision and announces it | Manager 'sells' decision | Manager presents ideas and invites questions | Manager presents tentative decision subject to change | Manager presents problem, gets suggestions, makes decision | Manager defines limits; asks group to make decision | Manager permits subordinates to function within limits defined by superior |

Source: Tannenbaum and Warren (1973).

Figure 4.2　*Continuum of leadership behaviour*

or highly complex. In such circumstances, it would be wise to focus on the job, not your relationship with the team, and, even if you normally prefer a democratic style, the situation may require for a time that you tell people what to do whilst simultaneously trying to persuade and motivate the team towards goal achievement. As with so much in management, flexibility is the key.

Hersey and Blanchard (1982) have further pointed out that another situational variable is the *maturity of the team*. The concept of 'maturity' is a nebulous one, but a group's psychological maturity might be portrayed, for instance, by their willingness to help one another. (In groupwork with service users we recognise the strengths of a developed group as one where there is strong commitment, open relationships and balanced perspectives.) On top of this is task maturity (that is, being able to do the job). Working with a defensive team, for example, a person-centred style may not work and you will be in trouble if you have only one leadership style to call upon.

Using power responsibly

A common classification into seven bases of power is that set out by French and Raven (1959) and modified by later writers:

- *reward power* (the ability of the leader to give and take away praise, funding, promotion, resources and so on)
- *coercive power* (the ability to reprimand and discipline, also to withhold career development opportunities)
- *legitimate power* (conferred by position or office held in the organisation; a Weberian idea – see Chapter 2)
- *expert power* (the use of superior skills and knowledge)
- *referent power* (this is closely tied to charisma, where others desire to seek the leader's approval).

To this list might be added *information power* (also called 'gate-keeper power') where we become interested in having the information which others keep to themselves, and *connection power* (through being seen to have close contact with influential people within the organisation).

As well as asking themselves which of these kinds of power they now possess (and what kinds others in the hierarchy are using), new managers also have to question the degree of *perceived power* they hold and whether others are vying for it. Informal leaders, for example, act as if they are powerful even though they do not have the organisational authority to back them up, while some actual, appointed leaders allow others to usurp their influence by defaulting on the exercise of their authority and responsibilities. Furthermore, power does not only operate 'top down'. Everyone in the team has access to negative power, for example, which can be operated through means such as deliberate absenteeism, delaying urgent work, or stalling in the implementation of improved practices. The effective manager may well have to tackle some of these phenomena, perhaps as part of changing the overall culture of the workplace.

Power can, then, be both used and abused. If managers are to harness their position in order to become effective leaders, it is vital that they do not exploit their authority and that they are particularly aware of the ethical aspects of decision-making. The responsible use of power cannot be taken as given merely because we work in the human services. As social workers, we are still capable of being less than humane in our approach to each other and to service users. There are also deviant ways of acquiring power and exercising it. Some people may gravitate to senior positions in order to fulfil a need to control others; they are more likely to be overbearing and bullying in manner, and to manage by fear rather than by mutual respect. Equally, others do not feel comfortable holding power and may attempt to minimise what it means, perhaps leaving all decisions to the team and counting on group norms to maintain standards. These are stereotypically masculine and feminine styles, though both men and women can be observed operating in either style (see Chapter 7).

For the manager who wants to make a show of his or her power, the contemporary fascination with surface appearance opens up all the possibilities of power dressing, carrying the computerised personal organiser, and so on. Some of those who start off with status disadvantages in terms of gender and/or skin colour may be all the more likely to appear in slick business suits with large shoulder pads because they know they have to become visible and credible to more traditional managerial colleagues. But there are more subtle ways of winning respect and increasing our influence.

For those who are underselling themselves in the power stakes, it may feel more acceptable to think about increasing your influence rather than increasing your power. With subordinates, you can encourage others to do what you want by creating certain norms and by carrying these through with personal authority (thus using 'normative', rather than 'coercive' or 'remunerative' power). With those above you in the hierarchy, personal presentation is still an issue but it has to mean creating a style that suits you, not necessarily wearing dark suits or high heels. It also involves correcting negative verbal and non-verbal signals, such as not apologising whenever you start to speak, not fiddling nervously, and making eye contact more often. Some of the more job-oriented ideas for increasing personal influence within the organisation include:

- consciously taking on key roles or projects, while
- saying 'no' to things that will have no personal pay-off and should be done by more junior people
- joining and fostering influential networks
- making presentations at high-profile meetings
- taking office in key groups
- documenting your achievements
- developing skills that other people need to call upon
- taking advantage of presentational and personal effectiveness courses

- assisting your team to perform to a high standard and win accolades
- doing favours for people so that you can call on them in turn when you need help, and
- being flexible (which means only ever standing on your dignity or holding to a fixed stance if your position would otherwise become untenable).

These are all ways of becoming more visible and hence more influential without overstating your claims or being underhand. In these days of multiagency partnerships, it can also be a good idea to be the person who undertakes key aspects of liaison, though not if this makes you so specialised that you become marginalised and dispensable. None of these suggestions is restricted to SSDs or even to paid posts. The trustee or volunteer committee member of a charity, for example, may be equally interested in developing a power base from which to influence the future direction of the organisation's work.

In order to have time to think in this broader way and to take on the additional tasks involved, it is vital to be able to *delegate*. Otherwise you are likely to become bogged down in the day-to-day work of the team in inappropriate ways. The essentials of delegation include:

- creating a culture of *participation and mutual respect*
- using *staff development opportunities* to maximise the abilities of all team members
- *trusting staff* to exercise those abilities
- building this gradually into *career opportunities* for people so that they will welcome the new experience and the extra work
- providing considerable *support* when people take on a new task and reducing this to some extent over time
- building in *checks and balances* so that people cannot run on too far without errors or poor decisions becoming visible (e.g. regular reports to you, careful monitoring of all forms of management information by other relevant people)
- allowing people to *learn from misjudgements* without suffering unreasonable penalties (or they will never try again), and
- *never doing other people's work for them.*

The one exception to the latter 'rule' is where you discover someone in immediate danger or an unsafe working practice that requires instant rectification. Burton (1998) gives the example of mopping the dangerously slippery floor in the residential home lavatory yourself, assuming the person who normally does it is not immediately to hand and free to do it, *before* you put your manager's hat back on and go to find out how it came to be left like that and how this can be avoided in future.

Overall, it should be the end product and the performance standard that matter, not (within limits) how the staff member achieves these – they may well have a very different working method to your own and should be given the freedom to pursue it. You can reassure yourself along the way by structuring in progress reports. Delegation can fruitfully build on staff's own interests but should also challenge people to learn new knowledge and skills; otherwise, people will not develop in the rounded way that will equip them to seek advancement in due course. (It is noticeable, for example, that people tend to ask to go on courses about things they already know about and can do well – i.e. in their areas of special interest, not their areas of weakness where new learning might help most.) In delegating you are, after all, also mentoring and coaching more junior employees. Finally, the more people who can see a task through as a self-contained project, and understand its relevance to the organisation's work as a whole, and the more they can draw on information and guidance from the sources you yourself would have used, the more they will feel empowered to do a good job and the more the whole team will benefit.

Although there will always be business conducted and decisions reached in the gents' loo or the locker room (where not all of us can go), and although sub-cultures and cliques to which we do not all belong and unspoken rules and expectations we are not all party to will persist, it should still be possible to be noticed doing a good job and to be rewarded for it. Perhaps it is akin to presenting yourself at work like a walking CV – not afraid to say what you have done and what you are good at. And it is often to the benefit of the team and the organisation when a manager does well; remembering this may make it easier to adopt a less self-effacing style.

Some of the situations in which people do acquire too much power or abuse it are where:

- there are loose supervision arrangements and few external controls
- an organisation is undergoing change (decentralising its operations, for instance) and is temporarily destabilised
- control is gained over critical resources, be it by one manager having sole say over allocating resources, or an administrator holding the key of the stationery cupboard
- the employee is an expert in a needed field and does not share this knowledge (for example, the mystery surrounding computer know-how); and
- obligations are created so that others feel beholden.

The manager who observes an abuse of power by another may find it easier to start by considering how to alter the situation in which the power has been assumed or has apparently become legitimised – for example, by analysing it according to the above list, rather than by personally confronting the individual concerned as the first course of action taken. The ideas in Chapter 3 on 'managing change' might also be useful, for example in seeking allies who have noticed the same problem and who would work with you to change it, or in considering what aspects of the current situation are maintaining the status quo and which could be used to change it (as in a force field analysis). Where there is harassment of staff or an unacceptable response to service users, however, the more formal channels to take action against the person concerned may have to be used straight away. It may be helpful to think about this in terms of 'standard', 'discretionary' and 'forbidden' areas of power. There is a difference between those people who are doing a job we do not happen to like, those who are exercising their room for manoeuvre in slightly unpleasant ways and those who are actually perpetrating some form of misconduct. It may also be possible to seek confidential advice from a human resources manager without naming the person you are concerned about, before deciding what to do. As soon as you do voice dissatisfaction about someone or take action against them, you may begin closing down some options and opening up others – so it is as well to have thought things through in advance.

The use of *persuasion* deserves a final word as a potent (if overlooked) skill when used responsibly. Persuasion relies on: being able to communicate effectively; knowing how to monitor and control one's own tone and behaviour; monitoring and thus maximising other people's understanding and acceptance, including by finding out what matters most to them; and consciously conveying a relaxed, calm manner. It is often possible to influence others, including in multidisciplinary settings, by offering a single, firm proposal (you have to know what you want before you can get others to want it); building on this, and coping with disagreements like 'It won't work' in an open way; welcoming the voicing of concerns by other people and talking them through fully, not blocking their expression; testing for understanding; giving and seeking information; and summarising the points which are being made by all parties. Again, we saw many of these ideas in Chapter 3, in relation to managing change.

Leadership tasks

Control

The task we tend to think of as synonymous with management is that of controlling the work of others on behalf of the wider organisation. To the newly appointed, first-time manager, this will be an unfamiliar responsibility – sometimes more difficult than just getting on and doing the work oneself. But, of course, this is not possible because there is not time to do both. The number of staff who report directly to the manager is called the 'span of control' (see Chapter 2). The more rigid the hierarchy, the smaller the span, but 'leaner, fitter' organisations have been shedding middle-tier managers, thus making spans wider. In social work, managers do not have the freedom to appoint deputies to help them with their workload, but they can feed into reviews of staffing structures where there is clearly too much work to do and they can also seek to have staff seconded or allocated to carry out particular projects where important tasks would otherwise not get done.

Of course, the manager is not left to tell others what to do on a whim. He or she will be working within all manner of mechanisms and requirements established by the organisation to ensure that work is overseen effectively. It is well worth getting hold of all available written procedures, policies and other documentation, as well as identifying the key administrators within the organisation who are responsible for their oversight and who can advise on when and how to apply them in practice. The normal internal monitoring channels will include budgetary forecasts, reports and audits, management information on service delivery and staffing matters, feeding into committee reports on specific topics, feedback to one's peers and one's own managers, conflict resolution mechanisms (see below), and periodic overviews of particular areas of work (Pettinger, 1997). There are also external procedures to which all managers are answerable. For local authorities, these include joint reviews by the Social Services Inspectorate (SSI) and the Audit Commission (Jones, 1999c) and, for the private sector, inspections by registration and inspection units. These are currently run by the local authority but their functions are soon to be taken over by the General Social Care Council in England (Brand, 1999), the Care Council for Wales, the Scottish Social Services Council and a regulatory council in Northern Ireland. There will be commissioners with jurisdiction over children's homes, homes for older people and adoption services, whose aim will be to establish a higher and more consistent baseline standard of services. Consultation with local service users and carers constitutes a growing part of all such exercises, with service users also involved as inspectors, for example by the SSI, and due to be well represented in membership of the new Councils, as well as more fully consulted by local authorities as a key element of establishing 'Best Value'. Partnership with health, education, housing and the voluntary sector is also increasingly emphasised.

In social work and social care, within an overall project to 'modernise' social services (Department of Health, 1998a), regulations and standards are increasingly being set nationally by central government. The ultimate sanction for serious or persistent failure to meet them, under the Local Government Act 1999, is Government intervention to hand responsibility for running the department to, for example, a neighbouring local authority. This inevitably creates additional pressures on managers in expecting all staff to meet externally determined requirements and monitoring the extent to which this is achieved. It also means that managers nowadays are less often involved in setting standards from scratch, except in relation to particular quality or change management initiatives (see Chapter 3), and more often in measuring continuous improvement against externally determined criteria.

In the field of child care, for example, the governmental 'Quality Protects' initiative is based on published national objectives that local authorities are required to meet, together with more detailed sub-objectives and exhaustive performance indicators to measure outcomes for children. These tend to be numerical in nature, aiming, for example, to reduce child protection re-registrations by 10 per cent between 1997 and 2002, to increase by half the number of children in care leaving school with at least one GCSE pass, and to minimise the waiting time in care before adoption (Department of Health, 1999).

While no one would question the Government's aim of improving children's life chances, it is questionable whether such a mechanistic and regulated approach can truly respond to the qualitative aspects of their lives. For example, a rush to get children adopted can lead to separating sibling groups and eroding contact arrangements (Mullender, 1999). The numerical measures themselves are also open to criticism; why, for instance, should children only be expected to gain one GCSE pass just because they cannot live with their own families (*Community Care*, 14–20 October 1999)? Similarly the checklists in the Looked After Children (LAC) documentation may impose middle-class norms instead of capturing the diversity of family and community expectations and of young people's own identities (Garrett, 1999). Standards in other fields, such as the Government's performance indicators for adult services and national service framework for mental health, are open to equivalent criticism, while the whole idea of setting standards as a way of improving working relationships between social services and the voluntary sector, in the form of a 'compact' (Thompson, A., 1999), is perhaps a little strained. Nevertheless, such a compact now exists and has its own benchmarks, which require the statutory sector, among other things, to build in voluntary sector participation in planning and delivering services, to make proper internal organisational arrangements to ensure that this happens, and to review and evaluate the results.

The expectations introduced across the whole of social services work in local authorities, in the form nf a Performance Assessment Framework (Department of Health, 1999) cover strategic objectives, costs and efficiency, effectiveness of service delivery, quality of services and access to them for both children and adults. Inevitably, all such attempts to regularise and standardise practice through national priorities and objectives create more administration and bureaucracy at the local level. For the manager, an emphasis on outcomes imposes fresh pressures and additional work because the changes are being introduced within a management-led model and, not least, because 'league tables' are now published as to how local authorities perform. However, this does at least offer clarity as to precisely what is demanded, where previously there may have been only a vague sense of 'must try harder' or of the goalposts shifting with every external inspection or audit. It does also generally bring an influx of resources – for example, the special grant for children's services payable for three years until 2001–2 – and, even if this is largely intended to pay for the information gathering and outcome measurement involved, these are vital to the organisation in tracking what is actually happening to children in the looked after children system. It is also an important advance that the social care workforce is now being regulated for the first time, with recognition of qualifications, codes of conduct for all staff and removal or suspension from the register of those considered unsafe to practise (Jones, 1999b). The imposition of central directives upon standards is therefore probably a mixed blessing.

Conflict resolution and dealing with disciplinary matters

It has been estimated that managers in business and industry spend up to 20 per cent of their time resolving conflict (Anderson, 1985). They are not alone. Staff in group care, for example, who work in close proximity with one another and often with service users' distress may encounter considerable conflict, too. Early theorists such as Weber and Taylor, whose ideas were examined in Chapter 2, viewed conflict as undesirable and believed that it destroyed morale. More recent thinking suggests that it depends on the amount of conflict and how it is managed (Fisher and Ury, 1983). Disagreements might assist problem-solving and hence should be dealt with rather than suppressed.

The organisation as a whole will have all manner of procedures and regulations to ensure equity and clarity for staff and service users, communication channels to air issues that need resolving, and managers in fields such as human resources who can advise on rights, precedents and problem-solving tactics. The agency will also have mechanisms in place for dealing with serious eventualities such as harassment, grievances and disciplinary matters. The line manager's role is to try and ensure that problems are dealt with without needing to go through any of these channels – and not simply by keeping the lid on any area of difficulty. Indeed, a manager can usefully spot trouble brewing by noticing that someone's performance is declining or that morale is low in the team. Higher than average staff turnover or sickness absence can also be indicators that all is not well.

The manager's first task on suspecting a problem is to diagnose where the disagreement or dissatisfaction is occurring and why. Most commonly, everyday falling out arises from personality clashes, personal–professional boundary transgressions leading to inappropriate behaviour, differing goals, questions of rewards and the pressure of work. Informal staff subcultures can also upset people through gossip, unhelpful attempts to set agendas or exercise authority, vying for influence, or oppressive attitudes towards others.

Your dual aims as a manager are to resolve the conflict if at all possible while maintaining your working relationship with the people concerned. If a manager responds to conflict by ignoring it or withdrawing, she or he loses on both counts since avenues of communication are shut off as people build up resentments. Alternatively, someone who forces a resolution can thereby lose their working relationship with those who are obliged to comply. Smoothing or suppressing conflict could maintain the relationship but does not fulfil the other aim of resolving it. A compromise or bargaining approach accomplishes the two aims but, later, the parties to the conflict may feel that they gave in too much. Thus securing an nutcome vhich resolves the conflict and keeps relationships intact requires positively confronting and being honest with people. To reach this optimal position, management texts exhort us to see conflict as an *opportunity* rather than a problem – frustrations have to be reframed as chances to 'clear the air'. Although we saw in Chapter 2 that this thinking has been around for a century or so, it may be easier said than done, especially for those of us brought up to be overly polite or to fear retaliation. Additionally, getting involved can be draining of one's energies for other tasks. But it *is* true that conflict signals the impetus for change, as we know from groupwork and crisis intervention with service users as well as from management experience.

When the opposing parties are brought together, the skills are, first, to reveal the issues. This is done by: deciding what the conflict is really about; distinguishing between people's values, wants and needs; working at getting people to understand one another's way of looking at things and to overcome their own anger in order to become empathic; and exposing discrepancies in definitions of the problem. Conflicts may arise from matters as wide-ranging as the organisation, the way work is organised within it, industrial relations, management style, or an individual's own values or beliefs (Pettinger, 1997). It may be ideological, career-related or job-related. Any conflict involves clarifying who are the parties to the conflict, what is actually at issue, the dynamics of the situation (including what has happened up to this point and what it will take to put it right), and the best way for management to respond in order either to remove the causes of the conflict, or to contain and control it so that it does not cause damage, or to harness it into some useful energy for change. Uncontrolled conflict is often a sign of poor management on a wider scale.

Having 'rolled out' the issues, the next tasks comprise:

- separating the *people* from the *problem*
- jointly teasing out multiple, creative options for *problem-solving*
- getting to the *real source* of the problem so as to eliminate it (for instance, great conflict ensued when residents in a home for people with learning difficulties were allowed to make their own drinks and sometimes had accidents; the issue was really a difference of staff opinion about dependence/independence goals)
- seeking a *'win-win'* outcome in preference to one with winners and losers
- knowing that every situation is *unique* and judging, therefore, whether to use the strategy of ignoring the conflict, or of smoothing it over, or of actively confronting it.

More serious is the process for formal disciplinary action outlined below. Disciplinary matters are handled by senior managers but it does no harm for first line managers to study procedures, since any staff member at any time could become the subject of, or witness to, an enquiry. Disciplinary action is most often intended to encourage an unsatisfactory employee to improve so as to safeguard the rights of service users and/or of other staff. It is clearly necessary for social work agencies to have such systems in place in order to ensure that standards are maintained, even though the whole area is an unpleasant one to tackle. The quasi-judicial nature of this duty may cause some managers sufficient unease for them to avoid taking action even when it is sorely needed. Or they may take inappropriate action such as continually sending the poor performer on courses, long after it is clear that this will not bring them up to standard, in the hope that someone else will take the decision to fail them and draw attention to their shortcomings. But, although social work is a 'caring profession', it is not a sign of caring to let someone struggle on in a post to which they are unsuited and in which they are causing harm to others. If attempts to solve the problem with a staff development or staff care approach (see Chapter 6) have failed, then disciplinary measures may be needed. Useful information on these matters is available from the Advisory Conciliation and Arbitration Service (ACAS), whose general approach is summarised below. It is important, above all, however, to work with your Human Resources Manager and to suggest that the employee concerned may wish to involve their trade union and/or professional association at an early stage.

The first stage is always to ensure that the individual *knows there is a problem* and precisely what it is, and to obtain his or her own view and explanation. In order to observe the principles of natural justice, senior managers should:

• ensure that they could not be accused of *bias or involvement* – i.e. that they are the right person to deal with the case
• gather all the *relevant information* promptly before memory fades
• take *statements* and collect *documents and records* of any previous warnings, together with evidence of their impact or lack of it and accurate dates wherever possible
• be clear about the *complaint* and make sure this form of action is necessary (in some cases the employee might be willing to accept internal or external help to overcome a problem within an agreed timescale, or may elect to resign)

- prepare carefully for any disciplinary interview and advise the person of their *rights*, giving time for the person initially to state and then to prepare to defend her/his case
- consider *adjourning* the hearing before reaching a decision on any penalty
- finally, inform the individual of the *decision* and the reasons for it, record the action and monitor its *implementation*.

Besides careful preparation for a disciplinary interview and making sure that an employee has time to prepare his or her case, managers need to arrange for a time and place where there will be no interruptions, and to ensure that someone takes notes and that, if required, an interpreter is available. It is important for the manager who is chairing the interview to start by explaining its purpose and how it will be conducted (even though it may not run to plan if feelings are running high) and to introduce everyone by name and role. Then he or she should state precisely what the complaint is about, obtain the employee's reply and any witnesses' comments, encourage general questioning and discussion (adjourning if necessary at any point), ensure that the employee has a full and fair hearing, and summarise the main points of the alleged shortcoming before adjourning to take a decision so as to allow proper consideration of all the matters raised. As chair, he or she should remain firm but polite throughout.

In the case of a minor misdemeanour, the individual should be given a formal oral warning and measures put in place to prevent a recurrence. Where the problem is more serious or there has been an accumulation of minor failings, a formal written warning should be given. Further misconduct or unsatisfactory performance may warrant a final written warning. It is because there may be these various stages to go through that it is important not to delay taking action and not to fail to record the salient details along the way. Suspension without pay and dismissal require further guidance, and, again, advice from the Human Resources Manager regarding rights on the termination of employment should be sought. In the personal social services, in the case of gross misconduct such as abuse of a service user or dishonesty, these stages may be leapfrogged in order to protect the public. An appeal can be made, however, at each stage of the procedure.

It is not surprising, perhaps, that at times staff are relieved when action such as this is taken as a way of trying to improve the performance of, or occasionally to remove, a difficult colleague. The aim, after all, is reformative, not punitive. One manager's team effusively thanked him for finally doing something. In another case, a skilled and talented employee decided not to leave her job when her harasser was formally confronted about his behaviour, at which time other problems with his work also began to emerge. Had no action been taken, the good worker would have gone and the problematic one would have remained, unchecked. More usually, though, the failing is a minor one and is unnoticed or 'carried' by the team, such as making too many private telephone calls, poor timekeeping, inaccurate word processing and so on. What do we do? Most managers dread having to tell someone off, while a few bullies get an inappropriate kick out of it.

The dynamics of oppression may make it more difficult to deal with these matters, not only in cases where the manager (being white and male, say) could be accused of oppressing the staff member (if black and/or female) but also where, for example, a black senior social worker or one who is considerably younger than the team member in question cannot assume that they will be respected or listened to. Being assertive is part of the skill of being an effective manager, rather than being passive/ aggressive in relating to team members. But, here too, there is an interplay with oppression. At one assertion training workshop, for example, a black woman officer-in-charge said she had tried being assertive in her job but had been misperceived as aggressive and awkward. A female senior probation officer at the same event had found that all her team had seen her as 'bossy' when she quite properly instructed a team member to bring records up to date.

Above all, one has to make clear not only the behaviour which offends and why, but what is expected of the worker in terms of improvement and of the team as a whole in terms of acceptable standards of performance. Not only is this fair to the individual employee, but groups, including teams, perform better when they see everyone treated alike, with no favoured colleagues and no mood swings on the part of the team or group leader that mean a behaviour is acceptable one day and not the next.

Nowadays, it is not only managers who need these skills but all workers. Implementing care plans, for example, may involve monitoring contract compliance on the part of a service provider or overseeing the work of a volunteer. If confrontation is necessary, first of all, try not to let your emotions get out of control and be aware of the other person's emotional state. In order to cope better, spend time thinking what you might say beforehand. Second, do not delay voicing dissatisfactions because these may then become disconnected from the specific behaviours which offend and appear as a personal hobby horse. The focus should be on specific, unacceptable standards and conduct of work. If you stick to the problem, stay firm, and do not make personalised attacks, then most staff can accept constructive criticism. Third, another important tip is always to be ready (once the initial problem has been stated) to explore what might help put things right. Again, most people can recognise reasonable suggestions as helpful, provided they are not in a state of anger or other heightened emotion at the time (which might make it preferable to return to the subject on another occasion). But take care to build into this an agreed means of monitoring future performance, with a stated timescale and so on, so that you are not 'fobbed off' with promises of improvement which are not then carried through. Fourth, an offer to help solve the difficulty, emphasising the person's good points, is useful, as is a statement that you do not harbour grudges. It is important for a manager to be seen to be consistent and fair; unequal treatment, as we have said, is soon picked up by the team.

One tip that can prove helpful if you are in conflict yourself is to offer the other person a way out, and never, ever to back them into a corner where their only options are to respond with defensiveness or attack, rather than through logical problem-solving. This technique is useful because it leads to a 'win-win' situation where the desired end is obtained without anyone losing face. It can be particularly helpful if you have to challenge someone more powerful than yourself within the organisation because it focuses on a *possible solution* rather than on an apparent challenge to their overall authority and presents them with a problem you have already half sorted out.

Finally on this subject, we do clearly recognise nowadays that there can also be very grave abuses perpetrated in social work and social care settings. Complaints procedures for service users, appraisal mechanisms to oversee the work of staff and much clearer performance standards generally in agencies (including where service providers carry out work under contract) are all intended to help gather the evidence of unsatisfactory performance where necessary. It is also the case that whistleblowers (Hunt, G., 1998) will occasionally quite properly draw attention to serious problems that somehow have fallen through all these safety nets and that they have certain legislative protection in doing so. Part of the manager's role may then be to ensure that the person who 'blows the whistle' does not come off worse than the person who has been causing the problems because others close ranks around the accused party. Some of the problems that come to light may actually have taken place some years before, as in child abuse scandals in residential care, when there was less oversight of standards and more scope for individual exploitation of position (and, of course, less awareness of the prevalence of child physical and sexual abuse) than is now the case. But abuses do continue to occur, and managers continue to have to face the stresses and strains of dealing with them, assisted, fortunately, by increasingly clear procedures.

Conducting meetings

Social workers often feel as if they spend their lives in meetings. If, after two or three hours we are left wondering what we have achieved, we will find ourselves wishing they were chaired more thoughtfully. In a recent instance encountered by one of the authors, for example, the chair had not ensured that all the necessary people were in attendance (or contacted for information in advance) and almost every item had to be deferred. In this way, he wasted the time of everyone there.

Social workers go to many kinds of meeting, such as daily work allocation meetings, ward rounds, or regular staff meetings. Occasionally, there are additional task group meetings set up for special projects. At one time, these acquired a particularly bad name, with workers saying of a problem that was inevitably going to be shelved: 'Let's set up a working party!' The advice offered below about more routine meetings, could also avoid some of the wasted effort amongst *ad hoc* groups. It applies whether there is a fixed chair for every meeting (e.g. the team leader chairing team meetings) or whether a group has decided to rotate the chairing role.

As an effective chair of a meeting, you will do all of the following:

1. Ensure that a meeting is *really necessary* and that the matters could not be resolved by a memo, a circular with a response deadline, telephone or e-mail, or by seeing one or two key people separately.
2. Make sure the *size* of the meeting is workable for the intended purpose; about 12 people is a maximum if everyone is to take part (otherwise, scan the agenda to see if everyone has to be present for each item).
3. Indicate on the agenda the *function* each item is intended to fulfil (for example, 'for information', 'for discussion', or 'for decision').
4. Make the agenda items *self-explanatory*, not vaguely stated as, say, 'Budget'.
5. Order the items in such a way that the meeting starts with a lively concern and, if possible, ends with one which *unites* the group.
6. State the *starting* and *ending* times.
7. *Circulate* the agenda and brief supporting papers, neither so far in advance that people lose them nor so late that they cannot read them in time for the meeting.
8. State at the outset what the meeting *intends to achieve*, assist in achieving these goals, and keep your own intervention to a sentence or two on any item.
9. Always start the meeting *on time*.
10. Give prior thought to the *order* of agenda items. Meetings, however briskly chaired, are more likely to give full attention to items in roughly the middle two quarters of the agenda (and to get their collective teeth, somewhat randomly, into one or two of these as they gather steam); they are not warmed up for the opening items, and tend to rush through the last ones in order to get finished. The smart chair can select those issues that need the most consideration, as against others that need wide-scale agreement without protracted debate (for example where they have been 'done to death' in previous meetings).

11. Give *clear signals* that 'We must move on' or that it is someone else's turn to speak when any one person hogs the discussion.
12. Ensure that everyone *understands the issues*, writing on a board or flipchart (or asking someone else to do so) if the item involves details or needs analysing into separate parts.
13. Briefly *summarise* at the end of each item to help with minute-taking and show what has been achieved; also to agree what action is to be taken, by whom and by when.
14. Perhaps bring *senior people* in to speak only after a wide spread of views is known so as to prevent the inhibition of junior staff.
15. End by agreeing the date, time and place of the *next meeting* in people's diaries to save telephoning later (or do this earlier in the meeting if anyone has to leave).
16. Regardless of who has been assigned to write the minutes, still take responsibility for ensuring that they are both *accurate* and *complete* before they are circulated, consulting the minute-taker about any changes.
17. Use the *process* of the meeting as well as its *content* to good effect, for example by helping the team to gel or to collaborate, giving a sense of collective identity, producing shared ideas and plans, showing where contributions mesh, improving commitment to the decisions and underlining the manager's role as (democratic) leader.

Finally, because we are always being prompted to be efficient, effective and able to justify expenditure, it is sometimes worth reckoning up how much meetings actually do cost in terms of travel and salary of those attending. So late arrivals, low participation and constantly deferred items have to be tackled. On the other hand, it can be a false saving of time not to have an item out fully while everyone is present. The trick is in recognising which issues require team discussion, fresh commitment or change of direction so that they need to be brought to a meeting rather than circulated for information or for individualised feedback. As electronic communication takes on more and more forms, it is also worth considering whether an agency-based or interagency meeting is absolutely necessary or whether a three-way 'phone call, a pre-arranged telephone conference, use of a mailbase on e-mail, or even a video link-up could serve the same purpose.

Dealing with management information

Managing the day-to-day work of the team or organisation is only part of the story. Increasingly, it is recognised that an overview is needed over a period of time in order to plan ahead, meet targets, and improve on past performance where possible. This is where high-quality management information comes in. Only the manager who is provided with up-to-date statistics and also 'softer' information on every relevant aspect of work and organisational infrastructure will be in a position to gauge how well staff are doing and where improvements are most urgently needed. Prioritising spending and effort relies on this background picture.

When the topic of information is introduced, thoughts tend to turn immediately to computers and, certainly, producing the right statistical data, on time, and in a usable format is a key part of the process. But it is only one part. The existing software, or the uses to which it is put, may not be producing everything that the manager needs to know and, here, the manager's vision is essential in coming up with the right questions so that additional data can be produced – not all of it through crunching numbers, as we saw in the section on quality standards in the Chapter 3. Working closely with the computer staff and other information systems managers to discuss what can be learned is important, as is making good appointments to such positions. There are many stories of interviewers being overly impressed with technical qualifications and jargon so that they have ended up employing people who are either no good with people (computers attract such types) or who have no commitment to the overall work of the organisation.

In other words, information itself 'is a key resource which needs to be managed' (National Institute for Social Work, 1996), as are those who produce and use it. Statistics are not necessarily reliable just because they are on paper in black and white, and all information can usefully be 'triangulated' with other sources of data, as is done in research. Standards of accuracy will vary according to how information is gathered (and by whom). It is only in relatively recent years, for example, that front line staff have had to deal with financial assessments and budgetary targets, or that they have had to input these details straight into the computer. This may well be a better system than maintaining mountainous case files that frequently lacked or obscured basic facts. But computers can get things wrong as well as people, especially where a programme has gone through many modifications. Here again, a good computer manager can advise.

It is a good idea, too, to work with internal and external auditors so as to learn what they require. They will have a good understanding of what it is possible and reasonable to expect. At the wider level, authorities can club together to compare notes on baseline information so as to be able to set more realistic targets, charges and so on (*Community Care*, 14–20 January 1999, p.6).

Overall, then, it is important to manage information rather than being managed by it (Sapey, 1997). This requires strategic and principled planning, just as does every other aspect of organisational functioning. At all levels, including amongst basic grade practitioners, it is possible to move from seeing the data as a tool of management into regarding it as a helpful way of managing practice (National Institute for Social Work, 1996). This depends upon practitioners being given information outputs as well as being expected to make inputs. Staff themselves may come up with new ideas if they can see patterns of service take-up by different groups of users. They also always hold knowledge in their heads that is neither requested nor recorded by formal information channels. Sharing the management information picture with staff – the overall pattern of spending, the categories of users, priorities, needs and so on – and widening training beyond merely being able to input data into the computer, can generate fruitful discussion at the team level which may assist the organisation to rethink how effectively resources are dispensed and how user satisfaction rates can be increased.

A similar argument applies, of course, to sharing information with users and carers and with the wider public. Most people do not want to make unreasonable demands and they want to be proud of the local services which they help fund. Corporate newsletters telling residents what their council tax is spent on are commonplace but consultation exercises that feed into planning community care, children's services, community safety and ideas on Best Value could all be far more of a two-way information-sharing exercise than tends to be the case. These questions of ownership have always been present in social work and the possession of good quality information could just as easily open them up as close them down. There is no intrinsic reason why managers should hide behind their sheets of numbers.

For the new manager, the starting point is not to be afraid of the information systems or the data they produce but to regard them as being there to serve your needs and those of your staff and service users. You will require precise and timely information about types and levels of need, about the services available locally (in your own organisation and beyond), about costs, charges and budgetary targets, and about your staffing resources. You have a right to discuss the format in which this material is presented and the use to which it is put, as well as a responsibility to educate your team about gathering and recording information accurately and about the potential, in turn, for using it to raise standards and sometimes for making working life easier. A good example of this can be using the data as a basis to argue for extra resources or for changes of focus. It is still quite rare, for example, to record data on cases involving domestic violence and consequently even rarer to have designated staff in social services departments to deal with the issue. Another example could be feeding back to senior management how un-user-friendly the information systems commonly are, which is no incentive to staff to use them well, or any risks they may pose to user confidentiality when case records can be too freely accessed across the organisation.

Decision-making

Decision-making is the process of *choosing between possible courses of action* and is therefore something we all do all the time. In management it is of the essence, notably in relation to planning. Decisions may be arrived at unilaterally, by group or committee consensus, by a majority vote, through delegation, by a powerful minority, or by default – that is, where there has been no active process of decision-making at all and inertia determines what happens next. It can be very important to recognise that a decision to make no change, perhaps in the face of evidence that change is needed, is still a decision. Failure to listen to user demands for more appropriate services, for example, is a decision not to hear just as much as setting up an action group would be a decision to explore the potential for change.

However decisions are taken, conventional management literature recommends that they be based primarily on objective facts
and figures. In social work, however, it is important to emphasise
that values and assumptions always underlie the process. People's
value orientations might be theoretical (for example, knowledge
about child abuse might influence decisions about the allocation
of resources); economic (deciding if costs outweigh benefits); aes-
thetic (appealing to personal preferences for order and attractive-
ness); social (placing value on the quality of human relationships);
political (taking into account where power lies), ideological or religious (taking decisions according to beliefs about what is 'good'
or 'right'). In management decisions, just as much as in practice,
therefore, we need to be self-aware and able to analyse underlying
agendas.

A normative or rational procedure for decision-making would
take managers through the cycle of classifying and defining the
problem or issue → developing criteria for a successful solution →
determining the timescale and what process should be gone
through, including how participative this can be in the time available → gathering all the necessary information → generating
alternative solutions → comparing these potential solutions to
the criteria, including by means of a cost–benefit analysis where
necessary → selecting the most appropriate → implementing
the decision → monitoring the implementation → evaluating the
outcome(s). The resulting feedback would then be incorporated
into any new definitions of the problem and so on round the
cycle. The process should always include time for reflection (what
Pettinger, 1997, refers to as 'wait a minute'), so that the manager
can consider any 'knock on' effects, any implications for other
individuals or groups of service users or staff, relevant aspects of
agency policy and so on. It is easy to get 'bounced' into a decision
by someone who asks 'It will be all right if I just do this, won't
it . . .' and then to find that there are all sorts of unforeseen
consequences.

The trouble with all decision-making models is that they tend to
make it look as if the issue or problem is straightforward and not
beset with conflicting needs or values. The real world of social work
suggests that many decisions have to be made quickly, without all
the information being to hand and often in an atmosphere of uncertainty. We need only consider the dynamics of decision-making in

child protection cases to recognise how fraught the process can be. Management texts do recognise risk and uncertainty, and suggest minimising them by weighing up the relative impact of likely success and failure, involving those adversely affected in agreeing a way forward where possible (a care plan drawn up in partnership with parents; a redundancy package agreed with the workforce), and taking into account legislation and guidance, as well as the wider public interest (Pettinger, 1997). For larger-scale decision-making, the manager may be assisted by public consultation, establishing a sub-committee or working group, or buying in consultants to produce a report outlining all the options and a recommended solution. It may be necessary to keep relevant groups briefed along the way and perhaps to ensure they receive support if the eventual decision is likely to lead to major life changes.

Where concentrated and perhaps collaborative thought is needed, an amazing variety of *decision-making tools* can assist (see Leigh, 1983), such as decision tree analysis, brainstorming, the Delphi method and the nominal group technique, all of which are summarised below. Each of these is best suited to helping with one or more stages of the decision-making process so they can also be used in conjunction.

Superior decision-making might result from calling on the combined wisdom of a group. *Brainstorming* (see Figure 4.3) is an effective tool for creative problem identification. It involves a group of equal participants in face-to-face interaction, using free association of ideas to stimulate as many suggestions as possible. These are

Figure 4.3   *Brainstorming*

written down, as they come, without comment or discussion. The group then works together to draw out the common themes and to explore any points that 'don't fit' in order to see whether they also need to be part of the picture. This can lead to reformulating the problem. (These latter stages of the exercise are less well known than the first and are sometimes omitted, which simply results in an accumulation of free-floating suggestions that are not in usable form.)

Brainstorming can also be used to generate ideas on possible alternative solutions. A more sophisticated technique for thinking these through is *decision tree analysis*, a method of exploring alternatives with the outcomes that are likely to result. This can be useful when a manager has to choose between different courses of action in a climate of uncertainty, where parts of the decision rely on chance factors or on factors which lie beyond the manager's control, such as user satisfaction rates or changes in government policy. The 'decision tree' is so called because it resembles a tree (on its side). At any one time, two possible options represent branches off a larger trunk or branch, allowing a systematic appraisal of the opportunity each branch represents and the likely consequences of choosing it. It is an incremental model which allows each stage of decision-making over time to be plotted, illustrating the complexities of the choices involved, and the reality of what is ruled in or out once one option has been selected. Bamford (1982) illustrates a decision problem of where to make budget cuts; his simplified analysis is adapted in Figure 4.4.

The *Delphi* method (named after the Oracle at Delphi), unlike brainstorming, operates in an impersonal, anonymous setting in which opinions are voiced without bringing people together. The technique (see Figure 4.5) is really a way of collecting data from experts which is then coordinated through a central questioner (Bunning, 1979).

The *nominal group technique* (Ford and Nemiroff, 1975) is another creative procedure which combines the advantages of brainstorming and Delphi, using highly structured face-to-face group meetings. The group meets but members generate ideas and alternative choices separately. It has been found to be an effective tool in reaching decisions, the group voting on the range of choices before them while a coordinator records the decisions, as shown in Figure 4.6.

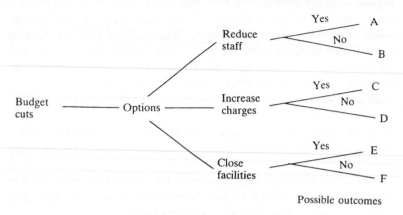

Figure 4.4 *A decision tree*

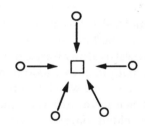

Figure 4.5 *The Delphi method*

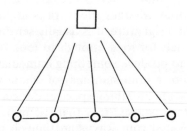

Figure 4.6 *Nominal group technique*

It is acknowledged that, when a team participates, it gives everyone a sense of ownership in the eventual decision. We would want to qualify this statement, however, in the following cases. First, where the team lacks trust, motivation and good communication, and where destructive relationships and attempts to control one another exist, then the team leader may not get true participation. Secondly, the other side of the coin is where the group is excessively cohesive and rarely engages in conflict, so that poor decisions may result due to 'groupthink' (Janis, 1971). People in such groups are afraid to offer a different point of view and the team leader consequently may have to act as devil's advocate and stir up differences of opinion in order to stimulate reliable decisions.

At the end of the day, the manager may have to make his or her own decision and live with the consequences, but it is generally useful to have explored a range of thinking beforehand.

Delegation

Delegating decisions and tasks is sometimes awkward when assuming a managerial role for the first time; decisions have to be made whether to delegate upwards, downwards, outwards or to keep the work oneself. At the same time, the middle manager in particular has to keep an eye on the work which is sent her/his way. If asked to undertake duties which have little relevance to his or her role, these may have to be 'fielded' back.

Delegating too much or too little irritates one's colleagues. It can be the result of pressure, or of not prioritising one's own workload demands. This may happen if staff get into a habit of pressurising you to do something immediately – you take the bait without giving yourself time to study whether the work is important. When staff rush in and ask for a signature, it is usually sensible to require that the document be left for long enough to look over it. If we ourselves are unable to produce something immediately, we may send a 'holding' memo or a brief summary of where we are up to, just to give ourselves some breathing space and show that we have not forgotten the task. It is a sad fact that the more you achieve the more will be delegated your way; sometimes it pays to let people know how hard you are working as well as with what good results.

The importance of delegating upwards merits emphasis; it is important to ensure that our own managers give us the support we need (and safeguard the organisation) by taking key decisions and reviewing potentially problematic issues or areas of functioning. The consequences can be disastrous if senior management are not kept informed of any major concerns. Once they know that a problem is brewing, however, they can draw upon the whole range of managerial resources to deal with it, take legal advice if necessary and generally ensure that the manager does not feel alone in tackling something quite beyond his or her remit.

As regards delegating downwards, this relies on having a good knowledge of staff members, including each person's level of competence, job description and current workload. It then involves weighing these against the task to be performed, the timescale and the standard to be achieved. In one sense, all management consists of delegation because the manager's role is to plan, co-ordinate and control the efforts of others. It is also sometimes necessary, however, to identify someone to take on an additional task or responsibility. Besides feeling uneasy at the first attempt at delegation of this kind, you might find that this does not result in the person doing what you have asked. It is no use just giving someone a job and then leaving them to get on with it; this fails to indicate the time by which tasks have to be completed, it ignores the need to check that the duties are clearly understood, and gives no scope for monitoring what progress is being made. It also overlooks potential resistance. You have to be very clear in saying what needs to be done and, if necessary, follow up a verbal request with a written memo. Also, when you delegate a decision you must allow for the following: (a) people have to work without interference (such as critical comments); (b) usually there have to be incentives for the person doing the work such as helping them build a CV or dropping another task to make space; (c) a delegated task must be accompanied by the time and resources to do it; and (d) delegated decision-making requires equivalent delegated authority. Although some of this takes more time initially, it is worth it in the longer term because it builds a team with whom the manager is able to share the work effectively. We have all known overworked managers who have failed to do this, at the expense of their own health and the well-being of their staff, not to speak of the work the manager should actually be doing in planning and forecasting, organising and co-ordinating. It is also good for employees to develop their potential and to become more involved in the agency's wider work. Satisfaction at work may be closely related to this kind of 'job enrichment' and opportunity for creativity.

Delegation always involves the manager retaining oversight of the task or project in hand and requiring progress reports; it depends upon a combination of *trust* and *control*. At all times, the buck still stops with the manager, not with the staff member – anything else would be abdication, not delegation of responsibility (Pettinger, 1997).

Conclusion

To say that an organisation is well managed implies *direction* and *intent*, from the overall vision and purpose at the top, through strategic and operational planning in the middle, down to effective decision-making in well chaired meetings at team level. Equally, one should be able to see a line of communication and feedback going back the other way so that the senior managers are in touch with what matters to staff and service users. Responsibility for public money, whether in the form of taxes in the public sector or charitable donations to voluntary organisations, deserves no less and only in this way will responsive and effective services take the place of outmoded practices that have persisted by default.

In the personal social services, even the best managers are only *facilitators*. It is a skilled and committed workforce which is the key to high-quality services. Chapters 5 and 6 will look, first, at the recruitment and selection of staff and then at staff appraisal, development and care policies, all of which should combine into maximising what the human resource – the people employed there – can offer to a well managed organisation.

5

Matching People and Jobs: Job Analysis, Job Description, Recruitment and Selection

Nowhere is the tendency towards tighter management in contemporary social work more in evidence than in recruitment and selection. Consequently, this whole chapter owes as much to texts from human resource management (McKenna and Beech, 1995; Torrington and Hall, 1998), as to social work sources or to the authors' own experience of appointing staff.

Selecting the wrong person for a post has implications not only for that individual, but also for those who use the services they offer and for their future colleagues. It may also be damaging to the organisation if the ill-suited postholder goes on to make errors, upset valued staff or incur complaints. In the worst case scenario, the considerable costs involved in disciplinary hearings, dismissal and renewed recruitment, even litigation, make improved selection procedures look cheap at the price. There are, of course, additional risks of attracting the wrong people in social work and hence further reasons for growing official interest in how staff are recruited (Warner, 1992; Support Force for Children's Residential Care, 1995; Kent, 1997). Direct access to children in some settings means that particularly careful screening of applicants and greater consistency between local authority employers are necessary, for example by enforcing the Warner Report (1992) recommendations. At the end of the day, all social workers are in positions of trust and have ample opportunities to exploit, rob or abuse vulnerable people.

To try and avoid mistakes, selection procedures have become more complex. There is a more managerial approach, with the emphasis on recruiting a flexible workforce to meet the organisation's constantly changing needs. To this end, a wider choice of *selection techniques* is deployed (with increased awareness of their respective strengths and weaknesses), and more use is made of outside agencies to recruit to top posts and to temporary positions. At the same time, recruitment handled in-house may be used as an opportunity to promote the organisation's image to the outside world as clear in its direction, concerned for the people it serves and a good employer.

When a post falls vacant or is newly created, there are a number of tasks to perform. First of all, a job analysis is required, on the basis of which are prepared a job description, a person specification (outlining the essential and desirable requirements for the post) and the advertisement. (Job adverts are also used nowadays as an opportunity to present the organisation's corporate image to the outside world.) In some organisations, the human resources management staff ('HRM', formerly known as 'personnel') undertake these tasks directly, in addition to their wider involvement in job evaluations, workforce planning, predicting the necessary skills mix, analysing turnover and so on. In others, the line manager or operational manager produces the documentation with backing from human resources to make sure that nothing contravenes industrial or discrimination legislation or agency policy, that best practice is followed, and that the highest calibre people are likely to be attracted without wasteful financial outlay. HRM staff are likely to deal with all the correspondence from enquirers and applicants, right through to formal notification of the outcome of selection, and to set up the shortlisting and selection procedures.

We will now look at each of the stages in turn.

Job analysis

Before a job description can be written, a *detailed job analysis* is needed, listing the duties of the post. In preparing this, it is clearly helpful to ask the departing postholder, or someone doing an equivalent job, to outline:

● all the work activities involved, procedures followed, and specific responsibilities

- whether the job requires any particular writing or computing skills, physical strengths or dexterity, or extensive reasoning and planning abilities
- whether detailed knowledge is required and, if so, in broadly what areas
- particular personal and interpersonal qualities needed – e.g. in working alone or in a team, or in building relationships
- working conditions – such as irregular hours or amount of travel involved.

The outgoing jobholder may also be asked to keep a *work diary* prior to leaving as a record of how time is actually spent in this post. His or her supervisor and immediate colleagues can also contribute to the job analysis in terms of what they expect and how the postholder will relate to them. The manager writing the analysis needs to work out whether any specific qualifications or experience are likely to be required for successful performance, and to check whether there are any agency policies on qualifications for this level of post.

Armed with the job analysis, and before filling the vacancy, it is wise to look at the *strategic needs of the organisation* and to ensure that this post, as currently designated, first, can be afforded and, second, can best meet the changing needs of the organisation – not only now but in the foreseeable future. In recent years, freezing vacant posts has been one of the few ways for social services departments to make sizeable savings. On a more optimistic note, we should remember that, with such a large proportion of the resources of a social work or social care agency tied up in its workforce, people leaving or retiring presents one of the rare opportunities to review how staff costs might be diverted into areas that need expansion or updating. Or there may be other ways to get the same work done – for example, through reorganisation, subcontracting, using the overtime budget or part-time staff or agency workers, or even volunteers (though, clearly, there would be industrial relations issues here). Or it may be that the post can be retained but is in need of significant rethinking to ensure that it not only meets current demands but is flexible enough to anticipate future ones. Finally, there may be people who need to be absorbed into posts, rather than looking for people from outside, either as a result of internal restructuring or because a contract has been won to do work formerly undertaken elsewhere. This latter situation is dealt with by what are known as TUPE (pronounced: 'chew-pea') transfers under the Transfer of Undertakings (Protection of Employment) regulations.

Job description

Following on from the job analysis comes the job description: a concise summary of information about *what the post involves*. This comprises an outline of the job, the responsibilities involved, the competences and skills required in the postholder and the broad terms and conditions of employment. It will include the job title, grade (which may be flexible, depending on level of experience, skill and responsibility), location in the hierarchy, experience and professional qualifications required, hours to be worked and pay scale. As such, it is a baseline both for the organisation's Human Resource Managers (in selecting the best person and determining their rights to remuneration, training, and so on) and for the employee, for whom it constitutes a written statement of what they can expect and what is expected of them. In preparing it, care must be taken to observe relevant legislation and EU directives on matters such as the minimum wage and working time.

Usually accompanied these days by further particulars in an information pack (increasingly in the form of a glossy recruitment brochure), the job description itself includes a short paragraph giving the general 'feel' of the job. When it comes to specifics, it has become more common to place the emphasis on the competences the applicant will need and the management standards expected than on the detailed tasks he or she will be called upon to perform, because these tend to change so rapidly. Although the broad responsibilities of the post are still normally listed, it is also common practice to include a 'catch-all' clause at the end, such as 'any other duties as directed by a supervising officer', so as to build in the possibility of *continuing development* and to avoid a situation where the employee could later use the job description to pin down the employer and resist change when restructuring was planned. (The eventual employee may be required to sign to say that he or she has understood and accepted the job description, again to avoid objections at a later date.)

Some employers have gone further, following Japanese management practices, and have chosen not to specify which team the person appointed will be joining or what precise post they will take up. This gives the organisation the utmost flexibility in moving people around as required. A social work example of this is for a large employer to undertake mass interviewing in the early summer when students are all emerging from local social work programmes, against vacancies which are bound to arise over ensuing months.

To sum up, a typical job description might include sections on:

- context of the job within the organisation
- job summary
- job content
- working conditions
- additional information
- the performance standards that the employer will expect (which, in social work, normally includes a commitment to equal opportunities and sometimes to anti-discriminatory or anti-oppressive practice).

Person specification

There are models available (Torrington and Hall, 1998, pp.224–5) as to what kind of things to cover in a person specification. In social work, the emphasis is on qualifications, competences and aptitudes, relevant personal attributes and any special circumstances that may pertain (such as preparedness to work shifts or unsocial hours), rather than on general interests, personal presentation (though there may be a dress code for appearances in court, for example), or physique (unless there will be heavy lifting or other physical activity). Referees are increasingly being asked to comment on sickness record because sick leave has become such a big issue for social services departments.

Against each of the headings selected as relevant, 'essential' and 'desirable' characteristics are listed. Like the job description, the person specification provides an important benchmark as to the qualities and qualifications the organisation needs and as to who should think about applying. Both shortlisting and interviewing are normally done against the person specification. Indeed, any major departure from it might give an unsuccessful candidate grounds to object. Where there is a surplus of candidates possessing all the essential characteristics, the desirable characteristics can be used to shortlist those who have more than the minimum to offer. It therefore makes great sense for applicants themselves to structure what they write around these characteristics, in order to help the selectors see precisely what they would bring to the post. This is especially helpful where there is a covering letter to write or a general section to complete, and not just a straightforward application form to fill in.

Recruitment

In social work and social care, recruitment is usually done through newspapers and relevant professional journals. The advert normally only includes: brief details of the organisation; the job and duties; key points about the personnel specification, such as qualifications required (e.g. Diploma in Social Work or equivalent, driving licence where relevant); the salary scale; and how to apply.

Lower-grade jobs are likely to be advertised in the local press and perhaps job centres, while professional and managerial jobs will appear in the social work and national press, with some employers feeling the need to use ever more eye-catching and upbeat advertisements to attract sufficient high-quality applicants from a nationwide catchment area. It can be good for the employer and the profession to bring people in from outside, so as to spread fresh thinking and new practices around the country. Internal applicants, on the other hand, offer the advantages of needing a shorter induction and, in the more senior posts, not having to be paid relocation expenses. Certainly, it is good anti-discriminatory employment practice to advertise all posts externally and it may also provide safeguards against the build-up of a negative culture – even an abusive network in residential settings (Levy and Kahan, 1991; Warner, 1992) – by ensuring that new and existing staff are not all previously known to each other or imbued with the same culture.

Social work qualifying programmes can have a very positive effect on their local social work agencies in attracting people from a distance who may afterwards settle in the area where they train, or those locally who want to combine a good education with a vocational opportunity. Regions without a local higher educational institution or further education college offering diploma and degree-level qualifications may feel its lack, and agencies have been known to work together to get a social work programme set up nearby, sometimes as an off-shoot of a more distant university. Over 90 per cent of the 4000 plus people emerging from social work programmes in the UK every year obtain social work posts within a relatively short time of graduating, giving social work education an exemplary employability record – as good as medicine's, for example. Social work has been slow to link workforce planning to the location and size of social work programmes, however, and it is notoriously difficult to build the independent sector into this equation, so recruitment shortfalls do occur.

Local authorities also use internal advertising ('job sheets') in case there are staff who are looking for a change of responsibilities, of working conditions (e.g. going part-time) or of location, whose needs can be met without being lost to the employer. In order not to discriminate indirectly against potential recruits from outside, however, this is typically combined with external advertising in some form.

Social work has a reasonably good record in attracting students and employees from minority ethnic communities, but more could still be done. Vacancies do not yet appear routinely in the black press or get actively disseminated through informal communication networks such as noticeboards in relevant community centres. A wider issue here is the status and image of the profession of social work which does not mark the pinnacle of 'making it' in Britain in the same way as becoming a doctor or a lawyer. When you add to this the fact that most people have relatively little idea what social workers actually do, there is a strong argument for publicising and promoting social work generally to whole communities, and not just to potential recruits through careers advice at school or in further or higher education. However, only jobs which are exempt from the provisions of the Sex Discrimination Act or the Race Relations Act can actually specify, respectively, the gender or ethnicity of the person sought (see Chapter 7).

A greater number of disabled applicants may be attracted if proof is offered at this stage of serious intent in adapting the working environment to their needs. Thus, for example, a minicom number can be provided for requesting application forms and these, in turn, can be made available in a range of communication formats.

In periods when the national vacancy rate is very high, employers may resort to additional means of attracting staff. Recruitment fairs or career conventions are now part of the national scene. They are attended by a combination of students in training, social work staff who may be thinking of changing employer, and a general interest audience who may be considering a move into social work or social care as a career. A high proportion of social work students are mature entrants who are making a career change, in fact. Again, this brings many strengths to the profession in terms of life and previous employment experience, be it in terms of another profession, such as teaching or the ministry, a previous job in a declining sector of heavy industry, or a move from a less demanding and consequently unfulfilling job in another employment sector.

Only top management jobs are likely to be placed in the hands of executive search consultants ('headhunters'), but there is an increasing use in social work of employment agencies which hold a pool of social work qualified staff to fill temporary vacancies. In some local authorities, and in some employment settings within authorities, the number of agency staff may rise to levels high enough to create concern about continuity of the service being delivered and the standards being met. In a residential home, for example, it may be very difficult for a floating body of staff to keep track of individual residents' needs or of the particular tensions and risks inherent in the context or the user group being catered for.

Shortlisting

The first question is who should carry out the shortlisting. Clearly, the initial consideration will be their roles in the organisation but the representativeness of the shortlisting panel (and of the interviewing panel later on, which may well be bigger), in terms at least of gender and ethnicity, is also relevant.

As has been mentioned, shortlisting is carried out using the job description and person specification as a profile of the ideal employee. This is a very fair way of proceeding. Indeed, the profession of social work and the local authority sector which is its largest employer are both normally rigorous in employment practices. Applicants are required, for example, to state if they have any personal connection with a member or officer of the council, must not make any contact which could be interpreted as canvassing support for their application, and may not serve as an elected member while holding professional office above a certain level in the same local authority.

The biggest variable in shortlisting is the total number of applicants – too few and it may be difficult to select high-calibre staff, too many and a time-consuming and hence costly process ensues of attempting to construct a shortlist of manageable size. The emphasis (perhaps in the face of high levels of unemployment and hence heavy rates of applications in some employment sectors) has moved away from undertaking an initial screening to rule people out (which may allow arbitrary and perhaps unlawful criteria to creep in after the essential criteria have been met) and towards looking for the positive aspects, the strengths in each application that argue for that person to be included. Some big businesses are even using computers or automated multiple-choice telephone responses to pick out applicants who merit moving through to the next (human) stage of selection. Once the essential points are covered, the criteria that were listed as 'desirable' may become crucial, as may other job-related issues such as overall approach and vision and length and range of experience. A panel may each draw up a personal shortlist on this basis and then construct a final one consisting of those applicants about whom everyone agrees and, if necessary, a sufficient number of others about whom consensus can be achieved.

The only dangers to be avoided are the inclusion of compromise candidates who offend no one but excite no one either, and the exclusion of maverick candidates who approach a job in a way no one else had thought of but which may be good for the organisation. A typical shortlist might consist of from three to six people, unless there is more than one vacancy to be filled. A good rule is to include no one on the shortlist who would not be really good in the post – i.e. no one who is just 'making up the numbers'. Either the interview will waste their time and yours or, worse, they may end up as the compromise appointment, thus losing the real strengths that others could have offered, in one area if not in all.

Applicants for local authority posts are typically required to present themselves to the shortlisters through the medium of a printed application form with standard headings (though commerce is beginning to move towards 'talking CVs' conveyed by digital camera and computer, and also personality tests conducted through the internet). Management trends in local government have meant that employers are keen to control the process of recruitment and selection, at the same time as streamlining it and saving time, by requesting information only as it relates to organisational needs. While the freestanding CV may give the candidate scope to present themselves in their own terms, and to show their abilities with computer presentation and writing skills, it is much more difficult for shortlisters to know whether the candidate had help with its production, perhaps even from a professional CV writer. Also, the only reliable way to obtain the same range of information from every applicant is to specify this in the application form, which also then becomes part of the record held by the employer on the individual eventually recruited. Obtaining information in a standard format and without gaps is also important in respect of detecting those with a history of abuse (Support Force for Children's Residential Care, 1995) or if a 'biodata' approach is to be employed in systematically analysing all applicants (Audit Commission, 1995).

There are equal opportunities issues involved in aspects of the information which may be collected. Some potentially sensitive questions can be defended. Current salary is declared since the new employer would, in a normal career progression, usually be expected to match or better it. Any unexplained breaks in employment record could potentially relate to periods of mental ill-health or imprisonment and will require clarification (Warner, 1992). All applicants should be asked to produce proof that they are entitled to work in the UK and should be offered the same list of alternative forms of doumentary proof to establish this. Issues relating to gender, marital or parental status, or ethnicity should *not* be enquired about in the form or the interview as this poses a risk of sex discrimination or racial discrimination which are proscribed by statute. (There may, quite properly, be a parallel process of ethnic or other monitoring, with separate, anonymised paperwork, which helps the organisation to evaluate the fairness of its employment practices over time.)

There is no such law covering either age or sexual orientation so that older workers and gay men and lesbians could find themselves subjected to prejudices against which they have no redress. Local authorities are not entirely free, for example, of the still widespread confusion between homosexuality and pædophilia, making child care not the safest job in which to come out as gay. Naturally, this can pose a dilemma as to whether to declare oneself at interview and know where one stands, but risk not getting the job, or keep one's sexuality concealed and fear being outed at a later stage. The only way round this, until such time as there is protective legislation, is for employers to make clear their stance on employing gay men and lesbians by incorporating it into their stated and published policy and ensuring that all interviewers are able to apply it fairly.

There is also a tension between gathering information which can help to identify those with a record of abuse (e.g. previous names) and that which might lead to discrimination since a woman giving a previous last name is most probably married, and since other reasons for changing one's name include religious and cultural affiliations.

For disabled people, the Disability Discrimination Act 1995 now places the onus on the employer to take reasonable steps to adapt the workplace, through the provision of necessary facilities or support, or to alter current working practices so that potential disabled employees are not discriminated against (see Chapter 7). Examples of such adaptations might include providing minicom equipment to enable deaf employees to use the telephone (and, at the same time, ensuring that other relevant staff are trained to use it) or a scanner to transfer documents into braille. It is important that individual needs are taken into account, however, since different equipment suits different people's needs. Shamefully, there are still constant reports that disabled people do not even get interviews for jobs for which they are eminently well qualified and it is these attitudinal obstacles which will need to be overcome along with the physical ones in the work setting. Now that the social model of disability is fundamental to social work service delivery, there is little excuse for it not to underpin employment practice in the same way and there is scope for this to receive far more discussion both in management training and in social work education, amongst the managers of tomorrow. Indeed, positive action can be taken, for example by shortlisting all disabled candidates who meet the essential criteria for the post.

In the meantime, shortlisters and selectors need to be very sure that their own prejudices are not impinging on their decision-making, and training can help with this. This can apply to areas in which interviewers need to be more rigorous, just as much as those where they may be blocking access to jobs unnecessarily. And, once a more diverse workforce has been recruited, there will be proportionately greater demands placed on the organisation's managers to manage diversity positively and creatively.

Selection

Selection is usually carried out on the combined basis of an interview, the application form and references, and perhaps psychometric or other forms of testing. Group selection methods are still found in social work education, because so much of the learning takes place in groups, and may be relevant for some work settings, such as group care. The more senior the post, the more complex and costly the process is likely to be since the organisation wants to make sure of choosing the right person to cope with present-day demands. For example, there may be an additional element to the procedures if some particular presentational or other skills are involved in the job – e.g. in a training post – which need to be tested on the day of the interviews.

Interviews

Interviews remain the most commonly used selection technique, despite frequently voiced doubts about their fairness or validity (that is, whether they are testing what they are intended to test or some other extraneous factors which creep into the process). Some of the doubts about interviewers' judgements include whether they are:

- too *subjective*
- based on *initial surface impressions* (favourable or unfavourable) of the interviewee's personal presentation or similarity

in background to the interviewer, rather than on their ability to do the job

- further affected by these subjective or superficial impressions being communicated to the applicant early on in the interview, through *tone or body language*, so that he or she performs more or less well under their influence
- based around looking only for material to *confirm a bias* for or against the candidate, formed in the first few minutes of the interview or even before it, so that the interview becomes a self-fulfilling prophecy.

Clearly, these factors can combine together into an upward or downward spiral, working in favour of or against that particular candidate. Looked at more closely, all the problems listed lie more at the door of the interviewer than in the nature of an interview as such, which would suggest that there might be ways round them.

The first of these potential solutions – which is a norm in social work but not in all sectors of employment – is to have a *panel of interviewers* rather than a single person. Each may form a different impression of candidates that counterbalance one another, and particularly where the panel reflects the diversity of the community to be served by the person appointed. As with shortlisting, the make-up of the interviewing panel is important and should be based on anti-oppressive as well as human resource management (HRM) principles. The involvement of service users is sometimes built in, notably in service provider settings, where those attending a centre or resident in an establishment may play a role either in serving on a selection panel or in formally feeding in collective views for the panel's consideration. There need to be clear parameters here. Unless the setting is entirely user-run, users would not normally see confidential information about candidates and, as far as young people are concerned, the Support Force for Children's Residential Care (1995) warned that they should not have a role in final decision-making about the appointment. Having said that, young people may be less taken in than adults by unsuitable people (Kahan, 1994). Of course, with several people present, good chairing of both the interviews and the ensuing discussion is essential.

Second, training in selection and recruitment should encompass not only employment and anti-discriminatory legislation and best practice in human resource terms, but also the *interpersonal skills and awareness* involved in interviewing. Ideally, the opportunity to rehearse posing questions and listening attentively to the answers, and to see a playback of themselves on video, would help interviewers to overcome some of the pitfalls. In local authorities, the potential for tension between officers and elected members on interviewing panels (or between paid staff and management board or committee members in the voluntary sector) constitutes a strong argument for joint training. If there is resistance, as mentioned above, the wide-scale exposure of abusive practices in residential and other social work settings could be suggested as a justification for the time and effort involved. Certainly, training for all selectors is recommended by the Audit Commission (1995). And training is equally important as a way of combating discrimination in selection practices (e.g. Commission for Racial Equality, 1993).

It can perhaps be taken for granted in a social work context that thought will be given to the following: reception and waiting arrangements; the lay-out of the interview room; having all the paperwork circulated to the panel well in advance and its members well briefed; introducing the panel to the candidate and helping him or her to relax; allowing uninterrupted and sufficient time with each candidate that is fair to each; asking questions that are relevant to the job (and not other matters, such as family circumstances) and ensuring that the answers have been understood; giving space for candidates to ask their own questions and to add anything they feel the interview has not managed to glean about them that relates to their ability to do the job; closing the interview smoothly and with mutual understanding about what will happen next; and, finally, making notes during or immediately after each interview, preferably on standard documentation provided, that would stand up at a tribunal as providing sound reasons for forming the judgements reached. Time needs to be allowed in the interview schedule for this note-taking, as much as for interviews that overrun.

Disabled applicants should be asked if they need any particular provision in the interview, such as a sign language interpreter and/or information in an accessible format, and, of course, the venue should be fully accessible. Members of some social groups, who may have been disadvantaged in education (including disabled people and members of some minority ethnic groups), may have more to offer in life experience than in formal qualifications or may have had an unconventional career pattern. Depending on the demands of the job and the training opportunities available within it, there may be scope to consider any equivalence in particular strengths they might bring.

EQUAL OPPORTUNITIES INTERVIEWING

As one means of seeking to improve interviewing, in recent years local authority and other social work panels have often decided to ask the same questions of each candidate, based on the *key competences* involved in the job (together with reasons for wanting the post, for moving jobs at this time, and so on), so that equality of opportunity is upheld. This procedure may even be organisational policy. At one time, this became an essentially mechanistic process, with each question asked, unembellished, like a mantra and with no follow-up. Yet the purpose of asking questions is presumably to find out more about the applicant's abilities and orientation to the post; this can scarcely be done if there is no content tailored to their particular circumstances or strengths.

Perhaps a useful distinction to be made is that between 'prompting' and 'probing'. Where one interviewee but not others is given prompts, or additional opportunities to go off in entirely new directions at the whim of the selector, this can be seen to be unfair. Where, however, further probing questions are asked, on the basis of what each person has already said or has written on their application, they are merely being allowed to do themselves justice in responding to the set questions, provided that this happens for all those seen and does not become too personally intrusive. Areas that will certainly need to be probed include any gaps in employment history and any concerns raised by the application or references. Where a candidate has had personal experience of abuse or other trauma, this could give them a great empathy with service users but it may be important to be clear that they are at a stage of readiness to help others (Barter, 1997), perhaps through conducting a preliminary interview under equal opportunities conditions (Warner, 1992). More generally, attitudes to power and authority, and to sexuality and other sensitive issues, should arguably be gauged for all candidates for posts in residential child care (Kent, 1997).

Furthermore, the quest for complete uniformity in interview procedure was arguably bound to fail. A selection panel might unwittingly influence the outcome in any number of ways: the skill with which applicants are settled down in the interview room, the tone in which questions are posed, the sequence in which people are interviewed (e.g. because of the degree of attentiveness from a panel that is ready for its lunch or is drowsy afterwards), and so on. Even if some device like interviewing in alphabetical order is decided upon, where a good applicant follows a poorer (or poorly interviewed) one – or vice versa – the 'contrast effect' (Anderson, 1985) can come into play so that perspective is lost on their actual performance. Nevertheless, the happy medium is certainly to retain some overall structure because it can be explained to candidates, facilitates comparisons between them and makes it easier to keep notes. The panel chair should ensure that decisions, and the grounds on which they were reached, are systematically recorded as a defence against any later challenge of unfair treatment and for evaluation purposes.

(For those who wish to pursue their reading in this area, particularly in the context of formal study, there has been some complex theorising about the dynamics of interviewing and the problems inherent within it. A Foucauldian analysis of the power relations in human resource management and of the discourses operating within it, for example, is offered by Townley, 1994.)

OTHER APPROACHES TO STANDARDISED INTERVIEWING

Other employment sectors, notably business, have experimented with different ways of trying to standardise interviews and to tie them more closely to the matters they are supposed to be testing. These include 'situational' or 'critical incident' interviewing, based around asking how applicants would cope with particular situations which might crop up in the job (the job analysis can help to identify these), and the 'patterned behaviour description interview' which probes a series of major life changes to try and identify whether there is a pattern in the way the candidate deals with problems and challenges. Both these approaches may tend to assume that there is one optimal way of reacting and that the panel knows what it is. Nevertheless, they are not entirely foreign to ideas that can be found in theorising social work intervention, they do attempt to stick to matters related to carrying out the job, and they may produce more valid and standardised results than less structured methods that leave the candidates free to talk about whatever they consider relevant in response to each broad question.

A final method that may resonate even more closely with current social work thinking is *competency-based interviewing* (Johnstone, 1995). Here, the focus moves from what candidates have achieved to how they achieved it, so as to identify the skills or traits that underpinned their achievements. Once again, the questioning starts from specific situations, this time in previous employment experience and asks what were the tasks, the actions and the results that ensued. This gives the acronym STARs: or *Situations, Tasks, Actions, Results*.

Whether or not one of these more structured methods of interviewing is followed, it is generally more productive to pose a hypothetical situation, or to ask the interviewee to tell you about a specific experience in their area of practice, than to ask closed questions with 'yes/no' answers. Asking someone whether they agree with anti-racist policies, for example, is of little help since they can hardly say they don't. Asking them to describe one occasion when these policies have created or eased tensions in their working life and what they did about it will be far more revealing.

PARTICIPATIVE INTERVIEWING

Despite the inevitable stress, a job interview should be an opportunity for *two-way communication* and, though there is unlikely to be the hard bargaining over pay and conditions in social work that is seen in business circles, the applicant does need the chance to check on issues that may be unclear or of particular personal importance and can make certain requirements clear. More than this, he or she should be given the opportunity to be actively engaged in the recruitment and selection process by being valued and listened to at all stages. A profession such as social work that prides itself on partnership should surely be keen to support this more reciprocal approach to selection, and not one that is based on assuming that 'management knows best'. At the end of the day, in hearing fully from candidates what they have to offer, we can show that we are 'concerned not only with the job to be done, but also with the work that is offered' (Torrington and Hall, 1998, p.222). The more information candidates have had about the job, the more there can be an element of *self-assessment* in what they write and say about their ability to do it.

When the panel comes to consider its decision, it may also take into account any feedback from the team the candidate would be joining, if a meeting with, or presentation to, its members constituted part of the selection process. After all, they are the people who will be working with the successful applicant and they are among the ones who will suffer most directly if a misjudgement occurs in selection. Care must be taken, however, that all candidates have an equal chance to present themselves to the team, and that feedback about the team's views is sought systematically on each, in order to avoid introducing unequal treatment into the process at this point. Involving prospective colleagues in this way also means that unsuccessful candidates for the post are not able to keep the matter confidential. It may therefore be sensible to advise the wider team, as well as the interview panel, about appropriate protocol.

Police and other checks on suitability

The panel should also be mindful of police checks if the job will involve contact with children. Child sex abusers may actively target residential child care and day care settings (Kendrick, 1997; Colton and Vanstone, 1998) and, although there are no certain ways of identifying them in advance of the abuse, the very least that must be done is to check with police records (in Scotland, the Scottish Criminal Records Office), including the register of convicted sex offenders, and with the Criminal Records Bureau, a proposed central access point for information about those banned by the Secretary of State for Health from working with children, whether in a paid or unpaid capacity, to replace the Department of Health's own index amongst other listings. (There is also a new index for this purpose in Scotland; see Scottish Office, 1998.) There is a further proposal, under the Sexual Offences (Amendment) Bill, to make it a criminal offence for a staff member to abuse a position of trust by having a sexual relationship with a 16- or 17-year-old in care or in detention. Attempting to work with children while being a 'banned' person would be similarly proscribed.

Although police checks can take some weeks to come through, an appointment should ideally not be confirmed until this happens or, at least, the appointee should not work unsupervised with children in the interim. For social work posts, it should be noted that convictions do not become 'spent' under the Rehabilitation of Offenders Act 1974.

The system is not problem-free, either as regards safeguarding children or in respect of the civil liberties of job applicants. The free movement of workers within the European Union is a matter of some concern, for example, because of the complexities it introduces into the checking procedures. There may, in effect, be no way of obtaining sufficiently detailed information from the other country or countries where the applicant may have worked, and not every state has reached the UK's level of awareness of the dangers of child abuse. On the other hand, the police checks that are made here do not only produce hard data on criminal convictions but also 'soft' information held by the police which might relate to more general concerns or to a possibly disguised identity. One of the authors has had experience of several worrying examples of details sent through by the police, including a lesbian student who felt she had been unfairly targeted by the police in a series of incidents which were now recorded on the police computer, and an Asian student with a common name which, when entered into the police computer, elicited confidential information about the convictions of several other people of a similar age living nearby! Clearly, we would want to know about anyone who, though not actually convicted of an offence against children, had already given rise to serious concerns but, in our eagerness to try and protect the public, we may be infringing the liberty of potential social work students and employees, not to speak of their neighbours.

A further concern is the possible lack of consistency with which interview panels and employing organisations act on police information once they have received it. In one recent research study, a hypothetical interview exercise led to a fictional candidate, described as having quite a serious conviction for an offence against a child, being considered by some people as appointable to a post with direct access to children (Smith, 1999). The people concerned, though role-playing in the exercise, were making the same type of judgement as they were called on to exercise in their actual jobs. There is no way of knowing how often this kind of laxity may be occurring in real life. Given the scandals in a number of residential child care settings (see, for example, Hughes, 1986; Levy and Kahan, 1991; Williams and McCreadie, 1992; Jones, 1996), it is perhaps little wonder that government is taking a more interventive line through the establishment in England (with equivalents elsewhere) of a General Social Care Council (GSCC) to regulate entry to and exit from the workforce according to appropriate conduct and practice standards. Indeed, many in the profession have long called for such safeguards. They will always be a case of shutting the stable door after the horse has bolted in the sense that they will operate to strike people off the Register after they have shown themselves to be unsuitable for employment in social work or social care. Those with a propensity to physically, emotionally or sexually abuse others, or to steal from or otherwise exploit vulnerable service users, do not have a badge on their foreheads to warn us that this is the case and no selection procedure, no matter how good, will ever be able to identify all those who present a risk.

Nevertheless, a number of official reports and reviews (Utting, 1987, 1997; Skinner, 1992; Kent, 1997) have made relevant recommendations to try and protect children in residential care. In particular, the Warner Report (Warner, 1992) and the *Code of Practice* from the Support Force for Children's Residential Care (1995) (following piloting by the Local Government Management Board, 1996) deal with recruitment and selection procedures for residential child care staff.

The use of tests in selection

PSYCHOLOGICAL TESTING

Psychological or psychometric testing has been growing in favour amongst social work employers, again as a reaction against the subjectivity of interviewing and under the impact of management training which may be less critical of pseudo-scientific techniques being applied to people than is social work itself. Tests in use in social work contexts are more likely to be designed to gauge personality than general intelligence (as defined by test designers). They include some which have been devised to test the suitability of candidates applying to work with children and even their potential to abuse. Since most of the abuser population is hidden, and since abuse is rooted in denial and minimisation, even to the self, it is hard to see how such tests have been standardised, though they claim high levels of validity. Nevertheless, it is understandable that employers would want to do everything possible to avoid placing trust in a likely abuser and recent government-backed advice (Support Force for Children's Residential Care, 1995; Kent, 1997) is that such tests, provided they are professionally assessed, may have a useful role to play.

Like interviews, tests do not always measure what they are meant to measure. Just as IQ testing has long been known to involve many elements of motivation and performance in a test situation, over and above the content of the test itself (and this has been suggested as one reason why some ethnic groups perform better than others), criticisms of psychometric testing include an accusation that they have been designed around white norms and that African Caribbean candidates may do less well (Skellington with Morris, 1992) and hence lose out on being appointed to posts for which they are perfectly well suited. (This also begs the wider question as to whether candidates must always be fitted for jobs or whether jobs might sometimes be adapted to benefit from the skills of less traditional candidates.)

Furthermore, the tests are useful only if they can be shown to relate to the skills and qualities actually involved in doing the job *and* if there is agreement as to which are the most advantageous of these. As we saw in Chapter 2, there is a strong move in some management quarters away from macho management and towards networking and teamwork. Thus the 'right' answers to a leadership test last week might be the wrong answers this week. And the job itself might change quite radically over time.

At the extreme, no organisation (other than one producing works of art, perhaps) desires an emotionally unstable workforce and motivation can certainly be considered more relevant to employment contexts than it is to measures of intelligence. So tests may not be all bad. Nevertheless, the other aspects of personality that tests purport to measure – such as risk-taking or playing safe, being controlling or submissive, and other areas of strength and confidence – might arguably be needed in some degree of balance within a team. A children's home might be an equally unthera-peutic place if all the staff were trying new ideas all the time as if no one was. And no team can survive if everyone is trying to lead it. The aim of the psychologists in creating a standard profile for each job may therefore be an essentially unhelpful one in social work.

Test designers themselves own up to certain flaws in the notion of testing, such as the chance of people giving dishonest or only socially acceptable answers. They attempt to build in safe-guards and to standardise their tests against randomised popu-lation samples so that other psychologists will accept them as valid (actually testing what they set out to test) and reliable (pro-ducing comparable results over time). Social scientists in other fields may draw a distinction between people's answers to hypo-thetical questions and what they do in real life, or may see human beings as a complex combination of characteristics affected by context and by interactions with others, rather than as a series of 'types' that can be neatly labelled and measured. We would all like to think that we know ourselves, and most of us love to score ourselves in magazine quizzes, but, faced with an emergency or a true test of leadership, we very often do not know exactly what strength of courage, resilience or resourcefulness we would find. The best test probably is how we have behaved in any similar circumstances in the past and we have already seen how an interview can focus on that.

Nevertheless, the use of psychometric tests as one part of the selection process is growing, especially amongst large organisations and especially for more senior posts. Given this fact, it is important to remember that the testing is not an objective, scientific solution to the vagaries of interviewing but actually has some of the same weaknesses built into it. Even where properly qualified occupa-tional testers are paid large sums to undertake it, they are subject to the same difficulty in getting the organisation to specify exactly what it is looking for, the same challenge in really knowing how to match an infinite variety of human beings to the narrow constraints of paid employment, and the same artificiality built into the whole selection process. There remain many aspects of individuals that *tests cannot measure* and the data they produce should always be incorporated carefully into the more wide-ranging information gathered by other means.

WORK-BASED TESTS

A different sort of test that may be combined with an interview is the 'work-based' or 'in-tray' test. This may give the candidate a representative sample of work to do, possibly complete with interruptions and emergencies, and ask how they would prioritise it and what tasks they would carry out, or it may be based around one case study in which a decision or a care plan is needed. This technique has certainly been used in social work selection though it is not widespread.

While closer to the 'real world' than psychometric testing, it is still devoid of context, and also subject to the candidate's interview nerves and other drawbacks of the artificiality of the situation. Always assuming that the selectors are skilled enough not to look for 'right answers' but for viable and professionally justifiable ones, there is still the issue of how they can use this one-off technique to evaluate what a candidate would be bringing to a job that may change considerably over time and in which the contribution of some intangible flair or vision might be advantageous. Nevertheless, this may be the closest social work practice can get (because it tests practice skills) to the almost universal requirement in education and training for applicants to demonstrate their practical teaching skills through a presentation to their potential colleagues.

Presentations can also explore a candidate's knowledge of policy and practice agendas, and ability to project ideas and personal vision for the organisation; hence they are widely used for management level posts. Certainly, there needs to be some attempt to evaluate the skills the candidate would actually use in the job if we are to avoid the 'Peter Principle' (Peter, 1970), whereby people are promoted to the level of their own incompetence – i.e. to the job above that in which they have already demonstrated they can cope (or at least avoid doing any real harm). Arguably, those who will make the best managers may not be those who made the best social workers, with the result that the profession may gain an inadequate manager at the expense of a competent practitioner.

APTITUDE TESTS

Where the employee will be called on to exercise particular practical skills such as word processing or desk-top publishing, there is every reason to set a pre-interview exercise that tests these quite specifically and that can be incorporated into selection decisions.

References

In a profession like social work, references as to past job performance and general good character are clearly essential. They should be derived from professional sources who have known the candidate in a previous professional or caring role, including the current or most recent employer, and should be conveyed direct to the recruiting organisation, not via the candidate so that there can be no question of the reference being forged or tampered with.

Each agency has its own policy regarding when selectors should read references, either before or after the interview; the same might be the case in relation to any necessary police checks. If taken up in advance, then any negative or unclear points from the references may be explored in the interview. References have, however, tended to become ever more bland since there have been legal challenges to their contents (which, if defamatory, can unfairly cost someone the job), and it can take a very great deal of reading between the lines to spot any dissatisfaction or unease. On the other hand, in social work, a future employer or service user could equally well have a case for damages against a referee who had failed to reveal adverse information about an applicant (Warner, 1992) from which some harm later resulted.

The main function of a reference is probably to verify that the applicant has the employment record they claim, and has not done anything in a recent post that has resulted in disciplinary action or other formally recorded outcome or that has given rise to concern. Thus, the reference is often made a condition of appointment in the new job, rather than a tool to assist the interviewers, and reading it may be left until after the candidate is seen so as not to bias the interviewers. This can be frustrating for the reference writer who takes care to express both the strengths and the weaknesses they feel should influence the matching of candidate to job – for example, a need for support or a protected caseload in a first post or a more developed level of skill in one type of practice than another. Practice may swing back towards reading references in advance in the light of views taken in the residential child care field, where it is increasingly felt that concerns should be probed in the interview rather than risking giving candidates the benefit of the doubt (Warner, 1992; Support Force for Children's Residential Care, 1995; Kent, 1997). Also frustrating for the conscientious referee is the trend towards 'tick box' references which seek to gauge the candidate's level of competence without offering the writer any chance to 'bring the person alive' though, again, they are arguably fairer as well as quicker to complete.

From the applicant's point of view, of course, it can be a worry to have one's future fate controlled by a current employer, tutor or practice teacher. There are many stories of managers who are said to write bad references for staff they want to retain, sometimes in jobs and at salary levels that vastly undervalue their potential. Certainly, any applicant should have the right not to have their present employer consulted for a reference until a late stage in the process. This is partly because it may be awkward to let the employer know that another post is being considered, and the individual may fear that annoying their current manager could affect not only the outcome of their application, but also the way they might be treated in their current workplace afterwards. Or, where the job seeker is a manager, having the team knowing that he or she is on the look-out for another post can have a destabilising effect, or can lead to jockeying for position as people wonder who will get the soon-to-be vacant job. Conversely, there are some employment contexts where an employee who is known to have been shortlisted for another job is more likely to be retained through internal promotion or other recognition. Much depends on the culture of the organisation and the value of the particular staff member in terms of skills and experience.

Just as with job applications, the advent of Human Resources Managers in social services departments has brought with it standardised reference forms designed to mirror the competences and qualities required in the job, and key aspects of what is known of the applicant from his or her last work setting. His or her sickness record increasingly features, alongside confirmation of post held, dates employed, nature of the referee's relationship with the

applicant – e.g. line manager, university tutor on social work programme, how long they have been known to one another, and so
on. Given the nature of social work, there cannot help but be an
element of the character reference in that any information that may
be known regarding criminal record or unprofessional conduct
ought to be declared. A fuller reference will talk about the candidate's performance in their last job or on their qualifying programme. Although the applicant nominates their own referees,
there is an almost unvarying requirement in social work to have
the last employer nominated and some agencies are very particular about the management level at which the reference can be
signed. This is intended to ensure that the next employer is not
falsely reassured about someone who has actually not been trust-
worthy in holding social work responsibilities.

It is the norm in the UK to require references and, far from
falling from favour as low on validity, they are being standardised
for management credibility along with every other aspect of the
recruitment and selection procedure. Indeed, referees may be
approached by telephone in relation to residential child care posts
(Kent, 1997; Utting, 1997) to ensure that they have had the opportunity to comment frankly on what they have written about the
candidate's strengths and weaknesses in relation to the job description and person specification. Once again, a potential tension can
be perceived here between users' rights (in this case children's
rights) and equal opportunities in the workplace since it might be
far more difficult to challenge something afterwards that had been
suggested over the 'phone than written down in a reference. At the
very least, applicants should be told that the employer reserves the
right to contact any previous employer. This can carry risks, though,
in that there has been a recent out-of-court settlement and also an
adverse local government ombudsman judgement concerning
information on a reinstated employee and on a withdrawn allega-
tion passed, in each case, from a current to a prospective employer
and later deemed confidential (*Community Care*, 16–22 September
1999, pp.6, 12). The same debates can be had as to whether written
references should be confidential or open. Currently, referees are
often given the choice, open references having formed part of a
wider trend towards freedom of information, but there may be
some evidence of a swing back to confidentiality (Kent, 1997) as
more likely to lead to a frank sharing of concerns.

Other outside information about the candidate which may be taken into account is a medical report which states whether their physical condition is considered suitable for the job and a declaration by the candidate of any previous criminal convictions or cautions, which would be followed up. Also, since it is now the employer's responsibility to establish the right to work in the UK, all candidates are now asked to produce documentary evidence that they possess this right. In order to avoid discrimination, it is important that all are presented with the same choice of documents that will suffice – not passports for minority ethnic candidates and evidence of their National Insurance status for others, to take a 'worst case' scenario. It is also a sensible precaution to check professional qualifications with the awarding body and to ask for proof of the applicant's current address.

Feedback to candidates

Organisations also vary in whether or not they give feedback to unsuccessful candidates. In the main, it is considered useful for people to be given constructive comments on how they came across and advice on how they might enhance qualifications, experience and so on. On the other hand, there is a constant fear in these litigious days of challenge through employment tribunal, and employers may fear giving opinions that could be actionable.

Then, too, the interviewers have only seen the applicant for a very short space of time, under highly artificial conditions. They are arguably much less well placed to advise on career development than the present employing organisation which has the employee's whole work record to weigh up. They have made a decision about who to appoint to a specific post, not what the other people seen should now be doing with their lives.

Internal candidates

Once a job is advertised, then staff within the organisation may apply. This can create dilemmas for the manager if an internal candidate is not appointed because it can lead to lowered morale and commitment, although not inevitably. Keeping a valued member of the team is possible not only through promotion but by ensuring their workload is sufficiently challenging and rewarding. Just as much stress occurs with underwork as overwork so that such a person might be asked if there were tasks which they would wish to develop so that everyone could benefit from fresh insights and ideas. If the internal candidate is successful, then it is vital that their existing commitments are taken from them; it is not uncommon for staff to be expected to cope, at least in the transition period, with two jobs.

Monitoring and evaluation of selection

Like any other aspect of the agency's work, selection should ideally be monitored and evaluated over time. This can include: asking both the selectors and the candidates to fill in a brief questionnaire about the process followed and whether it enabled the candidate to perform optimally and helped the selectors to obtain the information they needed about both the vacancy and the candidates; monitoring the progress of newly appointed candidates to ascertain whether they perform to the level expected; and comparing different selection methods to gauge which appear to have the greatest validity. Adverts can also be monitored to find out which were the most effective in attracting high calibre candidates.

Rites of passage

Two phases of working life sometimes ignored in management literature are those of orienting a new member of staff and of saying goodbye to one who is leaving. When planning an induction programme for a newcomer, the manager may want to decide, if appropriate, which areas of information can be left to the headquarters system to deliver and which areas are better handled by the team. Usually, others explain the organisational structure, where the person fits into it and what the regulations are (for instance, in relation to health and safety at work). It is helpful for the team leader to spend some time with the new worker, possibly giving a brief history of the team, its philosophy, how the workload might be reallocated to fit with what the person can offer, and perhaps explaining one or two procedures. Any adaptations that the person may need to their work station or pattern of work, if disabled, should be finalised at this time.

Too much information at this stage could be confusing and so the team leader might link the new member with close colleagues or an experienced member of staff for a short period. Introductions to key figures and resources can be undertaken by this colleague. Staff in group care are typically 'thrown in at the deep end'; whether or not this happens or if, in fieldwork, a ready-made caseload is waiting, immediate exposure is not necessarily harmful provided that there is a supportive climate in the establishment. What is unhelpful is seeing induction as a once-and-for-all event: someone's passage into an organisation has to be planned on an unfolding basis, where there is scope to learn and develop throughout one's career. It is also a two-way process. The organisation needs to set some parameters about expected standards of behaviour, and to familiarise the individual with their new job and working environment, offering any necessary training – for example, in using the in-house computerised recording system – but it is also important to hear from them what they need to know in the early stages and how they learn most effectively. Any manager who has previously been a practice teacher will have developed useful skills in settling people in in the most helpful way. It is also useful to remember that there is an informal as well as a formal side to induction. People form personal impressions from the way they are treated (at selection and after), from things they have read or heard about the organisation, and sometimes from past dealings with it. The formal induction may sometimes need to correct some of these impressions (Pettinger, 1997).

At the opposite end of a career, when retirement, obtaining another post, or even redundancy or redeployment through the ubiquitous 'downsizing' looms, similarly the manager's sensitivity is essential; a sense of loss generally accompanies each leaving, so a lunch or a gift tends to mark the occasion. Often, people are leaving to begin a new stage in their life – promotion, retirement, moving home, parenthood – which can be celebrated with them in a way which recognises that we do all have lives beyond the job and that we have valued one another's support and company as people, not just as colleagues. Even with an unsuitable worker there will have been some professional and personal strengths which can be acknowledged, so that positive factors are to the fore at the point of leaving.

But where an employee is suspended or summarily dismissed for misconduct (see also Chapter 4), there may be an embargo on others speaking to them outside of the formal procedures which can make it impossible to do the human things one would naturally want to do. Sometimes the person becomes so angry that even a neutral enquiry as to how they are coping might be misconstrued, or they are so upset that such an enquiry is turned into an inappropriate conversation about all that has happened. It is at times like this that other support structures such as trade unions and staff care services come into their own and it is usually advisable to leave them to support the individual who is being investigated. At the end of the day, the first responsibility of other employees is to the general public, including service users. This must outweigh allegiance to a colleague and perhaps friend who is thought not to have upheld the standards those services demand or who has shown in some other sphere of life that they cannot be trusted (not to be violent or dishonest, for example). Having said that, it is recognised that any suspension causes stress for the person under investigation and for all the others around them (including any who may be called as witnesses), all of whom will need support, and that it is potentially divisive for the team. Conflict resolution at an early stage or mediation through the BASW Advice and Representation Service (Dadswell, 1999) or through ACAS would be a positive step, if appropriate, though sometimes matters have already gone too far or the alleged misconduct is simply too grave.

Fortunately, many potential problems with employees can be avoided by adequate staff development policies and practices – with appraisal mechanisms and training opportunities feeding into one another in a positive way (see Chapter 6) – and by the provision of timely advice through guidance or warnings, incorporating stated targets and timescales for improvement. Above all, clearly stated performance standards and agency policies and protocols mean that there can be no doubt what is expected, though they do risk making social work practice more mechanistic and rigid than it used to be. And all disciplinary matters must be dealt with fairly, giving the individual a right to a hearing, consistent treatment, an unbiased decision with stated reasons, and provision for appeal.

These 'procedural rights' (Galligan, 1992) are the cornerstone of an individual's civil rights, in employment as elsewhere.

Conclusion

We have seen in this chapter how managerialism in social work has made its mark on the recruitment and selection process and also how (post)modern organisations deliberately recruit for a climate of flexibility and change. The workforce which is faced with these imperatives is bound to experience an increased level of job demands and stress which, in turn, makes policies of staff development and staff care all the more important. We shall move on to these in Chapter 6.

6

The Human Resource:
Meeting the Needs of Staff

The largest element of the budget in human service organisations is spent on staff salaries. This is why staff are nowadays referred to as the 'human resource' in any enterprise and are regarded as valuable – a huge step forward from the 'cogs in a machine' thinking we saw in Chapter 2.

An organisation's employees are a major asset, not only in themselves, but also because the organisation's whole reputation and future success depends on them. Consequently, it could be regarded as a very false saving to skimp on the ways in which staff are supported or their skills developed. These are arguably the most direct ways to influence the quality of organisational performance as well as retaining and fostering the best employees. It is better value to invest in and motivate a workforce than constantly to recruit and train replacements. This is most notably recognised in the Investors in People Scheme to which many local authorities have subscribed.

As befits the husbanding of a precious resource, 'getting the best out of staff' is a concern for the whole organisation, not just the immediate line manager. Good supervision by the line manager in social work combines management, education and support. The organisation as a whole needs frameworks which encompass these same three elements which, on this larger scale, become: performance appraisal, staff development and staff care. Each of these will be looked at in turn in this chapter, which will conclude with consideration of some additional ways in which staff themselves can promote their own development and well-being at work and in which the enlightened manager can encourage them.

Since supervision combines elements of all three of the main ways organisations relate to their staff, it will be dealt with first.

Supervision

In the days before managerialism wrought such a transformation on social work organisations, virtually everything that was known about what a social worker was doing with his or her 'clients' was conveyed to the organisation through supervision. Now, however, work is recorded on computer, thus becoming accessible to a whole swathe of managers, and is subject as much to budgetary as to professional oversight. As a team leader remarked: 'I am supervised by my manager but the person who I need to see the most, and this is no reflection on my manager, is the Principal Finance Officer' (Harris, 1998).

Nevertheless, supervision in social work continues to serve several purposes at once. These may be listed as: managerial, educational and supportive (or enabling). Many accounts of supervision tend to present all this as a problem. Lishman (1998, p.98), for example, sees these competing claims as a 'potential dilemma and danger of supervision' and Turner (1995, p.127) as a subversion of professional staff development into 'a means of controlling or instructing staff'. It is certainly true that these various functions have to be held in tension, with the achievement of stated outcomes now essential in all spheres of work, but it could equally be seen as a remarkable achievement of the social work profession that it has so tidily combined several different complex requirements into one process, with such economy of time and effort. And to such a degree has this been taken for granted, that we have never even crowed about it. Few work settings can claim a mechanism which, at its best, so smoothly combines the oversight of work undertaken, staff performance appraisal, staff development and staff care considerations.

Because it is the norm in social work to hold these functions in a fruitful tension, the biggest shift for the newly promoted manager in fieldwork or group care is in having to face in two directions at once – both towards the staff they are supervising, to meet their support and development needs and to help them exercise judgement wisely in their assessments and interventions, and towards their own managers, so as to meet the needs of the organisation in getting the work done appropriately and managing the human resource.

Becoming a supervisor for the first time can be daunting. It is all too easy to feel that experienced staff are more skilled than you are or the newly qualified more 'up' on the new ideas, that you have not been trained in professional supervision, that staff see what you offer as merely checking up on them, or to ask why you should bother to supervise others when you yourself do not receive adequate support or supervision. Supervision has also fallen somewhat into disrepute and even disuse in social work because it focuses on inputs to social workers rather than outcomes for users, can become associated with merely checking that procedures are complied with, and is seen as part of the woollier days of social work before there were other ways of holding staff accountable for standards (Kearney, 1999). Front line managers nowadays may see their job as lying more in balancing budgets and gathering management information than in spending time with individual staff.

Yet one of the greatest joys of any manager's work is to foster the skills and talents of others, to see people achieving their full potential and flourishing over time and to assist them in giving a good and professional service to others. And sometimes all it takes to do this is a listening ear, a few questions to draw them out, some words of praise or guidance, and ensuring that you yourself keep on top of what is happening in the wider agency and, preferably, in the profession as a whole. More positive trends that may support managers in offering supervision are those of 'reflective practice', which relies on practitioners being given opportunities to stand back from and question their approach to their work, and a project at the National Institute for Social Work on the 'management of practice' (Kearney, 1999). This has revealed a lack of overall supervision policies in a majority of social services departments and has demonstrated that supervision needs to go beyond checking up on managerial objectives and supporting individuals in developing better practice. This also resonates with the constant calls in inspection reports for higher standards of supervision.

So the manager can fairly make demands of their agency to help them learn to supervise and mesh supervision into broader agency strategy. He or she can also reasonably ask the individual staff member to be well prepared and to work at getting the most out of supervision (Knapham and Morrison, 1998).

Supervision: purpose and methods

The overall purpose of supervision must be to enhance the standard of work undertaken so that, in turn, vulnerable members of the public will have an improved quality of life. This means that supervision should be grounded in the principles of anti-oppressive practice and aimed at offering a 'Best Value' service to the organisation's 'customers'.

More specifically, supervision is intended to:

- *Meet managerial and administrative needs by*
    - assisting with *workload and caseload management* (for example, through reviewing and planning work)
    - monitoring the day-to-day work to ensure that it is carried out within the *policies* and *priorities* of the organisation
    - providing *a sounding board* for ideas, concerns, plans and strategies
    - keeping the staff member in touch with *developments* in resources, statutory requirements, departmental policies and so on, and the ways these relate to his or her work
    - giving *feedback* about performance
    - ensuring that *manual or computerised recording* is of the required standard and up-to-date (though computerisation increasingly means that there are instant ways of checking up on this and, indeed, that work cannot proceed unless the necessary entries have been made on the computer)
    - providing the supervisor with part of the *management information* needed to keep an oversight of the throughput of work in the team and the rate of resource allocation to carry out that work.
- *Meet educational and developmental needs by*:
    - promoting *professional and personal development*
    - providing *learning opportunities* so that staff can keep their knowledge and skills up to date
    - developing *awareness of role and responsibilities* within the organisational context
    - helping the worker acquire greater *understanding* of people, problems and situations
    - building *professional confidence*, creativity and new ways of working.
- *Meet support needs by*:
    - providing *emotional support* (e.g. by helping someone rediscover the rewards in their work where motivation has flagged, reviewing an overload of work, providing new

challenges so that staff continue to grow in their jobs, helping
the practitioner express and deal with the feelings content of
their work)

– keeping an oversight of *personal and professional boundaries*
to ensure that the practitioner can use him or herself in the
work but without personal needs or attitudes impinging
adversely on the way the work is handled
– talking through what to do if *personal considerations* do look
like getting in the way of doing a good job
– enabling the supervisor to ensure that *organisational policies*
on staff care, including worker safety, are operating effectively and that the employer's duty of care towards staff is
being observed.

If this looks like a tall order, it will serve to underline why the
social work profession has always placed such importance on
supervision, and why outside observers, for example in official
enquiries and inspections, have also regarded it as crucial and
called for improvements to be made.

At the practical level, nothing on the above list is achievable
unless supervision sessions:

• can be relied on to happen regularly
• take place in uninterrupted privacy
• offer enough time to talk (typically around 60–90 minutes)
• occur at prearranged times so that both parties can be adequately prepared and can contribute to the agenda.

Interpersonal considerations are equally vital. A mutually
trusting supervisory relationship will combine clear boundaries
of responsibility and accountability with the opportunity openly
to air practical concerns, ethical dilemmas and more personal
issues (in so far as these may impinge on the work in hand).
It is because there needs to be this mutual trust that power
dynamics assume such importance. There are clearly dangers in
supervision where members of oppressed groups are being
supervised. In so far as supervision can be seen as 'one of the
vehicles through which social work organisations transmit their
cultures and control their workforces' (Cosis Brown, 1998, p.79),
there is ample scope for personal or organisational intolerance to

creep in. Cosis Brown points out that the private nature of supervision means that it has 'rarely been opened up for scrutiny and evaluation through the processes of quality assurance'. In the context of writing about gay and lesbian staff in social work, she shows how the supervisory relationship can be anything from valuing and respectful to homophobic and repressive. Maintaining personal and professional boundaries means that the staff member must be clear about his or her own issues and needs and must not impose these on the service user. It does not mean that an employee who has experienced abuse or racism or homophobia at first hand cannot use this personal experience to understand the pressures in the lives of those who face similar kinds of social injustice.

Cosis Brown (1998) offers a balanced account of the dangers of over-identification – in overlooking abuse, for example – and of compensatory over-distancing – perhaps to avoid attack: 'You're gay, you should have understood' – either of which may affect professional judgement. A lesbian or gay practitioner working with a lesbian or gay service user may, she argues, be particularly in need of good supervision which they will get only where there is a mutually trusting and mutually valuing supervisory relationship. We would add that, where this is available, it can liberate excellent practice. Provided he has support, a gay worker may be the best possible person to understand the suicidal feelings of a young gay man who is being looked after by the local authority, and a well supported and self-aware woman worker who has herself been abused may be best able to undertake safety planning with an abused woman to keep her and her children safe.

Models and methods of supervision

Supervision can be individual or group, formal or informal, direct or indirect. Figure 6.1 shows that, working clockwise, and rotating the formal/informal pointer, this gives eight possible combinations to choose from. Thus a staff team discussing a case over lunch would be an example of informal, indirect, group supervision.

Individual supervision allows for the development of professional and personal practice, meeting each staff member at his or

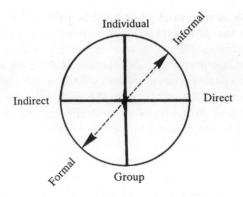

Figure 6.1 *Models of supervision*

her stage of experience and confidence and dealing with needs which cannot be met or which may be threatening in some way when talked about in groups. The individual can talk about problems which may be affecting their work and can also receive acknowledgement of work well done. This method has been the norm in social work settings and was traditionally undertaken by the first line manager, although this is decreasingly the case nowadays (Kearney, 1999).

Group supervision (see Brown, A. and Bourne, 1996, Chapter 9) might be chosen as the only way in which everyone will get the support they need given the time available, but a more positive rationale is that each person learns from all the others' experience and that this sharing strengthens the team, making it less reliant on top-down direction. There is greater scope in a group, too, for using different methods such as role play, case studies, sculpting and exercises. Ford and Jones (1987), referring to student supervision, add that groups reduce the impact of personality clashes or of the supervisor imposing ideas on the supervisee. In relation to staff in residential establishments and day centres, Atherton (1986) points out that the staff team in supervision might be able to rethink their approach by noticing when their own dynamics mirror issues among service users. He advises that, for this sort of learning to occur, the group should be as small as possible, that staff should be at more or less the same stage of professional development and that care should be taken to ensure that the sessions do not become management sessions or moaning arenas more appropriate to staff meetings.

Informal supervision in general is not seen as the most reliable model. *Ad hoc* chats do not allow individuals time to reflect on their work or to plan the agenda beforehand, and neither do these types of discussion usually get recorded. Unfortunately it is too easy for those trying to escape supervision to settle for this approach. But for someone who really wants supervision, it can breed resentment because there is rarely the chance to explore all their issues. It can be a perfunctory and dismissive form of support, keeping workers at a distance rather than using supervision to pull people together as a team.

The main advantage of informal supervision is that it is useful as an addition: either when the staff member is very newly in post and needs to feel he or she can 'pop in' for practical information or advice, or in a crisis situation when an individual needs immediate help. On occasion, too, the worker might be in the middle of an incident that holds tremendous learning potential which the supervisor witnesses; issues can be unpicked there and then, strengths pointed out, and the person returned to the fray with a clearer sense of what to try next.

Formal supervision, by which one social worker helps another to practise at an optimum level and in which the supervisee is formally accountable to the supervisor, is distinguished by three dimensions:

1. It has a *structure* which, for administrative reasons, is needed to ensure that there is adequate preparation, regularity, a flexible agenda, time boundaries and a record-keeping system of noting the planned agenda, points discussed and action to be taken.
2. It has a *focus* (that is, there need to be clear aims and objectives for the sessions, spelled out and reviewed from time to time; there may even be a formal learning agreement).
3. It has a *setting*, a context within which supervision is undertaken and which actually features as a basis for any discussions and strategies; again, as this book stresses, the organisational context has implications for practice and thus may be at the forefront of supervisory discussions.

Direct supervision is fairly new to field agencies, less so in residential and day-care establishments. It is now a requirement in all the professional awards in social work that there must be direct observation of the candidate's practice in order to verify the claim that competence has been demonstrated. 'Live' supervision and sitting-in supervision are further examples of gaining direct access to an individual's practice with scope, if appropriate, to correct any bad habits. Sometimes video/audio equipment or one-way screens might be available (especially useful for the development of micro-skills such as how to deal with hostility and so on).

Indirect supervision is normally the main approach which is available to most supervisors who cannot directly observe what contacts the staff member is making or what skills are employed (although in open-plan offices a great deal of information about staff's dealings with others is evident). The supervisor has to rely on free-ranging or topic discussion methods, reading through records and possibly some experiential exercises such as role play or simulations to help the supervisee.

Overall, methods can be far more innovative than is frequently the case. There is scope for critical incident analysis, assigned reading, role play, peer supervision and 'tag' supervision (supervisees supervise junior colleagues based on their own learning). An idea which could be borrowed from business is that of *quality circles*. Groups of between four and 12 staff meet once or twice a month for about an hour. They discuss how to improve the quality of their work but the immediate goal is to exchange fresh ideas, uninhibited by barriers of age, sex, status or qualification. The major benefits are that:

(a) ideas are used from everyone, at all levels in the organisation
(b) creativity and problem-solving are enhanced
(c) teamwork and team spirit develop
(d) commitment to the organisation is increased through involvement in decision-making and
(e) understanding grows between different work groups.

Core conditions are that staff have to have a modicum of knowledge and skill in order to contribute meaningfully; managers have to trust people by giving them sufficient information and leeway to follow through their ideas, and it is vital that there is a co-ordinator with groupwork skills in each quality circle.

The supervision session

Work in the supervision session, like any interview or group meeting, has both *content* and *process* elements. The task focus (the content) is on what the worker did, why and how. At the same time, a good supervisor recognises the processes within the supervisory relationship and the session itself as occasionally needing attention.

The task discussion, for each piece of work, proceeds through the following steps:

1. *Description.* Getting to know 'What happened?', letting the staff member describe each situation with the supervisor intervening minimally, just to check that salient facts have been covered and understood.
2. *Clarification.* Focusing on 'What did this mean?' and trying to understand the situation as the supervisee perceived it.
3. *Analysis.* Helping the individual make a pattern out of all the information that has been shared by asking 'How do we make sense of it?' This is the stage that needs to be grounded in relevant knowledge, policy, law and practice wisdom.
4. *Implementation.* Enabling the next step to be taken by first asking 'What are the aims in this piece of work?' and 'How can we begin moving in that direction?'
5. *Evaluation.* Asking 'How will we know when the aims have been achieved?'

The golden rule of the supervision process is not to overstructure or talk too much and thereby inhibit discussion. *Empathic listening*, establishing rapport at the outset, widening issues in the middle phase and ending the session with summarising are general guidelines. With a beginning, middle and end like this, the supervisor ideally will not get caught up in an individual's real anxieties right at the end of the session when there is too little time to do anything. Assuming that there is not a major problem with work performance, enabling staff to leave supervision feeling good about themselves and their work is an important aim. They should have a clear idea of any areas they could work on strengthening or gaps in knowledge that need to be filled (as well as how to do this and over what timescale) but with a general feeling of making an important contribution to achieving agreed goals. Over time, they may be able to think not just about their immediate practice but about the thought processes involved in improving it. There is great interest currently in 'reflective practice' (Schön, 1983; Eraut, 1994) which refers to this ability to capture our own learning experiences so as to generalise their benefits to our broader practice. Neither theory nor technical procedures can provide ready-made answers to the complexities that social workers encounter on a daily basis (Thompson, N., 1996, Chapter 20). It is the social worker who makes them useful by working out where they fit and what they have to offer. After all, we clearly do need something to move us beyond the dangers of a 'common sense' approach to any particular situation (every woman should leave violence immediately, child sexual abuse cannot possibly be widespread in the nurturing context of the family, newly disabled people should adjust to living a more limited life). Supervision is one of the key opportunities to stand back and think about practice at this level of abstraction.

The supervisor should find that he or she takes away an equally clear idea of any staff development or staff care needs the employee may have, as well as an overview of the person's workload, the extent to which performance standards are being met and any issues that may need taking up with another part of the organisation (e.g. about resource allocation or policy development). There may also be general lessons about how to make supervision more effective in future.

Performance appraisal

Management methods which promote efficiency, helping workers to organise, review and evaluate their efforts, go under the general heading of 'management by objectives' or 'MBO'. They include performance appraisal. Drucker (1954), the originator of MBO, believed that the process of planning agency-wide objectives should be one of *mutual goal-setting* between managers and staff. Unlike other planning devices such as workload and priority systems which frequently do not incorporate the views of those affected, the hallmark of MBO is that it tries to link each employee's goals to planned agency targets. Nonetheless, it is used by fairly large organisations in order to get everyone's commitment to top level goal-setting, demanding that team and individual goals be consistent within this. In other words, it is still control from the top. In that performance appraisal is a part of this process, it can make staff feel defensive, particularly if badly done. On the other hand, it ensures that supervision happens and that every worker has a clear idea of what is expected of them. Also, at its best, it can be used as the basis for keeping staff development and staff care needs under constant and focused review.

And 'top down' goals need not be arbitrary or even undemocratic. In the public sector, the agency's goals should mirror the felt and expressed needs of the community it serves (see Figure 6.2). In a local authority, for example, the views of local people are meant to inform the Community Care Plan, the Children's Services Plan, the Community Safety Plan and the authority's decisions about what constitutes 'Best Value'.

The other fear about appraisal is of *having one's performance judged*. Yet there is no workplace in which managers are not forming views all the time about their staff. Traditionally, these have

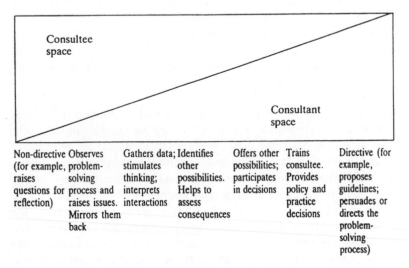

| Non-directive (for example, raises questions for reflection) | Observes problem-solving process and raises issues. Mirrors them back | Gathers data; stimulates thinking; interprets interactions | Identifies other possibilities. Helps to assess consequences | Offers other possibilities; participates in decisions | Trains consultee. Provides policy and practice decisions | Directive (for example, proposes guidelines; persuades or directs the problem-solving process) |

Figure 6.2 *The consultant: roles and activities*

been unspoken and subjective and have resulted in some people and not others being encouraged to apply for promotion, some people being put forward for training opportunities and some people being generally coached to 'get on' in the organisation. Individuals may also be put forward for pay awards in some settings. Performance appraisal formalises the process with a written record at the end. For the first time, every employee has the right to know what opinion is held about their chances of development and progression, every employee can be involved in gathering and discussing the information that underpins that judgement and every employee has the opportunity to use the normal channels of complaint if there is strong disagreement about the outcome. In social work and social care, those who undertake undervalued tasks – for example, those of physical caring – can as readily be included in the appraisal scheme as those who hold professional social work qualifications and, if appraisal is well conducted, this can improve morale in the workforce.

An effective approach to conducting appraisals can learn from social work in more respects than the fact that it usually consists of filling in complicated forms. These include adopting the following:

- A *partnership* approach, with agreed targets, open communication and shared tasks at the outcome.
- A *systemic* approach, with agreement on what information it is relevant to input into the process, measurement from planned performance right through to outputs and outcomes, and feedback to the individual so that future performance can be further improved.
- A *task-focused* approach, with agreed and prioritised goals, clear timescales (including for a follow-up meeting), shared tasks designed to reach the goals, and specificity about the purpose of the evaluation, its results, and any problems as both see them.
- A *problem-solving* approach, with clear agreement as to any area of performance where competence is not demonstrated or where improvement is possible; wherever possible tackling the immediately rectifiable ones through a personal action plan and the longer-term ones through staff development; keeping the focus very clearly on strengths and weaknesses in performance, not on personal characteristics.

- An *interpersonal* approach, the use by the appraiser of active listening skills to help the staff member identify problems, reflecting back and reaching a shared understanding; also, building self-esteem through positive feedback and ending on a note of accomplishment, as well as building a positive self-image in someone who is, or is becoming a valued member of the organisation.
- An *empowering* approach, encouragement to employees to voice their own opinions about all elements of the process, building in self-appraisal and actively seeking comments on how the appraisal system might be improved.
- An approach based on a *written agreement*, noting agreed solutions and goals for future reference; summarising clearly.

Appraisal techniques

McKenna and Beech (1995) provide a listing of ways of conducting appraisals, from a human resource management (HRM) perspective. The middle manager in social work is unlikely to be given a choice of these, but the more senior manager may wish to influence his or her agency's appraisal system for the future. The most common mechanism is a written report, often through the completion of a standard form or forms. This should not prove too taxing for social work managers because they are used to form-filling and to writing about people's strengths and weaknesses – more so than many managers in industry, in fact. Management by objectives (MBO) gains a separate listing by McKenna and Beech, as an appraisal approach in its own right.

Critical incident analysis can be used in appraisal, just as it can in selection (see Chapter 5). In the appraisal context, it is used to gauge strengths and weaknesses from actual behaviour (which can be evidenced) rather than from more general self-report. The staff member may be asked to keep a 'critical incident log' which is a narrative, running record of incidents handled well or badly (see Dessler, 1985).

Again like selection, the search for *objectivity* has pervaded appraisal. Rating scales can be used, ideally with performance indicators for each point on the scale (making it a 'behaviourally anchored rating scale') so that each appraiser knows exactly what they are looking for when trying to rate factors such as teamwork, punctuality or initiative on a scale from 1 to 5.

Another way of finding something to measure against – but this time in a relative rather than an absolute sense – is to make a '*multiperson comparison*'. This can be done through ranking each individual in turn from best to worst (individual ranking), or through a group ranking which places the person in the top 10 per cent (or wherever), or in a series of paired comparisons so that each individual is compared with every other individual and rated as either stronger or weaker than they are until an overall picture is formed. It is hard to regard this approach as applicable in social work where teamwork requires a range of different strengths, where the competitive ethos of business has never really impinged on the management of groups of staff and where such comparisons would probably be considered odious.

Other approaches to appraisal that, similarly, have not yet spread from industry to social work include the use of a 'development centre' to put an employee through the whole gamut of mechanisms over a period of several days, with a multirater comparative evaluation being undertaken by trained assessors. This is the ultimate recognition of investment in staff and might be undertaken, for example, before deciding who to send on an expensive training programme or who to put on a fast track route to further promotion.

There is no reason why *self-appraisal* cannot play a major part in several of the other systems, including MBO, starting with forms that are designed for the appraisee to complete the major part. It is an important part of staff development that people should learn to assess their own performance against agreed goals. The weakness in the approach includes the fact that many people in Britain tend to be modest about their own achievements and highly self-critical, with some groups more so than others – notably women (see Chapter 7). It has been found in both higher education and industry that students and workers tend to be harder on themselves than their normal assessor would be, so the appraisal needs to operate within a shared approach with the appraiser helping the individual to recall evidence of strong points and good outcomes.

Another exciting prospect would be *upward appraisal*. Here, the subordinates appraise the manager, on the grounds that they know more about his or her detailed strengths and weaknesses over time than anyone else. Pooling their views should make the process fairer. If staff are trained to use the method, and are confident that their views will be valued and acted upon without reprisals (individual views could be anonymised but might then be less fair), than it can work well. It clearly requires a major culture shift towards two-way trust and influence, however. A variation on the theme, of relevance in social work, is to involve *service users* in performance assessment or appraisal. In practice teaching, for example, there is growing interest in obtaining user feedback on student performance and there is no obvious reason why evidence of users' views could not feed into routine staff appraisals.

A critical analysis of appraisal

As with the assessment of competences (Ixer, 1999), appraisal is only as fair as the degree to which it is possible to state what must be achieved or to agree both about this and about how to measure it. An appraisal scheme is likely to increase the power of the appraiser over groups of staff who may be operating from different sets of assumptions – and who are also more likely to be overlooked in the organisation – as a result of ethnicity, gender, sexuality or other social status. Indeed, in social work, the whole question of performance appraisal can be a vexed one; *competence is not the same as effectiveness* (as they say about medicine: 'the operation was a complete success; unfortunately the patient died'), immediate, tangible results are rare, and the notion of 'success' is saturated with uncertainties such as the intervening variables which can affect outcomes – most notably, what service users and carers do for themselves as opposed to what help we give them.

It is important to be clear whether the appraisal is attempting to measure behaviours, the performance of technical tasks, attitudes and interaction (motivation, teamwork), practice knowledge and skill, quality of work, volume of outputs, delivery of outcomes, meeting organisational requirements or a combination of these. Furthermore, if an agency grasps for objectivity by using measuring instruments such as rating scales, checklists or critical incident logs, remember that these are still subject to the person making the judgements or writing the record, and the same is true of direct observation. In one interview, for example, the observer thought the practitioner should have spoken more clearly, whereas his strong local accent could have been seen as giving him an immediate advantage with service users. Even where factors taken into account are at their most quantitative – number of cases dealt with or particular outcomes achieved, extent to which budgetary targets were observed – these are easier to measure but no easier to decide on, and not always fairer since cases vary so much. Despite the original intentions of MBO, it is rare for staff at all levels to be involved in identifying what matters most in which roles, or in agreeing ways of monitoring this.

Then, too, in all work contexts there is a wider tension between using appraisal chiefly to measure individual performance in the technical aspects of the job, on the one hand, or to foster and develop the workforce, on the other. These two approaches are known as 'evaluative' and 'developmental' (McKenna and Beech, 1995). In social services departments, appraisal interviews do tend to feed into promotion procedures whereas, in some other settings, the emphasis may be on staff development and personal career planning, with perhaps even a choice of appraiser. Either way, it should be possible to build on strengths so that the organisation can 'grow its own' high-fliers and future managers from among its existing staff. Appraisal that is linked with *progression* also provides an opportunity directly to reward an individual's good performance in the job (though not by means of individualised performance-related pay, as may happen in business under a system of 'reward management'). Overall, it can promote a *performance-orientated culture* through setting aims and providing feedback, motivating staff being the holy grail of current theories of organisational behaviour.

Anyone who is called on to act as an appraiser (now that this is a line management rather than a specialist function), no matter what the model adopted or the techniques to be used, requires training and should insist upon it within their organisation. It is not a bad idea for appraisees also to be offered an orientation session on the operation and purpose of their organisation's appraisal scheme. As management moves increasingly into a cult of 'techniques', it is important that everyone understands both the benefits and the dangers. Certainly, the particular scheme to be applied needs to be well developed and properly executed, with ample time and attention given to its use in practice. The normal channels of trade union support, grievance procedures and so on are available for use in extreme cases.

Staff development

Staff development used to come under the far more limited heading of 'training' and was very much an 'add-on' in most social work organisations. The training officers in social services departments and large voluntary bodies used to offer mainly short courses in-house and allocate funding for attendance at external conferences and training events. Staff could largely choose what courses they attended, with occasional suggestions from their line managers, and the allocation of places was a case of 'first come, first served'. The only exception was when a new piece of legislation came into force or when a major policy change was made, such as computerisation, at which point there would be a strategy to put all relevant staff through the necessary training process.

The successors to the old-style training officers, the staff development officers or staff development commissioners, are now involved in drawing up thorough-going developmental policies for the whole workforce. At their most sophisticated, these become part of a system of performance management (Horwath and Morrison, 1999) whereby all staff development resources are targeted towards corporate objectives and the performance of all employees is measured against the organisation's operational and strategic plans. For this reason, as well as the wider ones of bringing out the best in the workforce and keeping all staff up to date, all managers need a broad understanding of their agency's staff development strategy as well as how it relates to their specific area of responsibility and to the staff they manage. They may also be asked to feed into the development of the strategy from time to time, both in detail (e.g. from conducting appraisals which reveal learning needs) and in helping to determine its overall direction (through identifying priority issues, neglected staff groups, and so on). A wider understanding of systematic approaches to training in the social care sector is also invaluable (Horwath and Morrison, 1999).

In social services departments, the staff development plan is not only under the oversight of senior managers and of the social services committee. It also has to be submitted to the Department of Health on an annual basis. The achievement of agreed targets and setting of appropriate new ones triggers a significant part of the funding for the following year through the Training Support Programme or 'TSP'.

What all this means is that, rather than responding to what an individual happens to be interested in at any one time or what happens to be on offer in the shape of outside courses, learning is planned according to what the agency intends to achieve over time – that is, the *strategic direction* of the organisation. Through the identification of individual and group learning needs, staff development can meet the shortfalls in the competences and knowledge-base of various grades of staff which might otherwise present obstacles to achieving organisational goals. As we saw in Chapter 4, in relation to recruitment, it may not be the skills required to carry out a specific job that are emphasised in staff development planning, but the skills, across the combined workforce, to carry forward a mix of tasks as these change over time. To inform this planning, it is essential that the processes of staff appraisal we considered in the last section and the vision of operational and strategic managers as to how services will develop in the future should both feed into future staff development priorities. Other factors may also be relevant, such as equal opportunities for particular groups of staff. Then, to complete the staff development feedback loop, learning is evaluated in terms of its impact in the workplace and feeds back into appraisal and future learning.

One consequence of this latter point is that, instead of merely completing anonymised 'happy sheets' at the end of a training day, giving their overall satisfaction ratings with content, presentation, venue, catering and so on, staff are likely to find the spotlight turned on themselves. They may well have been asked to determine learning aims before undertaking the training and to have matched these with the learning objectives the trainers specifically undertake to deliver. Then, after attending the event or course, staff will be expected to put their learning into practice and to comment on the extent to which the intended learning outcomes are actually demonstrated in the workplace, often through a *recall event*. In other words, learning is not undertaken for its own sake but to help people do their jobs better. And whether it works or not can be measured. A bonus of this approach is that staff learn to critically analyse their own practice (see 'reflective practice', below), to provide evidence of how it develops over time (e.g. in a portfolio, a diary, or a critical incident log) and to identify when competence is demonstrated. They are *active participants* who take responsibility for their own learning.

Line managers have a clear role to play in this process in that, as well as helping staff develop the skills just outlined (sometimes through formal 'mentoring', for which training should be provided), they are called upon to 'verify' the evidence produced. Whether this is done through a simple countersignature, a short written report, direct observation of practice, or the production of additional evidence, it is a crucial way of proving that the claims made by the learner are genuine and – in particular – that the learning *has* been applied in the workplace in a manner appropriate to the practice undertaken there. Line managers may be called upon to collate information on the impact of training plans and activities to pass to strategic managers who need to see the overall picture at organisational and interorganisational level. Line managers may also find the need to feed back to the organisation aspects of practice which training has revealed could be improved – for example, the need to develop a policy on vulnerable adults or on heavy lifting.

All this may sound like more work, and it is. Training is no longer a passive process for those attending and it is no longer detached from the realities of practice. Rather, as government is certainly recognising, it is an inescapable part not only of managing staff effectively, but of delivering a high-quality service. The Department of Health has funded the production of evaluation guidelines which outline this further: 'Senior managers have the responsibility for relating the outcomes of the evaluation of training to the strategic objectives of the organisation and establishing the future direction of the next training plan' (Joint Initiative for Community Care, 1997, p.67). The same organisation has produced a guide (Joint Initiative for Community Care, 1998) for managers who find themselves responsible for commissioning staff development and training activities, which includes an outline of the National Vocational Qualifications (NVQs) in Care and sections on placing training contracts and evaluating tenders.

External influence over this process of strategic planning of staff development comes in the form of Department of Health support for national frameworks of education and training, including the S/NVQs (that is, National Vocational Qualifications and Scottish Vocational Qualifications) and the professional Post Qualifying and Advanced Awards in Social Work (the PQSW and AASW), including the PQ Child Care. SSDs are required by the Department of Health to set targets under the TSP for the numbers of their staff who will work towards these various awards. The work-based nature of much of the learning means that is can still be individualised, although the Government is also increasingly seeking to influence content, most notably to raise standards in child care.

In social services departments, there has been a clear shift in priorities. Most noticeably, there is great concern to move beyond the situation where the qualified social work staff, who have already had a considerable amount of public money spent on their education, absorb the bulk of the staff development budget while home care and residential care staff remain largely unqualified (National Institute for Social Work, 1998). SSDs are seeking to devote far more attention to the learning needs of the unqualified majority of the social care workforce. and to put increasing numbers through NVQs. The Department of Health is backing this intent with a considerable increase in funding for the TSP over a four-year period to 2001–2 (White, 1998).

Responding to the needs of the whole social care workforce is also a priority for the Training Organisation for the Personal Social Services (TOPSS), the employer-led organisation with strategic responsibility for education and training in the social care sector across the UK. The overall aim is a coherent training strategy, with a comprehensive qualifications framework mapped against National Occupational Standards (outlining what skills are needed to do each specific kind of job), for all 1.25 million social care staff in the statutory, voluntary and private sectors. This also involves: identifying skills shortages and gaps, as well as overall skills mix needs; forecasting future staffing requirements; linking training outcomes to service standards, so that the public as well as the staff and their employers benefit from the changes; and working closely with related National Training Organisations (NTOs) in areas of work such as the Voluntary Sector NTO and those for Health Care, Early Years and Community Justice (TOPSS UK, 1999a, 1999b). It is a tall order to encompass such a breadth of planning. There are fears that patchiness may result from the devolution of planning to separate committees in the four countries of the UK, and that bias towards employers' views, while it will 'get the job done', may lose sight of educational principles. Certainly, the global academic discipline of social work stands for more than a narrow delivery of on-the-job skills and education providers in general are seriously under-represented on TOPSS. Ironically, it could be that inclusivity of levels of staff comes at the expense of inclusivity of ideas.

Part of the reason why it has been such an uphill battle to include social care staff in the strategic planning of education and training is the traditional undervaluing of much of the work undertaken. Phillipson (1988) has helped us to understand that caring was for a long time seen as 'women's work' which women staff should be able to do naturally, without training, yet that, paradoxically, the nurturing model of caring women offer in the family is increasingly at odds with current thinking about the empowerment of service users. So, where training was offered to care staff, it was sometimes imposed almost punitively on those who were seen as blocking the processes of change sought by management. Phillipson devised a more empowering approach to training which resulted in two-thirds of the care staff in one authority's homes for older people starting work towards an NVQ level 2.

At the other end of the organisational spectrum, there is also a focus currently on management training. The main qualifications relevant to social work and social care managers are the MBA (Master's in Business Administration) or other Master's degree or diploma in management with a public sector specialism, S/NVQs in management and the Advanced Award in Social Work (AASW), either through the management route or a route combining management with one or more of the alternatives: practice, education and training, and research. Managers constitute a further group whose needs were not well met by the old-style in-house provision of courses mainly for professional staff. Yet their role is as crucial as anyone's in meeting corporate objectives.

Increasingly, SSDs make special provision for them and government, too, has spotted the need. It has instituted a 'Top Managers' Programme', consisting of 18 regionally-based learning sets (see below) managed by the Local Government Association and open to social services directors and other senior managers, issued a best practice booklet on management for the social care sector through the Department of Trade and Industry in association with TOPSS, and instituted a social services leadership development initiative through the Social Services Inspectorate (SSI) at the Department of Health. The Improvement and Development Agency for local government (IDeA), established in 1999, also offers learning and skill development opportunities for managers, staff and elected members, while the most senior managers are kept updated by organisations such as the Association of Directors of Social Services and SOLACE, a representative body for senior managers working in local government. UNISON, the local government trade union, through its Open College, has also commissioned an open learning package aimed at first line managers in social services (*Community Care*, 4–10 November 1999, p.8). 'The Caring Manager' is intended to provide a flexible route to a management qualification pitched at S/NVQ level 4. Produced by the Joint Initiative for Community Care (JICC) it has four units covering the management of activities, resources, people and information.

There has also been interest in career development for women managers (Foster, G. and Phillipson, 1994; Foster, G., 1996) who are frequently isolated yet highly visible within a male-dominated management culture which prevents them from placing their particular strengths at the service of the organisation (see Chapter 7). There is some evidence that women social workers are less likely than men to have been on management courses (Murray, 1997) and that women may experience more difficulties than men in accessing training of all kinds, with problems of being selected, being freed to attend and being funded (National Institute for Social Work, 1998). The National Institute for Social Work continues its interest in career planning for women managers with women-only workshops available, while the SSI has commissioned a guide to training courses, organisations and networks for women managers (Lance and Bunch, 1998). Coyle (1989) regards specific opportunities for women of management potential and current women managers as having opened up at least a little space for women to 'discover their power, to support each other, to help others and to effect change' (p.124), though she recognises that rising through the existing hierarchy does not fundamentally challenge gender assumptions, let alone issues of ethnicity, class and so on.

Government measures taken through the TSP, of course, reach only the public sector. The independent sector has to find ways of financing its own training, with the result that provision may be far patchier and costs incurred may be passed on in contracts for service or met out of fund-raising efforts which would otherwise go towards meeting direct services to users. There is at least an argument for government attention of both a stick and a carrot variety – that is, through taking account of levels of training and of updating in the regulation of standards as well as considering offering some direct support to training for social work and social care staff in the independent sector. Certainly, the new Training Organisation for the Personal Social Services (TOPSS) has the oversight of training and qualifications and can set targets across all sectors though, as an employer-dominated body, it may take a particular view of labour market needs.

It can be seen from the above that staff development is increasingly of concern to the whole organisation; training opportunities are no longer 'goodies' for individual staff but are built into the fabric of how staff are managed as one of the key ways of meeting corporate objectives. This gives rise to the concept of the 'learning organisation' (Argyris and Schön, 1978; Thompson, N., 1995). By this is meant, as was noted in Chapter 3, not only an organisation in which learning opportunities for staff are encouraged and promoted, but also one in which the whole organisation is open to new ideas, to learning from experience and, in social work, from user feedback and interdisciplinary working. It is a question of climate and culture in which continuous learning and self-development are valued, in which norms can be challenged and in which staff at every level are encouraged to question and to explore ideas.

As we have seen throughout this chapter, the effectiveness of the whole organisation, particularly in the face of rapid change, is seen as best served by *maximising people's potential*. The agency needs lively minds if it is to survive. Individual workers also need lifelong learning in order to keep up to date the portable skills that will help them to survive reorganisations or, if necessary, to pursue serial careers with a range of employers. These trends are at odds with repressive managerialism and a passive workforce. If the role of management were seen as to inspire rather than to control, then having a strong management presence need not be in tension with people learning to think for themselves. Learners now need to be responsible for their own learning and to learn *how* to learn, not just *what* to learn (Thompson, N., 1995).

Overall, an organisation is likely to be most successful if it undertakes a training audit or training needs analysis across all staff groups to determine what organisational and occupational as well as individual training needs will best help staff to meet organisational objectives while carrying out their roles effectively, and developing positive careers (Horwath, 1996).

Staff care

It is difficult to feel relaxed about one's work when a 'culture of blame' exists within social work and is heavily targeted against it. This was fuelled in the late 1990s by a succession of negative joint Audit Commission/Social Services Inspectorate reviews of individual social services departments (Department of Health Social Services Inspectorate and The Audit Commission, 1998), a string of revelations about institutional abuse and an almost uniformly negative press, with government ministers also joining the bandwagon from time to time and then responding with regulation and performance assessment. Only at the very end of 1998 did a new Minister, John Hutton, start talking about focusing on good practice and recognising that some authorities were doing an excellent job (*Community Care*, 26 November–2 December 1998, p.1).

One of the worst aspects of a blame culture can be that practitioners are scapegoated for problems and are left to feel that any shortcomings in service, together with their own emotional reactions to these, are their own fault. A blame culture is frequently also a 'fear of failure' culture which blights learning, confidence and morale. An effectively operating staff development and staff care system, on the other hand, would offer the worker whose case had not turned out as hoped: first, a supported opportunity to reflect in supervision and to analyse what lessons could be learnt individually and by the team and the organisation and, second, the necessary personal support (e.g. counselling) to cope with the personal and emotional fall-out. (This is not to be confused, of course, with a situation in which a staff member has committed a criminal or a disciplinary offence.)

We cannot work with other people's pain, grief and (sometimes violent) anger without an impact on ourselves. Although we learn to deal with them professionally – i.e. to focus on the other person's needs and not our own feelings while we are with them – this should not mean that we distance ourselves from human suffering or joy, so that we become cynical. In the face of chronically unmet need, social workers may negatively label service users and become rigid in applying rules. Yet 'battle fatigue' or 'working under siege' are metaphors from the workplace which suggest feeling at war with consumers in ways which managers in organisations could help to prevent. As was mentioned above, part of the purpose of supervision is to help the worker to talk about the personal impact of the work. It is not healthy to the individual or to their employing organisation to expect them to suppress their own emotions, avoid facing their own anxieties, or deny their own stress levels. Yet there are worrying signs of a macho culture in social work and social care in which responding to stress is seen as weakness and taking time off as a needless expense to the organisation.

Stress

Thus far, we have looked at a number of ways (e.g. appraisal and total quality management or TQM) in which organisations can protect staff from overload. This is not just about endless form-filling or lack of resources; in the human services, we often do not have the satisfaction of seeing the problems that we tackle solved and cannot rely on happy endings. With staff under constant pressure and perhaps with few intrinsic rewards, there is a risk that they will stop caring.

When organisational stress came to the fore, the literature in social work talked of 'burn-out' and tended to look for individual weakness to explain it. It explored the kinds of personality that might be prone to this emotional exhaustion (people without a fulfilled private life, 'workaholics', those with an unrealistic view of what social work can achieve, or those subject to breakdowns) and ignored the impact of organisational power structures and cultures. But, since stress-related problems rarely appear in only one person at a time, organisations need to examine in what ways their systems might erode their staff's ability to cope.

Some organisations actually do create a 'culture of stress' (Thompson, N. *et al.*, 1996) and hence put their staff at heightened risk. Workers exhibit higher anxiety and job dissatisfaction, particularly in terms of a lack of autonomy and of recognition for a job well done, as well as a feeling that the the job is not worthwhile because little can be done for service users within the time and resources available. The difference cannot be explained away by characteristics of staff or workloads. Rather, key factors appear to be line managers who have unrealistic expectations of what is possible, who give too little supervision and do not use it as an opportunity for praise, and who expect or allow work to seep into non-work time (late home visits, taking work home, and so on). They are poor at motivating and supporting their staff and at helping them to organise their work, almost certainly because the managers themselves are stressed out. Since this is only happening in some organisations and not in other, comparable ones, it must be preventable through implementing a *culture change*.

Similarly, managers can be aware that there are categories of job in which people are more likely to be subjected to violence and can take additional precautions for their safety. The European Commission's (1998) social action programme recognises that it is not enough to adapt to the demands of the modern world for constant change; organisations must also look after the workforce and create 'a safe and healthy workplace'. In addition to domestic legislation on health and safety at work, there are European Directives on matters as wide-ranging as heavy lifting and hours of work which may prevent some of the days lost and personal suffering caused in social work and social care through back injuries and overwork. SSDs are expected by the Department of Health to provide guidance, training and support (as well as appropriate equipment) to protect the health, safety and security of users, staff and premises and this is monitored by the Social Services Inspectorate (SSI).

It is the risk of violence which arguably faces social work employers with their greatest staff care challenge. Levels of violence in SSDs are unquestionably high (Balloch *et al.*, 1998; National Institute for Social Work, 1999). Developing a positive work culture to prevent and respond to the risk of violence means not waiting for incidents to happen. Staff can be routinely trained, with the emphasis on defusing potentially volatile situations and promoting their personal safety. There is now much greater awareness in social work of sensible measures that can be taken. These include physical adaptations to offices (security systems, panic buttons), workers carrying mobile 'phones and/or alarms when they go out on visits, always making contact with the office at the end of a visit and, where advisable, going out in pairs. Of course, it will not be possible to prevent all attacks. Where an incident occurs, staff must know not only how to report it, but also that something will be done about it and that they will receive support from management in the immediate aftermath. They may also need time off work as a result of injuries or emotional trauma and longer-term help in the form of specialist staff care services. There should ideally be a free, confidential and professional counselling service, funded by the employing organisation but independent of it and with no leakage of information across, even as to who has used the service.

There are also categories of people who face additional pressures of other kinds. Experiencing discrimination at work on account of ethnicity, gender or sexuality is enormously stressful and cannot be reduced by generalised action to lift morale (Friedman *et al.*, 1998). It has to be tackled at source through equal opportunities policies and a commitment to their effective implementation. Bullying and harassment have a similar impact. Women (and a few men, for example those coping with a dependent relative at home), may be at risk of additional stress from role overload (constantly juggling demands with never any let up), role conflict (a sick child on the day a case goes to court) and role contagion (thinking about the family while at work and taking work home) (Home, 1993). Finally, anyone who is in a situation where they have to decide whether to become a 'whistleblower' (Hunt, G., 1998) and to report clear abuse or wrongdoing that is being deliberately overlooked by management cannot avoid facing enormous stress.

To sum up, let us itemise the kinds of problems that can cause undue stress:

- too much to do ('burnout'), especially where overload is prolonged and unremitting
- too little to do (this has been called 'rustout')
- lack of control over the work, making one feel trapped
- discrimination

- harassment
- bullying
- aggression and violence
- ill-defined responsibilities or objectives
- unrealistic expectations
- lack of supervision
- a blame culture/lack of praise
- an inflexible and unreasonable work schedule
- poor or unsafe working conditions, environment or practices
- poor working relations with colleagues
- role overload and role conflict (juggling work and home life)
- new demands with inadequate preparation (e.g. computerisation)
- job insecurity.

Any of these can be responded to by management, with the aim of tackling the stress-inducing factors in the working environment. Stress and workload management courses may also be helpful but it should not be regarded as solely the employee's responsibility to change.

The nature of stress

A certain amount of stress is a natural part of life and we all experience an increase at times of exams, public appearances (giving a talk, making a speech), and so on. Our body produces more adrenalin so that we have heightened physical responses for a time. The problems arise when the stressful context continues day after day and when we remain in a physical state that our body is not designed to sustain. At first, there may be warning signs such as an inability to shake off a cold – indicating, perhaps, that we would benefit from a short break. If we do not get the break or some other form of relief, things escalate, perhaps into bursts of irritability. Finally, there is a build-up into some of the following symptoms:

- *Physical*
  - chronic tiredness
  - insomnia

- tension headaches and muscle pain in the upper body
- digestive problems
- reduced libido
- tightness in the chest
- heightened sensitivity to noise.

- *Emotional*
  - inability to shut off from work or to see how a break can possibly be taken
  - irritability
  - constant worrying – e.g. about work, health
  - feelings of failure and of inability to cope, fear of the future
  - lack of concentration
  - loss of enthusiasm and sense of fun
  - anxiety and/or depression
  - mood swings
  - feeling guilty, looking for others to blame
  - feeling swamped by the job
  - loss of caring concern, cynicism.

- *Behavioural*
  - withdrawal
  - communication problems
  - inability to make decisions, loss of creativity
  - disorganisation
  - poor timekeeping
  - absenteeism
  - resorting to drink or drugs
  - overindulging in food or loss of appetite
  - declining job performance
  - forgetfulness
  - accidents – e.g. clumsiness, car accidents with no apparent cause
  - untidy personal appearance
  - inactivity

With all of the above, it must be emphasised that we are talking about an otherwise unexplained change in the person's normal state or behaviour. Where someone has been a good employee and they suddenly begin having unexplained absences, make mistakes or drop below par in their performance, it is reasonable to suppose that something is wrong, either at home or at work.

Responding to stress

If a problem is clearly job-related and the problem is dealt with at an early stage, it may prevent someone experiencing a breakdown in their mental or physical health which could cause them untold distress and be very costly for the organisation. In other words, it is better to deal with the *cause* rather than the *symptoms*. There may be solutions such as an internal transfer, a change of responsiblities perhaps including a new challenge, a holiday or period of unpaid leave to travel overseas, or a move to part-time working, or there may be sources of support which can be tapped, either inside or outside the organisation.

It is now clear that the onus is on the employer, where it is already known that a stressful job has been having an adverse effect on someone, to take action to reduce the risk to their future health and safety. In a well publicised case (*Walker* v. *Northumberland County Council* 1994), John Walker, a social work manager, was supported by his trade union in making a successful personal injuries claim against his social services employer. This was for breach of a common law duty of care in that the organisation had failed to take reasonable steps to avoid exposing him to a health-endangering workload after it was already clear that his mental health was suffering. This moves us well beyond the realm of personal coping with stress into organisational measures such as workload management (see below), clarity of priorities and procedures, adequacy of supervision, availability of resources, staff care in the face of violence and trauma, and the overall culture of listening to staff's concerns and valuing their contribution. This stems from a recognition that work-based stress cannot be understood outside of the working context (Pottage and Evans, 1992). Other public sector cases have raised further issues that employers may reasonably be expected to tackle, such as carrying an unreasonable workload, lacking the level of qualification and training needed to do an effective job, and suffering bullying and intimidation in the workplace (Schwehr, 1999). All require an organisation-wide culture that sets clear expectations and supports staff in their work.

Some specific methods of mitigating the stress of working in distressing and frustrating jobs include the points listed below:

1. training staff, both experienced and newcomers, in *preventive techniques* such as stress management and time management (see below)
2. *rotating tasks* and providing clear guidelines by which team members may negotiate 'time out' (that is, work which is less demanding than constant service user contact)
3. introducing *flexitime* to give staff control over the pattern of their working day and help them balance work, family and other outside demands
4. *streamlining paperwork and computerised recording systems* so that they help the work get done rather than feeling like additional obstacles
5. assisting teams to become *cohesive and consistent* in responding to service users, without losing compassion
6. helping staff to identify their *coping styles* (for example, warning 'sprinters' that 'long-distance runners' fare better)
7. orienting workers' families to the job's inherent *frustrations, rewards and importance*
8. passing around *tips for survival* to one another
9. promoting *physical fitness* by lunch and after-hours exercise, perhaps either arranged or publicised in the workplace
10. encouraging employees to join *networks outside the office*
11. working on *personal career plans* or new projects for those who feel 'stuck' in their job
12. improving *salary levels and promotion prospects*, including for older workers, women and black staff
13. engaging in *participatory management* so that staff feel part of the overall enterprise (see Chapter 3)
14. making it clear that *intimidatory behaviour* will not be tolerated through a published code or codes on harassment and bullying
14. ensuring that the overall management style is not a bullying one but one in which individual and team contributions are *respected and valued*
15. having *grievance and harassment procedures* in place for staff who feel they have been unfairly treated or discriminated against
16. offering a *staff care* or 'employee assistance' programme (see below).

The essence of staff care begins with a workplace culture in which staff can voice their worries and in which they are listened to, including in regular and effective supervision, so that those concerns can be addressed. A line manager can tactfully ask an individual whether there is something particular on their mind; there may be an obvious explanation for them looking unwell or stressed out, such as family illness, or they may say that the job is getting them down. It is always worth advising the person to have a medical check; illnesses such as chronic fatigue syndrome (or post-viral fatigue syndrome, formerly known as ME) (Shepherd, 1997), anaemia or an underactive thyroid can produce extreme lethargy, many conditions can affect concentration, or there may be a treatable depression.

Antidotes to occupational stress begin at the interpersonal level. Managers have to be prepared to listen and to show that they care about their staff, making reasonable allowances if, for example, someone's health is temporarily below par or they are preoccupied by a bereavement. Equally, compliments on work well done are essential; managers sometimes behave as if workers were disposable. Feedback should not be reserved for times when something has gone wrong. Overall, it would seem self-evident that cared-for staff are more likely to care for the users they serve.

Clearly, though, managers must draw boundaries around their role in relation to staff and not see themselves as counsellors (which can be a temptation when you are social work trained). A test as to whether to 'say something' to an employee who appears to be having problems would be, most importantly, whether or not the problem appears to have been caused or exacerbated by the working environment, or to be having an impact on the work of this individual or others. Other factors to consider would include whether the person concerned has sought your help, and whether or not they are already accessing appropriate systems of help and support outside. To take a tricky example, but one that satisfies the test of having an impact on the work of others, where someone's body odour is causing others to stay out of their way, a 'quiet word' is certainly called for. An example of being asked for help could be where one worker tells you that a colleague is constantly offloading work onto them; here, it would seem expedient to try and resolve these unhelpful relationships, perhaps through a team meeting on workloads and roles or through a team-building exercise. Where the situation clearly lies outside the office – if someone appears to be drinking rather heavily, say, but is already getting help and their work record is improving – this might be one to monitor from a distance unless the timekeeping or the standard of work starts to slip again. A balance always needs to be struck between ducking out of intervening and getting over-involved.

Another layer of boundaries between manager and staff comes into play where the employee needs to seek confidential advice or support. A staff care or employee assistance service, funded by the employer but with nothing reported back to the organisation – not even who has used it – can play an invaluable role. People need to know that the scheme can safely be approached for personal support and counselling and that it will not affect their chances of promotion or others' confidence in them as a good worker. The services offered may include short-term counselling and staff support groups. If several agencies join forces, this can be a feasible way of protecting workers' physical and mental health. Instances where it may be useful to have such a scheme, accessed outside the organisation but paid for from within, are where a worker has been the victim of violence or the subject of an investigation into their conduct, where they constantly deal with stressful matters such as sexual abuse or terminal illness, or where they have personal problems which it would be inappropriate for the team manager to try to handle.

In addition to managers looking out for signs of stress in individual staff (and in themselves), and offering individual support schemes outside, comprehensive management information can be gathered which may indicate that the organisation as a whole has a problem. This can include a marked increase in any of the following: sick leave, accidents at work, staff turnover, use of grievance and harassment procedures, and complaints by service users, as well as poor results in audits and reviews, evidence of poor teamworking, new ideas not getting off the ground, objectives and targets not being met, and a generally worrying picture emerging from appraisals and staff development evaluations. The response may need to be a complete culture change in the organisation, with the focus on valuing, developing and caring for the workforce, as well as on organising work sensibly without taking away the rewards of personal autonomy in the exercise of skill and judgement. Occupational health also requires a systematic approach, with issues such as safe lifting, the effect of VDU screens and keyboard work, attitudes towards smoking and alcohol use, the need to educate staff about HIV/AIDS and problems with 'sick buildings' all potentially as relevant in social care and social work as stress (Pettinger, 1997).

Worryingly, there are some signs of organisations using their management information to become more punitive towards individuals rather than more aware of their own responsibilities. Throughout the 1990s, for example, there was growing concern about levels of sick leave (Francis, 1992; Daly, 1998) but the use of the word 'absenteeism' to refer to this appears to place the blame on individuals who may, in fact, be affected by stress or unsafe working practices. Some of the sickness monitoring procedures are experienced by staff as a first warning in a potential move towards disciplinary action, rather than as a way of finding out about underlying problems. And referees are asked to give information about employees' past sickness records so that a move to a new job to escape unreasonable stress may also become more difficult. It is possible to combine rigorous sickness monitoring, instead, with health promotion, good staff care and an awareness of the relevance of team and workplace culture (Daly, 1998).

Workload management

There is evidence that *workload review and measurement schemes* can help keep workers' stress levels down (Orme, 1995). They assist employees by protecting them from overwork and unfair demands, at the same time as helping the organisation allocate work fairly and get the best from all staff.

Everyone manages their own work to some extent by using their diary to plan commitments and making constant decisions about when and how to perform tasks. More formal workload management, however, involves a systematic weighting of cases or other pieces of work, allocation of these up to an agreed limit for each worker and monitoring progress. It naturally involves more work for the front line manager, including being involved in prioritising work, allocating it and balancing workloads. As with so much in contemporary social work, this brings home the lesson that employee time is a *resource under pressure* that has to be rationed, just as much as places in residential care and cash budgets.

Over and above the handling of the routine workload, there need to be procedures in place to cope with emergency and other unplanned demands, ebbs and flows in the work coming through, and the whole question of unallocated cases when there are simply too many users needing services from too few staff. One busy child protection team, for example, has to operate a duty system just to deal with matters that arise in unallocated cases in parallel with the one taking new referrals.

Workload management has links with supervision, because that is where the progress of work is tracked, with staff appraisal, in that employees need a good fit between the work they are doing and their own skills and abilities, with staff development in terms of opportunities to grow into new areas of work and with staff care because people may occasionally need a temporary lightening of their load, for example. The auditing and management of work-loads also relates, of course, to the collection of statistical data by the organisation – and, indeed, to all aspects of strategic and operational management in that it regulates the point at which these are translated into a service to the public.

In a profession where levels of risk and violence are high, any measures that enable team members and managers to moderate the pressures placed upon them, and to manage these within a system owned and agreed by the whole organisation, must be all to the good. On the downside, they may involve saying 'no' more often to service users and leaving some categories of work to stock-pile. But at least we live in an era where audits of community need and the publishing of criteria, targets and achievements place this balancing act in the public arena and, in the local authority context, submit it to political judgement. This implies greater equity both for staff and for service users and means that the practitioner is not left to work harder and harder to keep up with impossible demands.

Grievance procedures

Where an individual employee does feel that they have been unfairly treated, in respect of workload or any other matter, they may wish to register a grievance. This is an action internal to the organisation, as opposed to using the courts or an employment tribunal to seek some form of compensation or other righting of a wrong.

As with disciplinary procedures (where, conversely, it is the organisation that is dissatisfied with the worker), any manager who is involved in the build-up to what might become a grievance would generally do well to see whether the issue can be resolved in a more informal way. This will give the staff member a more prompt response and sometimes be more likely to lead to the graceful apology or localised change that the employee really wants than can happen once interests become polarised and concretised by a more public airing. At this stage, it is important for the manager to know the limits of their own flexibility to act (Pettinger, 1997) since there may be things they can do to rectify the situation swiftly and without fuss.

It is equally important, though, not to leave the staff member feeling that their issue was not taken seriously and important, too, for the organisation not to leave unresolved a matter which might have wider implications. Once into a grievance, there will be both internal procedures to guide the manager and legal standards against which these will have been prepared, as well as advice from other quarters on personnel and legal matters. The manager's own dealings with the employee should at all times follow the principles of natural justice and the individual should be informed when there is the right of appeal to a higher level within the organisation.

The more that organisations work to agreed procedures and standards, and the more that managers can ensure these are followed, including in the treatment of staff, the fewer grievances, complaints and disciplinary procedures there should be to deal with. But we live in a litigious age and it is also possible to argue that, because workers and service users increasingly know their rights, they may be more likely to question the way they are treated. Either way, managers can do a great deal to create a climate in which misunderstandings can be talked through and in which concerns can be considered promptly and fairly without being 'allowed to fester and rankle' (Pettinger, 1997, p.343).

Self-help support and self-directed learning

Thus far in this chapter we have looked at what the good employer should do to ensure that the workforce is developed and supported.

Whilst it is every employee's right to expect that the employer's duty of care and good management practice will result in these mechanisms being offered as of right, they represent a 'top down' model which can usefully be supplemented by actions that employees take for themselves. In addition to joining a trade union (and thus benefiting from a system of support, independent of the workplace, which has played an important part in this country in ensuring more humane and enlightened treatment of workers), and perhaps a professional organisation, staff can take some steps of their own to protect their own well-being, assess their own abilities and potential, and develop their own learning and hence their career opportunities. Chief amongst these are the establishment of informal support groups or more formalised employee network groups to supplement staff care, and self-directed learning mechanisms, such as courses taken in the evening, to supplement staff development. Because consultancy stands outside the line management structure and is crucially affected by 'ownership' issues, it will also be covered here, even though it may be paid for by management in many instances.

Support groups and employee network groups

Support groups in the workplace are perhaps not as common as once they were. This is a shame because they can raise morale amongst members of staff who would otherwise feel isolated in their respective work settings. There are two reasons why support groups might be ripe for a 'comeback'. One is that networking is currently in vogue (see Chapter 8) and the other that the idea could be reinvented through being imported with the American human resource management literature as 'employee network groups' (see below).

In the UK context, groups typically combine support, opportunities for personal and professional development, empowerment and the development of a strengths-based approach. A group which is open to all those who define themselves as black, for example, will operate from a black perspective or perspectives. This means that it will work to base practice on knowledge that derives from the experiences of black people as articulated by them, will place understanding within the context of the historical subjugation of black people and of continuing racism, will relocate black people from the periphery of provision to the mainstream, and will work for racial justice and equality in staffing and service delivery (Sigamoney, 1994). A group which operates within such a philosophy will provide an opportunity for black workers to feel more powerful within their own support networks, to develop a collective black identity, to critique and monitor white-dominated approaches to practice while developing alternatives, and to identify and challenge overt and covert racism within the organisation (Stubbs, 1985; Dominelli, 1997).

Some groups have to think about how inclusive they want to be. A combined group for gay men and lesbians, for example, might not be an entirely comfortable place for those lesbians who prefer an all-women environment, and there is also a decision to be taken by the group as to whether bisexual men and women will be welcome. Similarly, a black support group will be faced with decisions about those who are of mixed heritage and those who are 'politically black' – that is, who face discrimination because of their ethnic or national origin or their religion, but not on account of skin colour (e.g. Middle Eastern, Irish people).

Over and above these questions, support group members may need to challenge one another where appropriate to recognise the interactions between the various forms of oppression. Women's groups, for example, need to ensure that their agendas are not set only by young, middle-class, white, heterosexual, able-bodied women but that diversity and difference are acknowledged and celebrated in an inclusive membership and debate. Provided this inclusivity can be achieved, members of the group may find it an intense relief to relate to others in a single-sex environment where they do not have to compete with men to be heard or to have their views valued. Topics they may feel freer to discuss might include women's life and career choices, life-cycle issues, sexual harassment and sexual violence in the workplace, appropriate service delivery to women users and carers, and assertiveness for women professionals and managers. Women returning after a career break, those who work from the isolation of home or in an intensely male-dominated environment, and those who have had to take up a harassment or sexual discrimination case may be among those who particularly appreciate the support. Male managers have a particular responsibility not to belittle women's groups or to make unfunny jokes about them, white managers not to undermine black groups and so on. It is to the benefit of the whole organisation if they thrive and flourish. Women's groups have proved to be a particularly useful form of support system amongst workers whose feminist perspective is at variance with the dominant stance of their agency (Dominelli and McLeod,1989).

The value of support groups is in helping staff members feel less isolated and vulnerable. They facilitate personal and professional learning about the significance of ethnicity, gender and sexual orientation in social work practice and opportunities to explore their personal significance so that staff's identities in the workplace will be confident and secure and they will, in turn, be more effective practitioners, managers and so on. Support groups provide an opportunity for people to relax as themselves, not to have to be on guard against hurts or misunderstandings, to talk in a rapid short-hand based on shared understanding and to get to the heart of issues which others try to block in mixed forums. These encompass the additional pressures faced, for example by black staff who are expected to be culturally (and often literally) bilingual, who experience high-profile visibility, who are expected to be 'race experts' whilst simultaneously being overlooked and bypassed, and who face racial harassment, racist comments from service users who sometimes refuse their intervention, and the risk of racial attack. Encouraging the formation of support groups in work time, and providing a meeting place, is one way in which an organisation can offer support commensurate with these demands and stresses. Groups will also need to decide whether or not they wish to have facilitation, and managers whether or not they are able to finance this.

A lesbian and/or gay support group may need a level of confidentiality and privacy not requested by other groups (though there can be a 'backlash' against membership of any group) since it cannot be assumed that all those who would potentially benefit from support are 'out' in the work setting, or would even want to be. Nevertheless, the group should be well publicised and respectfully spoken about in the organisation in order to convey that the low visibility of its meetings (perhaps out of work time and not on work premises) do not make it less important than other groups which meet more openly. In social work education, it is quite common to publicise a gay, lesbian and bisexual student support group to all students without waiting to be asked and certainly without expecting to know who attends it (Logan *et al.*, 1996). Employment settings could usefully follow suit.

The group may sometimes find that it needs to direct members to other well established networks of individual personal support for lesbians, gay men and bisexual men and women if it is not to become overwhelmed. It may, for example, wish to retain a focus on work-related issues. Such a group will provide an important opportunity for lesbian and gay staff to meet together in a context where no one has to keep their sexuality a secret, where no one is hidden or isolated and where there is a feeling of collective strength. Members will thus be empowered to discuss the common issues which relate to their roles in the organisation. These are likely to include the question of what it costs to be 'out' at work: weighing up the provision of positive role models, for example to young people, against personal vulnerability in a homophobic society which provides no specific employment protection for gay people. Overall, members will have the chance to discuss political, personal and professional aspects of their own sexuality, with the ultimate aim of developing stronger, more resilient and better informed gay and lesbian staff.

In the USA, support groups are known as 'employee network groups' and are defined as 'groups of minority or female employees that meet occasionally for social and career support' (Friedman *et al.*, 1998, p.1156). The networks take a strengths-based approach, pool the resources of their members for mutual support and are under the control of the members, not of management. Network groups in corporate America are formally recognised by the employer, with office holders and rules. Some UK support groups do operate in this way – for example some black workers' groups negotiate with management over issues raised by the membership. Dominelli and McLeod (1989) also mention women's groups as a channel for commenting on agency policies. This is not just self-help, then, but an attempt at organisational change. Women's groups, black workers' groups and gay and lesbian groups may also want to look beyond the organisation to campaign for legal changes or in support of individuals (benefits for lone mothers, deportation cases, the age of consent). There may come a point at which such campaigning would be better organised from within a trade union or other independent base, although a cross-agency grouping that meets outside of work time is clearly a different matter from a support group meeting within the context of an organisation that has to be politically neutral and uninvolved (this affects both local government and charitable bodies).

By way of a critique of support groups, there are one or two points to mention. First, since potential members are free to choose whether or not to attend, there may be a backlash against those who do. For example, men often do not like women having a space to meet which they are not allowed to enter. Members of women's groups and black groups may be seen as troublemakers. Second, support groups may help people to cope with their present job, rather than helping them to advance in their career. Social interaction at work cannot be separated out from the power dynamic. Thus, when members of minority groups seek the mutual support of interacting with one another informally, they are unlikely to be meeting with others in powerful positions and are still likely to miss out on the informal communication that can help majority group members learn the score about organisational politics and opportunities for advancement. Perhaps the ideal is to have support groups running alongside many other opportunities for personal support and professional development. Research conducted by Friedman *et al.* (1998) suggests that belonging to a black network group can make people feel more optimistic about their career, it would appear by making them better able to use mentoring and less uncomfortable with a white mentor. Perhaps this is because, where support needs are being met by an all-black group, the mentor is free to play a more career-focused role. The groups they studied did not change organisations, however, and could not remove feelings of discrimination where there was a real problem in the workplace.

Special interest groups

Establishing a special interest group (SIG) for interested individuals across teams, agencies and/or disciplines provides an opportunity to pursue an issue in depth. BASW provides an umbrella for a number of SIGs relating to specialist areas of social work practice and research, for instance its Project Group on Assisted Reproduction (PROGAR) and its Mental Health SIG. Freestanding national bodies also spring up from time to time – for example, for those with a special interest in certain methods of intervention such as family therapy or task-centred work. There may be a national newsletter and perhaps meetings organised.

Where an agency cannot offer inspiring supervision in a specialist area, other ideas are to set up a peer support group, a peer supervision scheme, or a formal or informal consultancy arrangement, as well as to attend relevant conferences, courses and practice exchanges. Any of these forms of networking can assist with the isolation of sustaining or moving into a new area of practice by assisting in developing the required skills and handling organisational constraints without losing the integrity of the work.

One particular role for a special interest group might be for white people who want to recognise and challenge racism, for heterosexuals to confront their own and the organisation's homophobia and heterosexism, or for men who want to take responsibility for tackling sexism and patriarchal assumptions in male-dominated institutions – not as something 'out there', but as something with which all men collude and from which all men benefit. In such a group, practitioners can consider what actions they can take to raise their own awareness and to effect positive organisational change. As with support groups, difference and diversity need to be recognised. A men's group, for example, may include black and white, gay and straight, older and younger, disabled and able-bodied men, and members from various social class backgrounds. Social injustices across all these divisions need to be acknowledged so that no one feels shut out of the group by difference, at the same time as not allowing them to escape from looking at their own sexism. The oppressed role can become a hiding-place, sparing oneself from looking at one's own oppressiveness. A group like this may benefit from facilitation to prevent it from becoming collusive.

Learning sets

As was mentioned above in relation to governmental support for management training at the highest levels in social work, 'action learning sets' or 'managers' learning sets' are an idea of the moment. They are like a seminar group discussing work-based issues. They have been developed for social work at NISW (the

National Institute for Social Work) and, though there are various models available, tend to share the following characteristics: discussion of work issues, with time slots for each member; aiming for practical outcomes; a facilitative environment (probably with a learning agreement or ground-rules); external facilitation; and member-owned agendas (Darvill, 1998a). Although there is no external training input, outside expertise can be brought in in the form of written materials that individuals have found useful or that the facilitator may suggest.

As well as offering all the obvious benefits of mutual support and shared problem-solving, learning sets can help to foster a climate of high service standards and good management and a feeling of shared responsibility and potential to promote these. They can be run with new, middle or experienced managers, or for those in more specialist posts in the hierarchy, but it is probably best to keep each of these separate so that agendas are sufficiently held in common and stages of learning are similar. Having said that, there could still be vast differences in, for example anti-sexist and anti-racist awareness which might mean the facilitator working quite hard, together with the more aware members of the group. The facilitator will also have a key role in maintaining a group process that maximises learning, and in ensuring that the feelings content of work can be appropriately aired and explored as it relates to management dilemmas. For these reasons, an unfacilitated set is less likely to be successful and so there are resource implications, even if a room and refreshments can be made available at little or no cost. There may also be questions as to whether this kind of learning provides as much value as the theoretical updating and research-generated knowledge offered by more formal educational opportunities.

Self-selected learning opportunities

As was explained above, staff development and training opportunities in social work increasingly serve organisational priorities. There has been a shift from 'education' to 'training' (Thompson, N., 1995). For those who want to learn purely for the love of learning, and particularly where the interest is in delving deeper than the technical, skills-based level increasingly involved in competence-based training, it may be a case of paying your money so that you can take your choice. But, once the self-funding nettle has been grasped, there has never been so much choice of part-time degree and non-degree level programmes available in every higher and further education college in the country, many of which can be pursued in the evenings, alongside a full-time job.

In that all learning influences who we are and hence the way we do our jobs, there is no subject which will not make the social worker see the world in a fresh way and virtually none which does not have some indirect relevance, whether it be modern languages improving communication skills, philosophy giving new clarity to ethical dilemmas, or sociology showing how the fabric of social life has developed over time. Learning how to learn is also important, as we saw in relation to reflective practice. For those with a social work qualification, awards obtained at Diploma in Higher Education level can now be topped up to degree level with one year of further full-time (two years' part-time) study. Those who already hold a first or higher degree may find that an interesting way of combining learning for its own sake with professional relevance is to take a taught higher degree that is also accredited for a professional award at post-qualifying or advanced level, or to combine elements of a taught Master's degree (e.g. MA, MBA, MEd) or the obtaining of a higher degree by research (MA, MPhil, PhD) with work-based learning and thus to pursue a PQSW or AASW award by the portfolio route.

Consultancy and mentoring

Consultation can be defined as an occasional event directed towards solving a particular set of problems or promoting a particular approach to practice without involving managerial power relationships. It can be undertaken with an individual or a group. Mentoring is typically offered to an individual and takes place over a period of time, sometimes with a particular aim in view such as the achievement of a professional award but sometimes directed at more general career advancement. Bhatti-Sinclair (1996, p.9) defines the mentoring role as being to 'provide a listening, counselling and empowering role'; there can also be educational and developmental aspects. She sees the consultant as having a more active validating and advocacy role, though this is not the only possibility. Thus, both consultancy and mentoring are separate from staff supervision and from line management. Often, consultation is requested by the person who receives it. Where it is 'prescribed' by management to tackle difficulties, it is unlikely to be as fruitful but there are also some enlightened managers who perceive instances where it could be useful and who negotiate this with their team.

Consultants who are experienced in the use of a specialist approach can open up fresh networks with like-minded practitioners through their own contacts. They may be the crucial links in the chain who turn the bright ideas of isolated practitioners into the co-ordinated development of a new practice-theory (Mullender and Ward, 1991).

Another use of consultation is for an individual, where their supervisor cannot meet all their support or developmental needs. Where a black specialist worker is supervised by a white line manager, for example, there could be issues that consultancy could explore which would simply not feel safe to raise first in supervision but which can then be taken up there as appropriate. It may be helpful for the organisation to offer black staff a black consultant or mentor without waiting for this to be requested. Then staff are free to take this up, or not, as they wish. There is evidence both from black students (Bhatti-Sinclair, 1996) and from women staff (Allan *et al.*, 1992) that personal consultation or mentoring of this kind can be invaluable for individuals who would otherwise have been isolated and unlikely to achieve their full potential. A formalised scheme may have the advantages of providing role models who operate within 'the culture, values and structure of the organisation' (Bhatti-Sinclair, 1996, p.5), of being properly resourced and efficiently run, and of being established after full consultation with all the 'stakeholders', including those who will use the service.

The knowledge and skills of a consultant are typically somewhat specialised and it may be hard for a manager to judge the quality of what they will offer. Nowadays, there are any number of freelance consultants available, both for individuals and for teams and organisations. It is sensible to take organisational help in drawing up a contract and choosing between tenders and to ensure that the tendering process includes asking for evidence of satisfaction from past commissioners.

Stress management

Although the section on staff care (above) quite rightly put the emphasis on managers and on organisational culture in general as being the key elements in preventing undue stress at work (and nothing in what follows should be taken to suggest that experiencing stress is a result of individual weakness), there are ways in which people can care for themselves and manage their own stress more effectively. We cannot prevent social work from being inherently one of the most stressful of jobs. Dealing with human problems and unpredictability is part of what makes it rewarding. But recognising that there will be stress and learning to read – and react to – the signs of its effects on oneself (e.g. constant minor illnesses, mistakes, irritability, problems with sleeping) are sensible precautions in handling the demands before they build up into illness or burn-out. Neil Thompson (1996) suggests the following personal effectivenesss tips:

- know yourself
- set objectives
- change your attitude
- be assertive
- keep control
- set boundaries
- learn time management
- use support
- avoid unhelpful coping methods
- be kind to yourself.

Stress in a workplace also feeds on itself, as we saw above, so a team or group of colleagues might usefully decide together to implement *stress reduction techniques*. These can be as simple as going to a lunchtime aerobics class once a week, stopping for proper coffee breaks, putting workload management on the staff meeting agenda, or arranging a talk on effective time management.

Time management

Since social work is labour intensive, one of its most valuable resources is *time*. Many managers confess to having difficulty with time management. Here again, there are some pointers which can help, including:

- Take time before a meeting or a telephone call to think what you want from it and keep this in mind throughout.
- Keep a note of everything you need to ask key people so that you can cover them all in one 'phone call.
- Have these notes to hand in case they should happen to ring you.
- Look ahead through your diary from time to time so that you can organise your time most effectively – for example, organising two meetings consecutively that involve a journey in the same direction, grouping activities to release useful slots of time.
- Have meetings at your office rather than always travelling to someone else's.
- Write up notes, make a first draft of documents (or jot down the headings) and so on while the material is fresh in your memory; this is much quicker than trying to remember it later.
- Follow up immediately on any promises made.
- Compartmentalise certain functions – for example, set aside slots for recording or telephoning.
- Never have any 'dead time'; make longer journeys by train and use for concentrated reading, use driving time to think through complex problems, recognise that time spent chatting over the kettle is valuable interaction with team members.
- Shut your door when you want to work undisturbed but ensure that staff know when you will be available.
- Never feel guilty about working at home: you will get through mountains of work and will do it carefully and well.
- Set aside time for planning and 'visioning'.
- Think in annual and other periodic cycles, not task by task (you should always know what regular work is coming up and when).
- Allocate time for administrative tasks in your diary.
- Wherever possible, only have a document in your hands once; either deal with it, file it, bin it, or pass it on.
- Where the last point is not possible, group paperwork into tasks and allocate time for each, with a deadline.
- With a longer-term project, try always to have one concrete step moving forward (e.g. doing the groundwork for the next meeting, making relevant phone calls) and work out a way for

your attention to be triggered if one of these steps grinds to a halt (e.g. if someone fails to get back to you).

In social work, there may not be many 'breathing spaces' in the day or week. And yet all of us would admit to ways of using our time unproductively. Allowing others to control our time occurs if we allow them constantly to interrupt us or to draw us into what are properly their own concerns, while putting off decisions can result in crises which take longer to sort out. Other common failings are concentrating on trivial, less important jobs and never knowing when tasks should be delegated to others, and habitually overcramming our diaries so that we have no time to chat or think. It is worth re-emphasising that the commonest causes of poor time management are doing *other people's work* and failing to *prioritise tasks*.

Ways of managing time are suggested by Zastrow (1985), including:

1. Conduct an *activity analysis* of how you are using your time right now, possibly drawing a diagram of a clock measuring which portions of time are devoted to various tasks, and then deciding if any are a waste of time or could be delegated to others. (One team leader was found to be spending large portions of time handling all the referrals for fuel debt because he had developed a contact at the social security office; an officer in charge of an elderly persons' home found that she was ordering the food, which should have been the cook's job, while another revealed that he was unable to assert himself with visitors who expected him to 'drop everything'.)
2. *Set goals daily* for what you want to accomplish. A 'to do' list would schedule really important goals and ensure that they got done; less important goals perhaps could be delegated or a start made on them; unimportant goals should lead to questions as to whether they really need to be done at all or could perhaps be delegated. (Fifteen minutes a day when you will not be bothered with telephones or interruptions, when your door is kept closed, when ideas are jotted down and not trusted to memory, can pay off. A senior who did this was firm in saying 'no' when, initially, her team resented her not always being available.)

3. Ask yourself if you are *procrastinating* over any particular task, and why. (Maybe someone else knows more about it and could advise you how to get started.)

Conclusion

This chapter has shown the range of ways in which social work organisations can foster their greatest asset, their staff, through maximising their potential, harnessing their efforts to the wider objectives of the organisation and observing the duty of care towards them. Without suggesting that any of these responsibilities be abdicated, it has also suggested some ideas through which staff can promote their own learning and well-being.

Most of the chapter has considered the workforce as if it were a homogeneous whole. Chapter 7 will explore difference and diversity in the workplace, as well as some more radical ways of celebrating a strengths-based approach to management and to organisational forms.

7

Managing Diversity

With over 80 per cent of the social services workforce made up of women (Balloch *et al.*, 1995) and major strides made in recruiting black students and staff to social work in recent years – not to speak of all the attention focused on anti-oppressive practice – we might like to think of social work agencies as being well ahead in terms of diversity. A closer look, however, reveals that there is still a long way to go.

Anti-discrimination legislation

Legislation provides the foundation for equal opportunities in relation to access to jobs, promotion and fair rates of pay. The primary laws in Britain aimed at protecting workers (and possibly ex-workers, following a landmark sex discrimination case in September 1998) from discrimination in the labour market (and also covering service delivery to users and carers) are the Equal Pay Act 1970 and Sex Discrimination Act 1975, the Race Relations Act 1976 and the Disability Discrimination Act 1995. The latter covers any physical or learning disability or mental illness with a substantial and long-term adverse effect. (Northern Ireland has separate provision.) There are no equivalent legal rights in respect of age, class or sexuality. The issue of older workers is now receiving attention, however, with a code of practice from the Department of Education and Employment and an active coalition of interested groups called Equal Rights on Age. Nevertheless, levels of compliance with the code are low – a survey in 1999 found that a third of employers had not heard of it and double that number had failed to act on it. Though there are no official plans to remove the compulsory retirement age or to introduce legislation instead of relying on a voluntary code, the situation is being monitored by government. European Directives are also relevant in some areas of equal opportunities, chiefly gender, with the European Union having established its own comprehensive legal framework on equal pay and equal treatment at work as part of an Action Programme on Equal Opportunities for Women and Men, 1996–2000 (European Commission, 1997).

Each of the major domestic Acts has been accompanied by a body to watch over the operation of the law. These are the Equal Opportunities Commission (EOC), the Commission for Racial Equality (CRE) and the Disability Rights Commission (DRC or Daras). Each exists to enforce the relevant legislation and to educate business and the community. They also provide guidance to individuals and investigate complaints of discrimination which may then go on to ACAS (the Advisory Conciliation and Arbitration Service) or to an employment tribunal. The monitoring undertaken by the two longer-established bodies, the EOC and the CRE, reveals that the position of women and of black workers has not improved as much as we might have expected. (It is too early to say what will happen for disabled workers.) Women in management and administration earn on average only two-thirds as much as men (Hunt, J., 1994). In a similarly dispiriting vein, by 1996, the CRE could report fewer than 2000 people having had complaints of racial discrimination supported by industrial tribunals or courts (Commission for Racial Equality, 1996) in a labour market in which black and Asian people remained twice as likely to be unemployed as white people (Commission for Racial Equality, 1997).

So what has gone wrong? First, a legal brief is inevitably narrow, and dependent on *proof and interpretation*, so that industrial tribunals may find it difficult to establish that discrimination has actually occurred.

Second, the Acts operate on the basis of *individual grievance*, meaning that one named individual must bring a complaint of differential, disadvantageous treatment, even where a whole category of workers is affected. Without the backing of the EOC or the CRE, this would, of course, be too costly and too daunting for most people to contemplate. Even with support, it is not a pleasant prospect and can be both distressing and embarrassing. So the majority of aggrieved individuals simply never take action.

Third, though indirect discrimination is also unlawful – that is, unjustifiably applying a condition which adversely affects one particular group – *proving* that it has occurred is yet more difficult. For instance, there are often hidden and not so hidden agendas when candidates are interviewed for jobs. Although the Sex Discrimination Acts invalidate questions about child care arrangements, it is hard for a woman to refuse to answer a question about this if she is really keen to get the job, though she is within her rights to do so. And, while equal opportunities interviewing has at least been thought about (see Chapter 5), psychometric and other tests may remain unintentionally ethnocentric in either their content or their process of operation. Because they are standardised around white test results, black people may find themselves valued only in as far as they conform to white norms and fewer may be appointed to posts as a result (Skellington with Morris, 1992).

Fourth, even if successful, the complainant may subsequently be *undermined* by colleagues or managers, being made to feel incompetent and patronised, and it is particularly hard to document attitudes and behaviour that pervade the very culture of the workplace or to take action when many people are involved. Research in Northern Ireland (Equal Opportunities Commission for Northern Ireland, 1998) revealed that, though most were pleased overall that they had made an enquiry or complaint, almost a third of the 859 respondents had experienced a deterioration afterwards in relationships with colleagues, one in three had suffered some form of victimisation, and almost a fifth had gone on to a period of unemployment following their complaint. A recent test case in England does now mean, however, that victimisation after challenging a decision or action based on racism or sexism is itself covered by the discrimination legislation (Letters, *Community Care*, 30 September–6 October 1999, p.17).

The issue of harassment lies on the boundary between the law and organisational policy because, for example, someone who has been harassed may feel forced to leave their job and may then have a claim against the organisation. It is important for every agency to have an effective harassment policy, to be willing to enforce it and to ensure that it covers all forms of harassment, including sexual and racial. Most members of socially oppressed groups have probably experienced harassment in the workplace and most take no action, not through weakness but after a conscious calculation that either nothing will be done anyway or that they are likely to suffer worse repercussions than their harasser (Coleman, 1991). This means that organisations face a huge challenge if personal harassment codes are to be worth the paper they are written on.

Fifth, there is a crucial difference between *anti-discriminatory* and *anti-oppressive* thinking. The former basically works from a position of treating individuals equally (in this case in the labour market), which usually means, for example, treating women more like men, whereas opposing oppression means tackling global injustice against women by a more fundamental rethinking of gender power dynamics. The announcement by the EOC in 1996 that, for the first time in its history, its annual workload included more individual complaints from men than from women starkly reveals the weakness of an individualistic anti-discriminatory approach. Equity-based European thinking has been even further wide of the mark with encouragement to men to move into traditionally female-dominated areas of employment, such as day and residential care of young children (Gensen, 1996), as part of evening up the numbers across all types of jobs without heed for the potential dangers (Pringle, 1992/3). The entrenched issues of violence, abuse and the exploitation of power are simply not on this kind of equal rights agenda.

In recognition of the limitations of a narrow, legislative approach, there has been a move, though only in respect of gender, towards 'mainstreaming' and this is now EU and UK governmental policy. It means that every policy discussion and decision taken should be considered for its gender implications, to ensure that it will not treat women or men adversely. A related concept is 'gender auditing' which is a way of looking for hidden discrimination within the functioning of an organisation and incorporating gender into strategic planning. There is no reason why this approach should not be extended to other areas of oppression.

Equal opportunities policies

Staffing

Every organisation should have an equal opportunities policy and can use it as a challenge to think beyond the confines of anti-discrimination legislation and towards implementing more widespread and innovative measures to assist oppressed groups in the workplace. For example, age discrimination and sexual orientation can feature in policy, even though they are not covered by the law.

It is important to recognise at this juncture that anti-discrimination legislation makes positive discrimination as unlawful as negative discrimination. To offer someone a job simply because they are female or black or disabled is not permissible (unless the post is exempt from the provisions of the relevant Act – e.g. because it is in a women's refuge, in which case the claim for exemption should be stated in the advert). To do so would give any man or white or non-disabled applicant who felt they had been passed over immediate grounds to claim unfair treatment. Also women, black and disabled staff themselves may be amongst those who feel most strongly that no favours should be given to particular candidates; they should fit the criteria and not have to feel less 'worthy' of a place or open to accusations or unspoken comments from others that they got on through patronage. Affirmative action quotas in the USA have come in for these kinds of criticism because it is felt that not all black students have got into university on equal merit, for example, and that some young white people have been kept out. Against a history in the States of slavery and segregation, and with a different legislative framework, it is important not to assume direct comparisons with the UK nor to underestimate what was achieved by this policy before it was challenged. Bowen and Bok (1998) argue that the black students achieved better outcomes than the excluded white students would have done (the latter being the least able of their cohort) and that they constitute vital 'social capital' for their nation. Nevertheless, the ferocity of some of the debates in America might give us pause for thought.

Positive action, on the other hand, is seen as an imaginative way forward in the UK and does not involve altering the rules in the same way as affirmative action (which here we call 'positive discrimination'). Crucially, positive action does not violate the principle of employment and promotion on merit becomes it implies reaching out rather than giving special treatment to the target population. Monitoring the workforce against the national and local populations gives a measure of which groups are under-represented in employment terms. *Targets* (but not quotas) may then be set as to the percentage of women and members of ethnic minority communities who ought by rights to be in the workplace, preferably with action timescales also. It is important to break down both the action and the intended targets by grades of staff since there may be, for example, a good number of black women in the workforce but largely confined to the lowest paid, low-status positions.

The next step is to design and implement measures to reach the targets that have been set. The two key areas are, first, those of outreach in recruitment and, second, staff development measures for those groups who do not currently make it to the top in numbers proportionate to their presence in the organisation. Both rely on effective monitoring of the workforce and of applicants for posts to ascertain which groups are under-represented and in what areas of the organisation.

The issue of outreach in recruitment was touched on in Chapter 5. The social work press, for example, often carries advertisements saying that the employer would particularly welcome applications from certain under-represented groups but efforts can go beyond this into publicising posts and raising the organisation's profile and credibility through local black communities, for example, or disabled people's organisations. Staff development was tackled in Chapter 6 and, again, there is an enormous amount that can be done, such as offering women-only courses and courses for black staff, support groups for those who aspire to get into management, mentoring and consultancy schemes, and opportunities to 'act up' in posts that otherwise might have seemed unobtainable.

Unfortunately, it is all too easy for employers to boast that they have an equal opportunities policy and to state this in job advertisements when, in reality, there may be no accompanying resources and no commitment to improve policy or practice. Even though the personal social services pride themselves on being caring organisations, when we survey their record in relation to employment, as we saw in Chapter 6, that caring may be seen not to extend to their own staff. Certainly, in relation to gender, other organisations such as banks (Nottage, 1991) are ahead of social work in providing child care facilities and in building in flexible working hours, career break schemes and returners' programmes, as well as term-time and home-based working. Overall, there is a considerable way to go before every social work and social care organisation has effective monitoring, codes of practice and other equal opportunities practices in place.

Service delivery

Equal opportunities extend beyond staffing considerations into service delivery. It is vital to consider whether the agency currently discriminates against any particular groups of service users, either wittingly or unwittingly, in its commissioning and/or purchasing of services. Here again, management information can be gathered as to whether men and women, members of different ethnic groups, residents in different parts of the town or out in the rural areas and so on, all use the service in numbers commensurate with their representation in the relevant population. With the more hidden populations it will be harder to gauge whether take-up is skewed but equally important to ensure that services are appropriately publicised and made accessible and acceptable to all. Thus gay and lesbian service users should be directly referred to in the policy and considered in the provision of all services and the training of staff. Would every group care setting give a warm welcome to a gay or lesbian partner of a resident or centre user? Does every children and families team value lesbian and gay parenting? These are concrete questions that will make an enormous difference to the quality of life of these groups of service users. Disability, age, marital status, religious affiliation and any other overt or covert areas of oppression should all be considered in a similar way.

For example, the staff of a mental health drop-in centre may be worried that they have not succeeded in attracting any Asian people to attend or a family centre may want to involve fathers. This kind of analysis of gaps in current provision, and generation of ideas as to how the quality of service to all potential user groups might be improved, can happen at team as well as organisational level. Has the team or establishment discussed the equal opportunities statement recently? If not, you may wish to instigate this at the next staff meeting and to incorporate the resulting discussion into an analysis and action plan which could be owned by management as well as being acted on locally.

It is, after all, very important that we do not neglect our own part in the culture of our employing organisation. The personal views of a staff group may well influence the service provided. Hardman (1997), for example, conducted a survey in a local authority social services department and a postgraduate social work programme using an attitudinal questionnaire and two case vignettes. The 75 respondents were predominantly straight white women, of whom six out of 10 said they had a lesbian colleague or friend and 35 per cent had knowingly worked with a lesbian service user. Although more than one in five had strong views that heterosexism is the main problem facing lesbians in society, it is extremely worrying to find that almost as many took a general view that lesbians should be referred for psychiatric help (with two strongly believing this) and one in 10 saying they would be afraid to be alone with a lesbian. Those in child and family social work were more likely than others to believe that lesbians should not be in charge of children, while the number of women respondents who were disgusted by the idea of two women having sex together does not bode well for the profession's general ability to counsel young people who may be confused about their sexuality. Further clear evidence of the persistence of pathological attitudes has been gathered in mental health settings (McFarlane, 1998). Fortunately, there is also a growing literature on gay affirming approaches to intervention (Burstow, 1992; Sanderson, 1993; Davies and Neal, 1996).

Overall, the need is no less acute than it ever was for us to consider how discriminatory or otherwise our own practice is and how we can go about making an active contribution to developing anti-oppressive practice in our work setting, as well as how to evaluate the success of any measures adopted for personal or organisational change, both in staffing and in service delivery. Researching the culture of an organisation, for example by conducting an 'equality audit' (Parkin and Maddock, 1995), might be a good place to start.

Representation in the labour market

Let us now look in more detail at developments in the staffing of social work and related agencies. Flexibility has tended to lead to the creation of more temporary and part-time jobs in all sectors of employment. Workers in these less secure positions operate on the 'contractual fringe' of the labour market (Handy, 1995, p.77). Women, as society's reserve army of labour, are likely to be disproportionately represented there. A good place to observe this is in university contract research, including in the discipline of social work.

In social services, many women have gained, in terms of the pressures of daily life, from employers' greater willingness to create permanent jobs with hours which fit in with domestic commitments – but this has not necessarily helped their promotion prospects and still has not given them as much leisure time as men (Franks, 1999). Nearly a quarter of field social workers work part-time, which includes more than nine times as many women as men, but the major expansion has been up to, and especially at, team leader level (Local Government Management Board and the Association of Directors of Social Services, 1993). Men still heavily predominate at the more senior managerial levels where part-time working would tend to be at the very least disadvantageous and usually still unimaginable.

Despite the fact that the pioneers of social work in the USA and the UK were women (Jane Addams, Bertha Reynolds, Charlotte Towle, Mary Richmond, Eileen Younghusband), and that there were many excellent women managers in the early days, for example in the children's departments of the first two decades of the British Welfare State (Carter Hood *et al.*, 1998), recent decades have seen a male takeover of the management of social work. In 1997, of 185 directors in Britain (England, Wales and Scotland), only 38 were women, or fractionally over 20 per cent. Scotland had a better record than England (with around a third, but still not a representative number of women) and Wales far worse (only one woman) (all figures extrapolated from Foster, J., 1997). Women have actually been losing ground in the metropolitan boroughs and in London, though gaining somewhat from a lower base in the shire counties. Sadly, the move to unitary authorities did not open up opportunities in any major way. The move away from having a designated director for social services as a separate sphere of responsibility and from organising social services as a separate department may increasingly blur this position in future, but is not likely to help women who are considerably less well represented in many areas of local government than they are in social work. The fragmentation of the personal social services across local government, not to mention the independent sector, is a further obstacle to implementing change. For example, Opportunity 2000 (launched by Business in the Community in 1991 and aimed at increasing the quality and quantity of women's contribution through a demonstrably better balanced workforce) was taken up early and on a national basis by the NHS Management Executive. No equivalent, one-off action would have been possible for social work, though some local authorities joined the campaign, beginning with Hertfordshire in January 1992.

Joy Foster (1997) has gathered evidence that women wait until they are extremely well qualified and experienced before applying for these top jobs, that they target their applications where they believe they have a chance of success, and sometimes adopt a male style of presenting themselves in interview (assertive language, power dressing) which is not necessarily their characteristic style of managing. Many still report encountering discriminatory attitudes during the selection process, particularly from elected members and especially during the informal stages, such as over dinner or lunch, when there may be a feeling of not being listened to or even dismissive comments passed. (See Chapter 5 for a fuller discussion of equal opportunities in recruitment and selection.) And, since some of the obstacles that work against women in other employment sectors, such as lack of qualifications and of permanent jobs, do not apply in social work, the key barriers to women's advancement clearly do boil down to these discriminatory attitudes and to unequal family responsibilities. Women who do make it in management are more likely to be single or divorced and without children than their male counterparts (Balloch *et al.*, 1995). New female entrants to the profession are no less ambitious than male (Murray, 1997), so the challenge is there for organisations to help them make it to the top.

Of course there remains, too, a scandalously low number of black senior managers in social work. For some time, one strand of implementing anti-racist practice has been seen as the need to employ more black and minority ethnic workers. But, instead of opening up mainstream opportunities for career advancement, the creation of 'section 11' posts (under the Local Government Act, 1966) to attract government funding for work in black communities has meant that many recruits have been 'locked onto career ladders with virtually no rungs on them' (Dominelli, 1997, p.145). Jobs secured under this arrangement have been temporary and somewhat sidelined, workers have been liable to be exploited at the lowest levels, and have become pigeonholed as the department's 'race experts'. Their presence in such posts has not solved the entrenched problem of failing to attract and promote more black managers. In the year to April 1998, Local Government Association figures show that there was only one black director of social services out of a total or 136 in England and Wales, and 18 black and Asian deputy and assistant directors, but a rising proportion of service heads at 6 per cent from ethnic minorities (*Community Care*, 14–20 October 1999, p.11). Although this latter figure is approaching representativeness of the population as a whole, it does not reflect the make-up in the areas covered by many individual authorities and indicates that a great deal more effort is still needed to achieve equal opportunities. The Association of Directors of Social Services does have at least one minority ethnic member on each of its committees, but this must mean a few people doing a great deal of work.

A similar phenomenon has happened with disabled workers who, where they have been thought about at all, have typically been recruited as the 'social worker for the blind' (*sic* – rarely 'blind people'), who also happens to be blind, or into a hospital setting where there is already good wheelchair access and little expectation of home visiting. Yet the Disability Discrimination Act 1995 makes it quite clear that there must be no barrier to a disabled people applying for or being appointed to any post for which they are the best candidate and that it is the employer's responsibility to take reasonable steps to adapt the workplace or existing working practices to remove such obstacles (Minister for Disabled People, 1996a, 1996b). It remains to be seen whether the Act will prove enforceable and whether its definitions will be more inclusive than exclusive of categories of disabled people. Certainly, its exemption of employers with fewer than 15 staff would appear arbitrary and unjust, and its provisions are weaker on transport and access than on jobs and services. Even there, there are bound to be test cases as to what constitute 'reasonable measures' to ensure that someone is not discriminated against. Nevertheless, as Britain's first civil rights legislation for disabled people, the 1995 Act is a landmark and, it is to be hoped, a foundation on which to build. It is also important in social work because it covers both employment and the delivery of services.

Those members of oppressed groups who do make it into the upper echelons may also encounter subversion or hostility from other staff. Black managers, for example, are likely to find that some white subordinates do not know how to relate to them as authority figures – double-checking their advice with white staff at an equivalent or even a more junior level to the black manager, reacting with particular surprise, mistrust or anger when a black manager draws attention to a weakness in their practice, and so on. The racist content in these reactions may be covered by a veneer of politeness, but it is deeply ingrained and it is undermining to black managers who need to be assured that white colleagues alongside and above them in the hierarchy do not collude with it. The organisation needs to find ways to make it clear that it requires staff to face such attitudes in themselves and to seek to change them because they will not be condoned, in however subtle a form. Unless the organisational culture moves in this direction, it is unlikely to offer an acceptable service to black users and carers or to provide a supportive and appropriate environment for black staff. The equivalent is also true for disabled workers and for women within the workplace. It is those who do not believe the new managers will do a good job who have the problem and who should be challenged if their remarks or behaviour make this apparent.

Opening up our thinking about work

So far in this chapter we have looked at ways of involving members of oppressed groups more representatively in personal social welfare organisations. The problem with this, if it remains the only change that is made, is that it can mean entering an agency's workforce on the terms set by those who got there first and who have already determined the agendas of assumptions, priorities, and even of language. This can lead to tokenism, harassment and continuing oppressive treatment. These, in turn, can mean that positive action measures do not work (because potential applicants are turned off by what they hear from others about the organisation or by their first impressions of it) or that people who take up jobs there do not stay in them very long.

Oppression is built into the very structures of many organisations because of the fundamental thinking on which they are based. The pure bureaucracy (see Chapter 2) is premised on the separation of the public and the private. Work becomes a place governed by rules, regulations and procedures. All that matters are technical qualifications to undertake a task and the maximisation of working efficiency. This model of rationality sees women as making a less worthy contribution, for example, if they take time off to look after sick children or need altered working hours to fit around child-rearing, since those matters are traditionally regarded as irrelevant to work-based considerations. '[G]ender, sexuality, reproduction and emotionality are outside organizational boundaries, continually and actively consigned to that social space by ongoing organizational practices'; as a consequence, '[c]omplex organizations play an important role . . . in defining gender and women's disadvantage for the whole of society' (Morgan, 1986, p.259). It is equally the case that black staff, gay men and lesbians, disabled and older workers or those from different social backgrounds may well not feel that they 'fit' the prevailing culture of the workplace or the image held in the minds of those who control promotion opportunities. The strengths of what they have to offer in terms of life experience, diversity and richness of contribution, and common understanding with whole groups of service users, simply do not get onto the agenda.

But pressure on bureaucracy to change has started to come from the recognition that the achievement of equality of opportunity for staff can, in turn, lead to a better service being offered and that this will require fresh thinking. Contrast, for example, the old, 'Don't bring your family problems to work' approach with the provision by enlightened employers of a workplace nursery or crèche; this allows people to bring, not the family problems, but the family to work! Organisations are, after all, not peopled by automata – people invest their personalities and feelings in the workplace and they are affected, in turn, by the way they find themselves treated there. Attracting and retaining the best staff, and encouraging them to give of their best, means not cloning the next generation of managers in the image of the last. Some of the moves towards quality and excellence that we saw in Chapter 3 allow more space for these considerations than either the ideal-type bureaucracy or new managerialism is equipped to do.

A celebration of difference: the feminisation of management

Earlier in this chapter we saw how an equal opportunities approach can fail to tackle entrenched oppression if it takes an individualistic, anti-discriminatory approach. A further shortcoming can be that it denies difference, both within and between groups, by seeking to have everyone treated the same, whereas there may be more to be gained from celebrating it. A celebration of difference can lead to the discovery of a great variety of new strengths and skills which a diversity of women, black people, disabled people, older workers and others can offer to the workplace.

An interesting example is recent thinking about the 'feminisation of management'. Just as the English language, until challenged, made women invisible for much of the time (chairman, headmaster), and continues to denigrate the female when visible ('goose', 'bitch', 'mistress' all have derogatory meanings while their male equivalents do not, Spender, 1990), so classical management theory concerned itself with men managing men in masculine ways while women disappeared from consideration (Hearn and Parkin, 1987, p.19). Or, where they became inescapably visible through pregnancy and motherhood, women were devalued because childbearing and child-rearing were regarded as obstacles to the search for ultimate efficiency through the imposition of universal rules.

Now, women's attitudes and behaviour are beginning to be valued in their own right. Opportunity 2000, for example, campaigned around the extent to which women could provide the solutions to the problems and challenges likely to be faced by organisations in the future. This represented a huge shift from previous thinking which saw women as the problem and organisations, at best, as needing to offer some response to their 'needs'. Thus the shift can be seen as part of a wider move to a strengths-based approach. What do organisations need and what do hitherto oppressed groups have to offer?

Certainly, contemporary organisations require highly developed listening and communication skills (Peters, 1988) in order to be responsive to their customers or service users. They also need empowering (Peters, 1988) and collaborative, alliance-building styles of management (Kanter, 1989) in order to cope with an ever-increasing speed of change. No manager can expect to keep up with the technological revolution single-handed, for example. He, or she, will simply *have* to listen to, and work effectively with, other people if the whole enterprise is not to suffer. This is sometimes summarised as 'emotional intelligence' (EQ) (Goleman, 1996) and encompasses self-awareness, managing one's own emotions and relationships with others, communication skills and personal style, as well as the more traditional self-motivation.

The research finding that, in single-sex conversations, women tend to take turns and to develop one another's thoughts, while men more typically adopt competitive posturing and try to dominate (Spender, 1990; Tannen, 1995), is beginning to be mirrored in management training courses. Single-sex tasks encourage participants to become aware of how they work together and how they might do so differently to achieve shared goals. Suddenly, women's talk is not 'gossip' but networking, not 'chat' but co-operative problem-solving. As the demands faced by organisations and the lines of communication they must maintain become more complex and less predictable, so women's ways of communicating, of co-operating in teams, of networking, and of drawing out each other's strengths rather than competing start to become ways of making organisations more effective. Thus women's more natural management style is becoming equated with 'good management'.

Up to now, there have been only disadvantages for women in the fact that, while men's talk involves 'bantering', self-promotion and putting others down, women tend to avoid what they regard as boasting, play down their own authority and help each other to contribute. Without a shift of perception about communication styles, women can simply be overlooked or be seen as less able in relation to actual or potential leadership roles. When men and women are in meetings together, too, women who do speak up tend to find that men repeat their ideas as if they have just thought of them and then take the credit. (Or, worse still, men simply look bored until they get a chance to interrupt.) But, looked at in terms of the good of the organisation rather than the ambitious individual, it may be the women who are putting forward the people who deserve to be noticed and who are helping the fruitful ideas to emerge from discussion.

Of course, this kind of observation is open to charges of essentialism or of biological reductionism. It is important to remember, first, that we are talking about male and female styles, not about all men and all women. Not all men operate in a male style, nor all women in a female style. Second, we are dealing with how women and men have been socialised to be – men competitive, aggressive, status conscious, territorial; women more self-effacing, good listeners, better with people – not how they potentially could be. But, until the social rules are changed, it is important to remember that those who behave outside the norm may lose respect rather than gaining it, with men being seen as 'wimps' and women as bossy. So the stereotype is hard to deny, even if it is neither biologically determined nor universally adopted. Third, diversity and difference within social divisions are as marked as those between them. Thus there is nothing to say that a black woman or a lesbian or disabled woman would automatically feel any more heard or assisted in a meeting by a white woman than by a white man. It is still likely to require personal and organisational efforts at greater inclusiveness and anti-oppressive working before true co-operation and shared decision-making can be achieved. But, whatever the complexities, the need to move away from harmfully 'macho' (and white supremacist) values in management is by now undeniable.

It is not difficult to extend this realisation into an understanding of some of the reasons why workplaces can be intensely uncomfortable for gay and lesbian staff members. Not only is there crude homophobia and heterosexism in much of the daily conversational interplay, and no legislative protection for gay men and lesbians who experience discrimination on the grounds of their sexuality at work, but there is typically a maintenance of rigid gender hierarchies which devalues women as women and rewards only those men who act out the expected sex role. There is beginning to be a literature on this. Hearn and Parkin (1995), for example, offer a broad discussion of sexuality as it is both expressed and overlooked in the workplace,

No doubt the ideal lies in taking the best from all styles. Thus the challenge for women – all women, including black women, lesbian women, older and younger women, disabled women and women who began life without socioeconomic advantages – is to be appropriately assertive without playing the competitive male game. And, in all of this, it will not just (or even predominantly) be women who need to change, but men – since they currently disproportionately hold the power in organisations. Here, too, there is beginning to be theorising about the ways in which managements and masculinities reinforce one another and about how both might be transformed

(Collinson and Hearn, 1996). There is also work which suggests that male practitioners should reflect very carefully upon how they operate in organisations, and even whether they should absent themselves from whole areas of work such as that directly involving sexually abused children (Pringle, 1992/3), or whether they have a special responsibility to establish groups and projects which work for change with sexually violent men and in all settings where young men could usefully reconsider prevailing models of masculinity (e.g. in probation, Bensted *et al.*, 1994; see also Mullender, 1996, Chapter 9, on the need for accountability to women in such work).

As mentioned above, it is by no means only women who enter a hostile world when they breach the environs of the manuals, flow charts and other rational management tools. Black managers may very well be seen as having 'sold out' by their own communities, on the one hand, and as over-identifying with service users if they speak too much about racism, on the other. Then, too, black managers may be resented by white staff who feel there has been a role reversal. This can operate quite subtly, with staff circumventing the black manager's authority or regarding him or her as aggressive or arrogant when a perfectly straightforward request is made. Attitudes of white supremacy, such as these, undermine the confidence and competence which managers are expected to convey; doubly difficult for a black manager who is already highly visible in the organisation. Additional pressures may come from black colleagues, young family members and others who look up to the black manager as a role model and for whose sake it becomes vital to succeed.

The stress of having to appear confident in the leadership role, together with the weight of carrying all the responsibility for developing anti-racist services on one's own or always being the one to draw attention to the agency's shortcomings in this regard, plus being perhaps the only or the most senior black manager in the organisation, can become overwhelming. Added to this are being on the receiving end of open (and unspoken) racial attacks from colleagues and service users inside and outside the agency, having to sit on one's justifiable anger and resentment or else experiencing the exhaustion of having to express them politely over and over again, while all the time seeing very little if any change in the surrounding organisation. It is little wonder that some black managers resign. Thus, while the agency might have a good record in recruiting people from black and Asian communities, organisations that leave people to struggle thereafter are likely to frustrate the new manager's ability to do a good job. If, on the other hand, what is seen as threatening about the black manager is turned into a challenge to the organisation to change, all sorts of exciting possibilities may be opened up (Bond, 1996).

There has been some useful work on ways of encouraging and supporting women and black staff to get on in their organisations. Starting with women, specifically for social work the Department of Health Social Services Inspectorate (SSI) researched first the scope of the problem (Nottage, 1991) – a preponderantly female workforce in local authority social services but only a small minority of women directors – and then the types of management development and training that women had received or would have valued (Allan *et al.*, 1992). Ideas that emerged included: help with career development and planning career moves; being very well prepared for each move, including through acting up in a more senior post, so as to overcome the problem of women often not believing in themselves; secondments, job swaps and project work as other ways of gaining relevant experience prior to promotion; and management training, including 'women into management' courses. Equal opportunities policies in recruitment and selection (see Chapter 5) were regarded as essential, while lack of child care provision and failure to value collaborative and participative styles were still seen as a problem. Many of the staff development measures we looked at in Chapter 6, such as mentoring, appraisal, support networks and action learning sets were mentioned as valuable.

The problem, then, is not personal but structural (see also Cockburn, 1991; Tanton, 1994). Both the SSI studies confirmed that: 'Women . . . do not lack ambition, but they often lack support and encouragement. They are more interested in doing a job to their own standards and exploring their own creative potential than conforming to (male) organisational expectations or seeking power or status' (Nottage, 1991, pp.25–6; see also Allan *et al.*, 1992, p.13). They may prefer to stay close to other women and to 'people-orientated' jobs, rather than accept the isolation, patronising attitudes and sometimes downright hostility higher up the organisation (Coyle, 1989). In the Nottage (1991) study, Black women were particularly keen on mentoring and external consultancies, no doubt because their daily experiences of racism and of being undermined were not well understood within mainstream line management support structures. The programme of SSI work led on to a helpful career development guide for women in social work and social care (Foster, G., 1996; see also Foster, G. and Phillipson, 1994). Coyle (1989) regards women-only initiatives, such as employer-sponsored management training courses, as valuing women's contribution and as helping participants become potential agents for change, both for themselves and for other women in the organisation. She acknowledges, though, that access to such opportunities may be controlled and that they do not inherently challenge existing hierarchies of gender, ethnicity or class.

Across the public services more widely, there has also been work on the development of black managers (Office for Public Management, 1995; Andrew, 1996). Black managers emerged as much more distanced than white from their organisations' training and equal opportunity objectives, even though those surveyed were people who had already 'made it' into middle and senior management posts. Black managers felt persistently undermined and that their credibility was doubted and any failures homed in on. Having just begun to arrive in middle management in any numbers, black managers felt they had been disproportionately affected by 'delayering' (cutting out the middle levels of management) and, more generally, the pigeonholing of black staff into equalities or race relations jobs had blocked career progression both through sidelining and because a wider lack of commitment to change meant they had had few successes on which to stake a claim for advancement. Over 70 per cent of black respondents perceived a lack of senior management commitment or desire to advocate the interests of black managers, together with the absence of a climate of openness around 'race' issues. This should spur us on to seek improvements, as may a few positive examples of what can be done in the wider organisational literature, for example of a black mentoring scheme in another work setting overcoming the legacy of negative educational experiences (Holder, 1995). Similar support for potential minority ethnic managers is now available in social services with the launch of a mentoring scheme for aspiring managers by the Association of Directors of Social Services (ADSS), in conjunction with the Local Government Association, the Improvement and

Development Agency (IDeA) and the racial equality organisation, REU (*Community Care*, 11–17 November, p.7). Directors and SSI staff are shadowed by rising black and Asian staff, both to develop career-building skills and access to high-level networks. The intention is to give individuals confidence to apply for the top jobs.

Once again, then, the structural issues outweigh the personal (both in problems and solutions), though it is no wonder that, in the light of all the above, lack of self-confidence and feelings of isolation within a hostile environment also take their toll for some. The barriers listed in the Office for Public Management study will require deep-seated change. They include negative stereotyping, marginalisation and tokenism, outright racist attitudes persisting in some quarters, backlash, excuses and dual standards. The commitment to change is seen as needing to come from the top, which inevitably equates with senior managers being prepared to give up some power and to avoid cloning themselves when making high-level appointments. In local authority settings, as mentioned in Chapter 5, it will also involve elected members being prepared to appoint people from social groups they have not previously seen doing the jobs in question (which links into the wider questions of ensuring that we elect councillors who are representative of their local areas and then training them to carry out their duties).

Revisiting organisational structures

But sometimes people get tired of trying to fit into an alien environment and simply want to work somewhere where their values and their philosophy of life represent the norm rather than 'the other'. A key aspect of the richness we can celebrate in UK social work is that organisations do exist which are run wholly by members of particular oppressed groups. Even though these have often arisen because of the vacuum in essential services left by the large public authorities, their existence has given the opportunity for the people most directly concerned to set their own agendas and priorities, sometimes with interesting organisational results. Such projects include black voluntary agencies like projects for young black people in care or black people with HIV/AIDS, all-women organisations including Women's Aid groups and Rape Crisis Centres – sometimes run solely by black women, as in specialist black refuge services, or by lesbian women as in lesbian helplines – gay and lesbian projects offering advice and help to young people or to wider populations who are coming to terms with their sexuality, older people's groups, disabled people's organisations, groups of young people in care, and locally directed projects in deprived inner city areas running credit unions, tenants' groups, and so on.

Though many of these developments are, as yet, little studied, others have spawned a fruitful literature, for example the field of women's community groups (see, for example, Hawxhurst and Morrow, 1984; Dominelli, 1990), where the distinctive organisational form has been that of the feminist collective. These have always stood as an antithesis to bureaucratic hierarchies (see Chapter 2) and their legacy includes practices now thought commonplace, such as rotating the chairing of meetings rather than competitively electing one person to hold that role at all times. Deliberately leaderless groups were ideal for sharing experiences and raising consciousness about their causes, but initially poor at agreeing how to take action for change (Freeman, undated). The principles of democratic structuring they eventually developed were the delegation of tasks to named individuals, the responsibility of those individuals to the whole group, the maximum distribution of authority and work around the group, the rotation of responsibilities in ways which helped people learn skills without monopolising control, the widespread sharing of all information and the equalising of access to resources (including skills). Women continue to value non-hierarchical forms of organisation and to find ways of making them work (Brown, H., 1992).

Some of the current interest in tribal/extended family group decision-making, according to Maori, First Nation American and other traditional cultural patterns (e.g. in family group conferences, Lupton, 1998), relates to a search for alternative means of working collectively or in partnership, often within a more holistic ethos than Western society retains – i.e. with material and spiritual values held in better balance (though the model as implemented in the UK has somewhat strayed from these origins).

All non-traditional organisations come under tremendous pressure from traditional ones to behave in ways the latter can recognise and understand and which they therefore deem preferable or 'more professional'. Often, there is simply no perception that others may deliberately be working to alternative ideas and values. If difference is noticed at all, it is registered as some kind of inferiority – as disorganisation, inefficiency or unprofessionalism – and, at the points where the two bodies need to interact, power may be used to force the smaller to become more like the larger. Hierarchical organisations complain, for example, when a collective does not have a named post-holder for them to telephone, or a recognisable line of accountability – not recognising in these facets the hard-won move to egalitarianism in organisational control. Then access to funding may be used to assert control over this and other matters. Increasingly, for instance, local authority contributions to the resourcing of posts in women's organisations have been accompanied by pressure to employ 'project directors' to manage groups that were formerly run as collectives. On a wider scale, this pattern of funder or service commissioner influence over the shape and ethos of long-established voluntary agencies is giving rise to considerable concern as the voluntaries compete for contracts to sustain their funding base and sometimes find themselves becoming distanced from their pioneering principles or campaigning roots.

This is by no means solely an issue for women. Just as many black people have set up their own small businesses, supported from within their own communities because white-run industry and finance refuse to take them seriously, and black communities also continue to foster a wide range of black welfare organisations in the voluntary section. Despite the moves towards anti-oppressive practice and the improvements this has brought about, much provision in both the statutory and the predominantly white mainstream voluntary sector remains, at best, inaccessible (lack of interpreters, lack of materials in community languages, lack of outreach), inappropriate and often unacceptable – and, at worst, racist (Sia, undated). Black organisations, on the other hand, typically work to principles which have been carefully developed and which may be highly significant in cultural and spiritual terms. (Though there is, of course, diversity here, too; an Islamic community centre and an Asian women's project do not necessarily share the same views about the incidence of, or the best response to, male violence, for example.) Ahmad (1990, p.80) urges social workers to learn about and build trust with the black organisations serving their area, to make referrals routinely to them but without using them as a 'dumping ground', to work in partnership to increase resources for black communities and organisations, and to learn from them how to make their own assessments and interventions more holistic. To this, one might add researching the specific needs of black communities, for example in relation to health (sickle cell anæmia, differential rates of contracting various forms of disease) and welfare (mental health assessments, the support needs of carers).

This kind of alliance is also important at the organisational level so that service commissioners do not simply exploit black projects by contracting services from them without any effort to understand either the philosophy underpinning the provision of those services or the shortcomings it might point to in their own in-house provision. The same is true when it comes to determining the performance standards against which services will be monitored and evaluated. As was mentioned in Chapter 3, there can be no quality without equality. Dominelli (1997) points out that respect for autonomous black organisations is not an argument for separatism but a recognition that influencing and controlling the service provision of choice is an important aspect of resistance against incorporation into the power dynamics of a white-run society. After all, to aspire to wholly separate provision would mean risking an under-resourced second class strand of welfare – and paying twice for the privilege since mainstream welfare is supported through taxation that we all pay, black and white alike.

The black voluntary sector has grown in importance to the point where umbrella groups have begun to spring up to safeguard and promote its interests. The Black and Ethnic Minority Infrastructure in Scotland (BEMIS), for example, has commissioned a survey of all 558 identified black and minority ethnic groups north of the border which reveals insecure funding that threatens their ability to plan ahead and even to survive (McKay, 1999). Important work is also undertaken by the REU (formerly Race Equality Unit) which, for a decade now, has been drawing attention to the shortcomings of the personal social services in the mainstream (see, for example, Butt and Mirza, 1996) and championing the cause of black projects (Jones *et al.*, 1992).

And, in the same way, there are gay and lesbian businesses and welfare organisations and for similar reasons – the former unacceptable or not credible to the mainstream (and/or not credible to its consumers if located in the mainstream), the latter serving needs which have typically been overlooked by the welfare authorities. Cosis Brown (1998) discusses the advantages for gay-run organisations in allowing gay and/or lesbian service users to define their own needs and retain control of the knowledge, skills and values that are perceived as relevant in meeting those needs. The Albert Kennedy Trust (working to ensure that young gay men and lesbians can find non-homophobic placements in the public care system and afterwards) and the Gay Bereavement Project are two examples she cites of autonomous organisations of this kind. Cosis Brown also reiterates that mainstream agencies still have a duty to make their services appropriate for all who are entitled to use them and that they can become more accessible through the images they convey, the language they use and the respect they afford to gay and lesbian staff and service users.

Naturally, the central argument has to be that overt and covert sexism, racism, disablism and homophobia in the funding and provision of services are unacceptable and that they must be eradicated, but this does not mean that the emergent women-only, black, disabled people's and gay and lesbian business and welfare organisations are not developing new frameworks which are innovative and exciting in their own right. Gay organisations, for example, have developed wholly new thinking on organisational principles such as confidentiality and recording, and new patterns of service such as buddying, in the context of AIDS projects. Some of these newly emerging methods have begun to spread into wider spheres of social work, for example telephone counselling groups. Similarly, it was disabled people's organisations that developed the social model of disability into concrete responses such as schemes for integrated living, peer counselling and disability equality training.

As with the women's groups in the early 1970s, which began to establish services to respond to women's priorities such as sexual (including domestic) violence, so the greater diversity of projects now, though beset by constant funding crises, reflects a more complex understanding of human need matched by more appropriate patterns of response. The challenge to the large public agencies is to listen, learn and emulate where appropriate, not to default on whole areas of service need because others are operating in that field – even where those others can attract commissioning funding from the public agencies through block service contracts – since that will leave the commissioners themselves, together with all the other service providers, uninfluenced by change. Complexity should not mean that we do not all learn from the best in what each of us is doing.

Conclusion

Unless deliberate attention is paid to the matters raised in this chapter, organisations are bound to take on the prevailing ethos of the dominant culture of the society in which they are located. It is ironic, to say the least, that just when large social work agencies have bought into the managerialist ethos of a generation before, management theory itself has begun to open up to feminised and otherwise far more flexible ideas on personal qualities to value, ways to approach problems and so on. It could have been so much more fruitful for the nation if social workers had continued to value their interpersonal and groupwork skills and had put these at the service of industry and commerce, rather than the influence having been all in the other direction, with private sector-style managerialism pervading the public sector while industry and commerce reinvent the wheels of listening, networking and respecting people.

But the social work profession, at the grassroots, does retain some priorities of its own. Organisations or departments established specifically to deliver social work or related services may be thought to have a special responsibility to consider issues of gender, of ethnicity, culture and religion, of age, disability and health, of class and poverty, and of issues affecting gay and lesbian people, since these are now recognised as essential considerations in the delivery of social work itself at the practitioner/service user level. They should also, therefore, be seen as essential considerations to social work organisations as purchasers or providers of services and as employers. The many levels at which these considerations become relevant provide us with our challenge for change in the future, both in management thinking and in the design of organisations able to be responsive to the full range of human need and potential.

8

Conclusion

So what of the future? Can the tremendous pace of change that has marked recent years in social work and social care be sustained in this new millennium or will we enter a period of consolidation? There is certainly no sign at present of things standing still.

In the first edition of this book, Veronica Coulshed was keen to persuade social workers why they needed to understand that they worked in organisations with concerns wider than their own day-to-day practice and, hence, why management and organisational theory was relevant to them. Today, no such persuasion is needed. Working in the mixed economy of welfare means that not only do social workers have a clear awareness of the overall remit and resources of their own agency, but they also gain the wider perspective that is born of complex links between purchasing and providing, and between statutory and voluntary agencies – and very often through multiagency working as well.

As this awareness has grown, the affinity with wider organisational theory has become more apparent. The importation into social work and social care of management thinking – with its targets, standards, management information and talk of people as 'human resources' – has also made public sector management feel like a much closer cousin of business and commerce than might once have been the case.

But does this mean that today's social work manager has to adopt the business ethos and be ruled by it, or does a study of the management literature reveal choices in the way things are run? It has been one of the intentions of this book to demystify much of the technical language and to reveal that, while psychometric testing, outcome measurement and the like may sound very scientific, any student of the social sciences is well equipped to perceive the limitations as well as the advantages of an overly managerialist approach to management and to decide how far to be influenced by it. Of course it is an advance to make clear statements to users and carers about what standards services aim to achieve and the extent to which this is managed, but people cannot be turned into simple numerical units without losing sight of much that is best about social work and the principles that have traditionally sustained it.

Personal style and principles: time to invent anti-oppressive policy?

It comes as a relief, then, to learn that there are other trends in management – that there is a choice of managerial styles to adopt, a range of visions to translate into practice, and even a contested approach to what it means to hold power and to be accountable for its exercise.

The real challenge for social work managers is not to emulate the stereotypes of the private business world in seeing who can run the leanest and fittest organisation, the tightest ship, the biggest empire, or who can hire and fire with the gayest abandon. Rather, it is to absorb those ideas emerging from the business world which suggest that success lies in valuing, fostering and listening to the workforce, in hearing and responding to the 'customer', in managing diversity not conformity and in seeking to build in flexibility at every stage. It is perfectly possible for a manager who is a 'people person' to build their own style around this, and for that style to be one that empowers others to give of their best, not to fit in with narrow diktats from above. The advent of computers in social work offices, for example, has made workers feel that they are filling in little boxes on the screen and being boxed in themselves in the process. Yet the lightning speed and infinite networks of the computer age could equally well be used to open up communication – to send ideas, insights and concerns speeding round the organisation to where they can be used in planning and improving services, and to draw in information from the internet so that policy and practice can be grounded in research-generated knowledge. It is frankly ridiculous to use such boundary-breaking technology only for recording and monitoring systems that make people feel like the lowliest pen-pushers of the Victorian era.

Similarly, the imposition of uniform standards into service aims and contracting, instead of being a levelling down to spread resources as thinly as possible, could be a levelling up to spread the principles of equality and social justice (because these do not always cost more but they do require more rigorous implementation). There is no reason why computerised case recording could not be used to make a note of every service user's first language and to ensure that interpreter services were pre-booked for each interview. There is no reason why women using every kind of service right across a local authority could not automatically be asked (in a safe and confidential way) whether they are experiencing domestic violence or why the resultant statistics could not be used to target an authority-wide policy and practice response. Nor is there any obstacle to collating information on the internal operation of the Disability Discrimination Act 1995 so as to make planned changes to working practices and workplace design, as opposed to incremental adaptations as the need arises.

In other words, when the principles of anti-oppressive practice are translated into anti-oppressive policy, they open up exciting new horizons for managers that could begin to make a reality of the rhetoric of social inclusion. Surely there can be no better reason to aspire to be a manager than to want to make one's mark in this kind of way?

And the world moves on

It actually felt very outdated still to be writing in Chapter 7 about the oppression of particular social groups as needing attention in social work organisations. We have known for many years what we ought to be doing about that and there is little excuse for the slow rate of progress. Social work is being outstripped in many commercial contexts (here and overseas) in provision for women returners, black managers, disabled employees, gay and lesbian staff and so on. We talk the talk better than we walk the walk in many respects.

Meanwhile, cutting-edge management theory has moved on to issues of social justice and human rights at a global and environmental level. From green audits of business and corporate environmentalism to micro-credit and entrepreneurship schemes that completely overturn thinking about investment and development (seeing poor women in the developing world rather than wealthy men in the West as the key investment for the future), interest in the ethical stance a business takes marks a shift towards 'values aware' management as making sound business sense. Many individuals now choose, for example, to invest their savings in accounts and trusts that have been specially selected to avoid socially and environmentally harmful products such as the arms trade and the tobacco industry.

Because the 'consumers' of social work typically do not have many choices about what services they receive, they are unlikely to boycott meals-on-wheels just because they are delivered in a petrol-hungry van, or to question whether the county council has its capital ethically invested. They do, however, expect the standards of central and local government, and of charitable organisations, to be transparently honest and to be based on 'ordinary common decency', not only in dealing with service users and staff, but also in pursuing the wider resposibilities of 'corporate citizenship' in the local community (Pettinger, 1997, pp.156–7). And it is also true that, these days, the threat of global economic meltdown or even of planetary climate change seems almost as likely to block the nation's ability to provide adequate welfare coverage in the future as do more localised considerations. Consequently, the manager of tomorrow may need to be able to see everything connecting to everything else on a scope the systems theorists never dreamt of. Organisational Gaia, perhaps.

Today's generation of social work students take an active interest in such widescale issues and, if the incumbent generation does not stifle their initiative and energies, they are well placed to make a difference in the future. The study of management and of organisational theory need not be about how to wear a suit and talk in statistics. It can be about how to work together, learn together and survive together in a world where every assumption has been turned upside down, where the only certainty is uncertainty, and where the most valued skill may be the ability to think on the broadest canvas, with the most variables in play, and the greatest respect for all the people whose well-being is at risk.

This is where principles and skills come together, in a way that confirms good social work as lying at the heart of good management. Every social worker has a part to play in management, and every manager – social work qualified or not – has a lot to learn from social work.

References

Adams, R. (1998) *Quality Social Work*, Basingstoke: Macmillan.

Ahmad, B. (1990) *Black Perspectives in Social Work*, Birmingham: Venture Press.

Aldridge, M. (1996) 'Dragged to market: being a profession in the postmodern world', *British Journal of Social Work*, 26(2), pp. 177–94.

Allan, M., Bhavnani, R. and French, K. (for the Department of Health Social Services Inspectorate) (1992) *Promoting Women: Management Development and Training for Women in Social Services Departments*, London: HMSO.

Anderson, C. R. (1985) *Management: Skills, Function and Organisation Performance*, Dubuque, IO: Brown.

Andrew, F. (1996) *Not Just Black and White: An Exploration of Opportunities and Barriers to the Development of Black Managers in Public Services*, London: Office for Public Management.

Argyris, C. (1957) *Personality and Organization*, New York: Harper.

Argyris, C. and Schön, D. A. (1978) *Organizational Learning: A Theory of Action Perspective*, Reading, MA: Addison-Wesley.

Armstrong, M. and Murlis, H. (1994) *Reward Management: A Handbook of Remuneration Strategy and Practice*, 3rd edn, London: Kogan Page.

Atherton, J. S. (1986) *Professional Supervision in Group Care: A Contract-Based Approach*, London: Tavistock.

Audit Commission (1995) *On Merit: Recruitment in Local Government*, London: HMSO.

Balloch, S., Andrew, T., Ginn, J., McLean, J., Pahl, J. and Williams, J. (1995) *Working in the Social Services*, London: National Institute for Social Work.

Balloch, S., Pahl, J. and McLean, J. (1998) 'Working in the social services: job satisfaction, stress and violence', *British Journal of Social Work*, 28, pp. 329–50.

Bamford, T. (1982) *Managing Social Work*, London: Tavistock.

Barter, S. (1997) 'Social work students with personal experience of sexual abuse: implications for Diploma in Social Work programme providers', *Social Work Education*, 16(2), pp. 113–32.

Bensted, J., Brown, A., Forbes, C. and Wall, R. (1994) 'Men working with men in groups: masculinity and crime', *Groupwork*, 7(1), pp. 37–49.

Bhatti-Sinclair, K. (1996) *Developing Black Mentors and Consultants Schemes in Social Work Education: A Guidance Handbook for Black and Minority Ethnic Students, Practice Teachers, Tutors and Programme Providers*, Southampton: University of Southampton, Department of Social Work Studies.

Bond, H. (1996) 'Tell it like it is', *Community Care*, 2–8 May, p. 10.

Bowen, W. G. and Bok, D. (1998) *The Shape of the River: Long-Term Consequences of Considering Race in College and University Admissions*, Princeton, NJ: Princeton University Press.

Brand, D. (1999) *Accountable Care: Developing the General Social Care Council*, York: York Publishing Services for the Joseph Rowntree Foundation.

Brown, A. (1992) *Groupwork*, 3rd edn, Aldershot: Ashgate.

Brown, A. and Bourne, I. (1996) *The Social Work Supervisor: Supervision in Community, Day Care and Residential Settings*, Buckingham: Open University Press.

Brown, H. (1992) *Women Organising*, London: Routledge.

Bunning, R. L. (1979) 'The Delphi technique: a projection tool for serious enquiry', in Jones, J. E. and Pfeiffer, J. W. (eds), *Annual Handbook for Group Facilitators*, La Jolla, CA: University Associates, pp. 174–81.

Burstow, B. (1992) *Feminist Therapy: Working in the Context of Violence*, Newbury Park, CA: Sage.

Burton, J. (1998) *Managing Residential Care*, London: Routledge.

Butt, J. and Mirza, K. (1996) *Social Care and Black Communities: A Review of Recent Research Studies*, London: HMSO.

Carnall, C. (1995) *Managing Change in Organizations*, 2nd edn, London: Prentice-Hall International.

Carter Hood, P., Everitt, A. and Runnicles, D. (1998) 'Femininity, sexuality and professionalism in the children's departments', *British Journal of Social Work*, 28, pp. 471–90.

Casson, S. F. and Manning, B. (1997) *Total Quality in Child Protection: A Manager's Guide*, Lyme Regis: Russell House Publishing.

Central Council for Education and Training in Social Work (1989) *Rules and Requirements for the Diploma in Social Work*, London: CCETSW. Paper 30.

Central Council for Education and Training in Social Work (1996) *Assuring Quality in the Diploma in Social Work – 1. Rules and Requirements for the Diploma in Social Work*, 2nd rev., London CCETSW.

Central Council for Education and Training in Social Work (1997) *Assuring Quality for Post Qualifying Education and Training – 1. Requirements for the Post Qualifying and Advanced Awards in Social Work*, London: CCETSW.

Chetkow-Yanoov, B. (1992) *Social Work Practice: A Systems Approach* Binghamton, NY: Haworth.

Clegg, S. R. (1990) *Modern Organizations: Organization Studies in the Postmodern World*, London: Sage.

Clutterbuck, D. and Crainer, S. (1990) *Makers of Management: Men and Women who Changed the Business World*, London: Guild Publishing.

Cockburn, C. (1991) *In the Way of Women: Men's Resistance to Sex Equality in Organizations*, Basingstoke: Macmillan.

Cohen, S. (1975) 'It's all right for you to talk: political and sociological manifestos for social action', in Bailey, R. and Brake, M. (eds), *Radical Social Work*, London: Edward Arnold.

Coleman, G. (1991) *Investigating Organisations: A Feminist Approach*, Bristol: University of Bristol, School for Advanced Urban Studies.

Collinson, D. L. and Hearn, J. (1996) *Men as Managers, Managers as Men*, London: Sage.

Colton, M. and Vanstone, M. (1998) 'Sexual abuse by men who work with children: an exploratory study' *British Journal of Social Work*, 28(4), pp. 511–23.

Commission for Racial Equality (1993) *Towards Fair Selection*, London: Commission for Racial Equality.

Commission for Racial Equality (CRE) (1996) 'Twenty years of action for equality', *CRE-Connections: Bulletin of Racial Equality*, 7, June, p. 1.

Commission for Racial Equality (CRE) (1997) '1997: Countdown to the millennium on racial equality', *News Release*, 629, London: CRE.

Community Care (1998) 26 November–2 December, p. 1.

Community Care (1999) 14–20 January, p. 6.

Community Care (1999) 16–22 September, pp. 6, 12.

Community Care (1999) 'Letters', 30 September–6 October, p. 17.

Community Care (1999) 14–20 October, p. 11.

Community Care (1999) 4–10 November, p. 8.

Community Care (1999) 11–17 November, p. 7.

Community Care (1999) 25 November–1 December 1999, p. 36.

Cosis Brown, H. (1998) *Social Work and Sexuality: Working with Lesbians and Gay Men*, Basingstoke: Macmillan.

Coulshed, V. and Orme, J. (1998) *Social Work Practice: An Introduction*, Basingstoke: Macmillan.

Coyle, A. (1989) 'Women in management: a suitable case for treatment?', *Feminist Review*, 31, pp. 117–25.

Dadswell, T. (1999) 'Under suspicion', *Professional Social Work*, February, pp. 6–7.

Daly, N. (1998) 'Care or scare?', *Community Care*, 30 July–5 August, p. 19.

Darvill, G. (1998a) 'Making the move into management', *Professional Social Work*, October, p. 14.

Darvill, G. (1998b) *Organisation, People and Standards. Use of Formal Standards in Social Services: Report of a Survey (ADSS and NISW)*, London: National Institute for Social Work.

Darvill, G. (1998c) 'Standards as knowledge', *Noticeboard: News from the National Institute for Social Work*, Autumn, p. 5.

Davies, D. and Neal, C. (eds) (1996) *Pink Therapy: A Guide for Counsellors and Therapists Working with Lesbian, Gay and Bisexual Clients*, Buckingham: Open University Press.

Department of the Environment, Transport and the Regions (DETR)

(1998) *Modernising Local Government: Improving Local Services through Best Value*, London: The Stationery Office.

Department of Health (1998a) *Modernising Social Services*, London: The Stationery Office.

Department of Health (1998b) *The Quality Protects Programme: Transforming Children's Services*, London: Department of Health, LAC(98)28.

Department of Health (1999) *The Government's Objectives for Children's Social Services*, London: Department of Health.

Department of Health Social Services Inspectorate and The Audit Commission (1998) *Getting the Best from Social Services: Learning the Lessons from Joint Reviews*, London: Audit Commission.

Department of Health Social Services Inspectorate and the Scottish Office Social Work Services Group (1991) *Care Management and Assessment: Practitioners' Guide*, London: HMSO.

Dessler, G. (1985) *Management Fundamentals*, Reston, VA: Reston.

Dominelli, L. (1990) *Women and Community Action*, Birmingham: Venture.

Dominelli, L. (1997) *Anti-Racist Social Work: A Challenge for White Practitioners and Educators*, 2nd edn, Basingstoke: Macmillan.

Dominelli, L. and McLeod, E. (1989) *Feminist Social Work*, Basingstoke: Macmillan.

Drucker, P. F. (1954) *The Practice of Management*, New York: Harper & Row.

Drucker, P. F. (1977) *Management*, London: Pan.

Dunnachie, Hugh (1992) 'Approaches to quality systems', in Kelly, D. and Warr, B. (eds), *Quality Counts: Achieving Quality in Social Care Services*, London: Whiting & Birch.

Ellis, R. and Whittington, D. (1998) *Quality Assurance in Social Care: An Introductory Workbook*, London: Arnold.

Equal Opportunities Commission for Northern Ireland (1998) *What Price Sex Equality: Making a Sex Discrimination Complaint*, Belfast: Equal Opportunities Commission for Northern Ireland.

Eraut, M. (1994) *Developing Professional Knowledge and Competence*, London: Falmer.

European Commission (1997) *Social Europe: Progress Report on the Implementation of the Medium-Term Social Action Programme 1995–97. Supplement 4/96*, Luxembourg: Office for Official Publications of the European Communities.

European Commission (1998) *A Guide 1998*, Brussels: European Commission Directorate-General V, Employment, Industrial Relations and Social Affairs (Leaflet).

Fisher, R. and Ury, W. (1983) *Getting to Yes*, New York: Penguin.

Ford, D. L. and Nemiroff, P. M. (1975) 'Applied group problem-solving: the nominal group technique', in *Annual Handbook for Group Facilitators*, La Jolla, CA: University Associates, pp. 179–82.

Ford, K. and Jones, A. (1987) *Student Supervision*, London: Macmillan.

Foster, G. (1996) *Getting What You Want: A Short Guide to Career Development for Senior Women Managers*, London: National Institute for Social Work.

Foster, G. and Phillipson, J. (1994) *Making Positive Choices. Career Development for Women in Social Care: What Women Can Do*, London: National Institute for Social Work.

Foster, J. (1997) 'A woman's liberation', *Community Care*, 4–10 December, pp. 18–19.

Francis, J. (1992) 'Sick staff syndrome', *Community Care*, 20 August, pp. 18–19.

Franks, S. (1999) *Having None of It: Women, Men and the Future of Work*, London: Granta.

Freeman, J. (undated) *The Tyranny of Structurelessness*, London, Dark Star Press (first published in the USA in 1970).

French, J. R. P. and Raven, B. (1959) 'The bases of social power', in Cartwright, D. (ed.), *Studies in Social Power*, Ann Arbor, University of Michigan.

Friedman, R., Kane, M. and Cornfield, D. B. (1998) 'Social support and career optimism: examining the effectiveness of network groups among black managers', *Human Relations*, 51(9), pp. 1155–77.

Galligan, D. (1992) 'Procedural rights and social welfare', in Coote, A. (ed.) *The Welfare of Citizens*, London: Rivers Oram Press.

Gann, N. (1996) *Managing Change in Voluntary Organizations: A Guide to Practice*, Buckingham: Open University Press.

Garrett, P. M. (1999) 'Mapping child-care social work in the final years of the twentieth century: a critical response to the "looking after children" system', *British Journal of Social Work*, 29(1), pp. 27–47.

Gensen, J. (1996) *Men as Workers in Childcare Services*, Brussels: European Commission.

Goleman, D. (1996) *Emotional Intelligence: Why It Can Matter More Than IQ*, London: Bloomsbury.

Grover, Richard (1992) 'Rest assured', *Community Care*, 3 December, p. 16.

Handy, C. (1993) *Understanding Organizations*, 4th edn, Harmondsworth: Penguin.

Handy, C. (1995) *The Age of Unreason*, 3rd edn, London: Arrow.

Hardman, K. (1997) 'Social workers' attitudes to lesbian clients', *The British Journal of Social Work*, 27(4), pp. 545–63.

Harris, J. (1998) 'Scientific management, bureau-professionalism, new managerialism: the labour process of state social work', *British Journal of Social Work*, 28(6), pp. 839–62.

Hawxhurst, D. and Morrow, S. (1984) *Living Our Visions: Building Feminist Community*, Tempe, AA: Fourth World.

Hearn, J. and Parkin, W. (1995) *Sex at Work: The Power and Paradox of Organisation Sexuality* (rev. edn, 1st edn 1987) London: Prentice-Hall/Harvester Wheatsheaf.

Hersey, P. and Blanchard, K. H. (1982) *Management of Organisational Behavior: Utilising Human Resources*, Englewood Cliffs, NJ: Prentice-Hall.

Hirst, J. (1998) 'Caught in the spotlight', *Community Care*, 23–29 July, p. 89.

Hofstede, G. (1980) *Culture's Consequences*, Newbury Park, CA: Sage.

Holder, J. (1995) 'Challenging racism: the BBC mentor scheme', in Itzin, C. and Newman, J. (eds), *Gender, Culture and Organizational Change: Putting Theory into Practice*, London: Routledge.

Home, A. (1993) 'The juggling act: the multiple role woman in social work education', *Canadian Social Work Review*, 10(2), pp. 141–56.

Horwath, J. (1996) 'Undertaking a training needs analysis within a social care organisation', in Connelly, N. (ed.), *Training Social Services Staff: Evidence from New Research*, London: National Institute for Social Work, Research In Social Work Education, 4.

Horwath, J. and Morrison, T. (1999) *Effective Staff Training in Social Care*, London: Routledge.

Hughes, W. H. (1986) *Report of the Inquiry into Children's Homes and Hostels*, Belfast: HMSO.

Hunt, G. (ed.) (1998) *Whistleblowing in the Social Services: Public Accountability and Professional Practice*, London: Arnold.

Hunt, J. (1994) 'Women's careers and the impact of public and organisational policy', paper presented by the Chief Executive of the Local Government Management Board to the Association of Women Senior Managers' conference, 14 October, Newcastle upon Tyne.

Hunter, M. (1999) 'A third way for charities?', *Community Care*, 7–13 January, pp. 18–19.

Itzin, C. (1995) 'Crafting strategy to create women-friendly work', in Itzin, C. and Newman, J., *Gender, Culture and Organizational Change: Putting Theory into Practice*, London: Routledge.

Ixer, G. (1999) 'There's no such thing as reflection', *British Journal of Social Work*, 29(4), pp. 513–27.

Jackson, A. C. and Donovan, F. H. (1999) *Managing to Survive: Managerial Practice in Not-for-Profit Organizations*, Buckingham: Open University Press.

Janis, I. L. (1971) 'Groupthink', *Psychology Today*, 5(6), pp. 43–36.

Johnstone, H. (1995) 'Beat the interview blues', *London Evening Standard*, Business recruitment feature, 8 March, p. 46.

Joint Initiative for Community Care (JICC) (1997) *Get Going: A Guide to the Evaluation of Training*, Milton Keynes: JICC.

Joint Initiative for Community Care (JICC) (1998) *Training for the Caring Business: A Manager's Guide*, 2nd edn, Milton Keynes: JICC.

Jones, A. (1996) *Report of the Examination Team on Child Care and Practice in North Wales*, London: HMSO.

Jones, A., Phillips, M. and Maynard, C. (1992) *A Home from Home: The Experience of Black Residential Projects as a Focus of Good Practice*, London: National Institute for Social Work.

Jones, D. (1999a) 'Frameworks for action', *Professional Social Work*, December, pp. 16–17.

Jones, D. (1999b) 'Regulating social work: key questions', *Practice*, 11(3), pp. 55–63.

Jones, D. (1999c) 'Surviving joint reviews', *Professional Social Work*, August, p. 17.

Kahan, B. (1994) *Growing up in Groups*, London: National Institute for Social Work Research.

Kanter, R. M. (1989) *When Giants Learn to Dance: Mastering the Challenges of Strategy, Management, and Careers in the 1990s*, London: Simon & Schuster.

Kanter, R. M. (1991) 'Change-master skills: what it takes to be creative', in Henry, J. and Walker, D. (eds), *Managing Innovation*, London: Sage.

Kearney, P. (1999) *Managing Practice: Report on the Management of Practice Expertise Project*, London: National Institute for Social Work.

Kendall, J. with Almond, S. (1998) *The UK Voluntary (Third) Sector in Comparative Perspective: Exceptional Growth and Transformation*, Canterbury: Personal Social Services Research Unit.

Kendrick, A. (1997) *Safeguarding Children Living Away from Home from Abuse: A Literature Review*, in Kent, R., *Children's Safeguards Review*, Edinburgh: The Stationery Office.

Kent, R. (1997) *Children's Safeguards Review*, Edinburgh: The Stationery Office.

Knapham, J. and Morrison, T. (1998) *Making the Most of Supervision in Health and Social Care: A Self Development Manual for Supervisees*, Brighton: Pavilion Publishing.

Kotter, J. and Schlesinger, L. (1979) 'Choosing strategies for change', *Harvard Business Review*, March–April, pp. 106–14.

Lance, H. and Bunch, C. (1998) *Choices for Change: A Guide to Training and Development Opportunities for Women Managers in the Personal Social Services*, London: The Learning Agency.

Lawler, J. and Hearn, J. (1997) 'The managers of social work: the experiences and identifications of third tier social services managers and the implications for future practice', *British Journal of Social Work*, 27(2), pp. 191–218.

Leigh, A. (1983) *Decisions, Decisions! A Practical Management Guide to Problem-Solving and Decision Making*, Aldershot: Gower.

Leigh, A. (1988) *Effective Change: Twenty Ways to Make it Happen*, London: Institute of Personnel Management.

Levy, A. and Kahan, B. (1991) *The Pindown Experience and the Protection of Children: The Report for the Staffordshire Child Care Inquiry*, Stafford: Staffordshire County Council.

Lewin, K. (1951) *Field Theory in Social Science*, New York: Harper & Row.

Likert, R. (1961) *New Patterns of Management*, New York: McGraw-Hill.

Lipsky, M. (1980) *Street-Level Bureaucracy: Dilemmas of the Individual in Public Services*, New York: Russell Sage Foundation.

Lishman, J. (1998) 'Personal and professional development', in Adams, R., Dominelli, L. and Payne, M. (eds), *Social Work: Themes, Issues and Critical Debates*, Basingstoke: Macmillan.

Local Government Management Board (1996) *Towards Better Selection of Children's Residential Staff*, London: LGMB/Department of Health.

Local Government Management Board and the Association of Directors of Social Services (1993) *Social Services Workforce Analysis: 1992 Survey. Main Report*, London: LGMB.

Logan, J., Kershaw, S., Karban, K., Mills, S., Trotter, J. and Sinclair, M. (1996) *Confronting Prejudice: Lesbian and Gay Issues in Social Work Education*, Aldershot: Arena.

Luciano, P. R. (1979) 'The systems view of organisations: dynamics of organisational change', in *Annual Handbook for Group Facilitators*, La Jolla, CA: University Associates.

Lupton, C. (1998) 'User empowerment or family self-reliance? The Family Group Conference model', *British Journal of Social Work*, 28, pp. 107–28.

Machiavelli, N. (1961) *The Prince*, Harmondsworth: Penguin (originally written in 1541).

Maslow, A. H. (1954) *Motivation and Personality*, New York: Harper & Row.

Maxwell, R. J. (1984) 'Quality assessment in health: perspectives in NHS management', *British Medical Journal*, 288, 12 May, pp. 1470–72.

McFarlane, L. (1998) *Diagnosis Homophobic: The Experiences of Lesbians, Gay Men and Bisexuals in Mental Health Services*, 34 Hartham Road, London N7 9JL: Project for Advice, Counselling and Education (PACE).

McKay, R. (1999) 'Scots open new umbrella group for ethnic minorities', *Community Care*, 4–10 November, p. 11.

McKenna, E. and Beech, N. (1995) *The Essence of Human Resource Management*, Hemel Hempstead: Prentice-Hall Europe.

Minister for Disabled People (1996a) *The Disability Discrimination Act 1995: Are You Facing Employment Discrimination?*, DL180 (from DDA Information Line: 0345 622 633).

Minister for Disabled People (1996b) *The Disability Discrimination Act 1995: A Guide for Everybody*, DL160 (from DDA Information Line: 0345 622 633).

Mintzberg, H. (1973) *The Nature of Managerial Work*, New York: Harper & Row.

Mintzberg, H. (1979) *The Structure of Organisations*, Englewood Cliffs, NJ: Prentice-Hall.

Mintzberg, H. (1989) 'The structuring of organizations', in Asch, D. and Bowman, C., *Readings in Strategic Management*, London: Macmillan.

Moore, J. I. (1992) *Writers on Strategy and Strategic Management: The Theory of Strategy and the Practice of Strategic Management at Enterprise, Corporate, Business and Functional Levels*, Harmondsworth: Penguin.

Morgan, C. and Murgatroyd, S. J. (1994) *Total Quality Management in the Public Sector*, Buckingham: Open University Press.

Morgan, G. (1986) *Images of Organization*, Thousand Oaks, CA: Sage.

Mullender, A. (1996) *Rethinking Domestic Violence: The Social Work and Probation Response*, London: Routledge.

Mullender, A. (ed.) (1999) *We Are Family: Sibling Relationships in Placement and Beyond*, London: British Agencies for Adoption and Fostering.

Mullender, A. and Ward, D. (1991) *Self-Directed Groupwork: Users Take Action for Empowerment*, London: Whiting & Birch.

Murray, C. (1997) 'Gender inequality in social work management: cause for pessimism or signs of progress?', in Keeble, L. and Fisher, M. (eds), *Making a Difference: Women and Career Progression in Social Services. Report of a National Seminar at the Social Work Research Centre, University of Stirling*, London: National Institute for Social Work.

National Institute for Social Work (1995) *Managing Information and Change*, London: National Institute for Social Work, *Policy Briefings*, 11.

National Institute for Social Work (1996) *The Social Services Information Agenda*, London: National Institute for Social Work, *NISW Briefing*, 17.

National Institute for Social Work (1998) *The Social Services Workforce Studies: Summary*, London: National Institute for Social Work.

National Institute for Social Work (1999) *Violence Against Social Care Workers*, London: National Institute for Social Work, *NISW Briefing*, 26.

Nottage, A. (for the Department of Health Social Services Inspectorate) (1991) *Women in Social Services: A Neglected Resource*, London: HMSO.

Nuffield Institute for Health and United Kingdom Homecare Association (1997) *What Do Users and Carers Want from Domiciliary Care?*, Leeds, Nuffield Institute for Health, Community Care Division.

Oakland, J. S. (1990) *Total Quality Management: A Practical Approach*, London: Department of Trade and Industry.

Office for Public Management (1995) *Setting the Agenda: Black Managers in Public Services. A Conference Held in September 1994 by the Office for Public Management*, London: Office for Public Management.

Orme, J. (1995) *Workloads: Measurement and Management*, Aldershot: Avebury.

Parkin, D. and Maddock, S. (1995) 'A gender typology of organizational culture', in Itzin, C. and Newman, J., *Gender, Culture and Organizational Change: Putting Theory into Practice*, London: Routledge.

Paterson, J. (1999) *Disability Rights Handbook: April 1999–April 2000*, 24th edn, London: Disability Alliance Educational and Research Association.

Pernell, R. B. (1986) 'Empowerment and social group work', in Parnes, M. (ed.), *Innovations in Social Group Work: Feedback from Practice to Theory*, Binghamton, NY: Haworth.

Peter, L. J. (1970) *The Peter Principle*, Harmondsworth: Penguin.

Peters, T. J. (1988) *Thriving on Chaos: Handbook for a Management Revolution*, London: Macmillan.

Peters, T. J. and Waterman, R. H. (1982) *In Search of Excellence: Lessons from America's Best-Run Companies*, New York: Warner Books London: Harper & Row.

Pettinger, R. (1997) *Introduction to Management*, 2nd edn, Basingstoke: Macmillan.

Pfeffer, Naomi and Coote, Anna (1991) *Is Quality Good for You? A Critical Review of Quality Assurance in Welfare Services*, London: Institute of Public Policy Research, Paper 5.

Pharr, S. (1988) *Homophobia: A Weapon of Sexism*, Little Rock, AR: Chardon Press.

Phillipson, J. (1988) 'The complexities of caring: developing a feminist approach to training staff in a residential setting', *Social Work Education*, 7(3), pp. 3–6.

Piggott, J. B. and Piggott, G. (1992) 'Total quality management (TQM): the way ahead', in Kelly, D. and Warr, B. (eds), *Quality Counts: Achieving Quality in Social Care Services*, London: Whiting & Birch.

Pottage, D. and Evans, M. (1992) *Workbased Stress: Prescription is Not the Cure*, London: National Institute for Social Work, *Discussion Paper*, 1.

Pottage, D. and Evans, M. (1994) *The Competent Workplace: The View from Within*, London: National Institute for Social Work, *Discussion Paper*, 2.

Priestley, M. (1998) 'Discourse and resistance in care assessment: integrated living and community care', *British Journal of Social Work*, 28(5), pp. 659–73.

Pringle, K. (1992/3) 'Child sexual abuse perpetrated by welfare personnel and the problem of men', *Critical Social Policy*, Issue 36, 12(3), pp. 4–19.

Professional Social Work (1999) 'New standards may leave social work out in the cold', February, p. 3.

Pugh, D. (1993) 'Understanding and managing organizational change', in Mabey, C. and Mayon-White, B. (eds), *Managing Change*, 2nd edn, London: Paul Chapman Publishing.

Qureshi, H. (1998) 'Outcomes and local authorities', in Balloch, S., *Outcomes of Social Care: A Question of Quality?*, London: National Institute for Social Work, Social Services Policy Forum, Paper 6.

Rosen, G. (ed.) (1999) *Managing Team Development: A Short Guide for Teams and Team Managers*, London: National Institute for Social Work.

Sanderson, T. (1993) *Assertively Gay: How to Build Gay Self-Esteem*, London: The Other Way Press.

Sapey, B. (1997) 'Social work tomorrow: towards a critical understanding of technology in social work', *British Journal of Social Work*, 27(6), pp. 803–14.

Schein, E. H. (1985) *Organizational Culture and Leadership*, San Francisco: Jossey Bass.

Schön, D. A. (1983) *The Reflective Practitioner*, New York: Basic Books.

Schwehr, B. (1999) 'Caring about stress', *Community Care*, 5–11 August, p. 27.

Scottish Office (1998) *The Scottish Office Response to the Children's Safeguards Review*, Edinburgh: Scottish Office.

Seebohm Report (1968) *Report of the Committee on Local Authority and Allied Personal Social Services*, Cmnd 3703, London: HMSO.

Shepherd, C. (1997) 'Research update note on ME/CFS', *British Journal of Social Work*, 27(5), pp. 755–60.

Sia (undated) 'The Black Manifesto: highlighting the needs of the black voluntary sector' (leaflet), London: Sia (The National Development Agency for the Black Voluntary Sector, Winchester House, 9 Cranmer Road, Kennington Park, London SW9 6EJ).

Sigamoney, E. (1994) 'Some features of the Black perspectives approach', unpublished teaching handout, Durham: University of Durham.

Skellington, R. with Morris, P. (1992) *'Race' in Britain Today*, London: Sage.

Skinner, A. (1992) *Another Kind of Home: A Review of Residential Child Care*, Edinburgh: HMSO.

Smale, G. (1996) *Mapping Change and Innovation*, London: National Institute for Social Work.

Smale, G. (1997) *Managing Change through Innovation*, London: National Institute for Social Work.

Smith, J. (1999) 'Prior criminality and employment of social workers with substantial access to children: a decision board analysis', *British Journal of Social Work*, 29(1), pp. 49–68.

Spender, D. (1990) *Man Made Language*, London: Pandora (originally published by Routledge & Kegan Paul in 1980).

Stock Whitaker, D. (1975) 'Some conditions for effective work with groups', *British Journal of Social Work*, 5(4), pp. 423–39.

Stubbs, P. (1985) 'The employment of black social workers: from "ethnic sensitivity" to anti-racism', *Critical Social Policy*, 12, pp. 6–27.

Support Force for Children's Residential Care (1995) *Code of Practice for the Employment of Residential Child Care Workers*, London: Department of Health.

Tannen, D. (1995) *Talking from 9 to 5: How Women's and Men's Conversational Styles Affect Who Gets Heard, Who Gets Credit and What Gets Done at Work*, London: Virago (also available in paperback, published in 1996, as *Talking from 9 to 5: Women and Men at Work – Language, Sex and Power*, London: Virago).

Tanton, M. (1994) *Women in Management: A Developing Presence*, London: Routledge.

Thompson, A. (1999) 'Shaping up for the future', *Community Care*, 25–31 March, pp. 22–23.

Thompson, N. (1995) *Theory and Practice in Health and Social Welfare*, Buckingham: Open University Press.

Thompson, N. (1996) *People Skills*, Basingstoke: Macmillan.

Thompson, N., Stradling, S., Murphy, M. and O'Neill, P. (1996) 'Stress and organizational culture', *British Journal of Social Work*, 26, pp. 647–65.

TOPSS UK (Training Organisation for the Personal Social Services) (1999a) *TOPSS: An Introduction*, London: TOPSS (Leaflet).

TOPSS UK (Training Organisation for the Personal Social Services) (1999b) 'TOPSS England training strategy to go public in October, with training cost estimates', 17 September, London: TOPSS (News release).

Torrington, D. and Hall, L. (1998) *Human Resource Management*, 4th edn, Hemel Hempstead: Prentice-Hall Europe.

Townley, B. (1994) *Retraining Human Resource Management: Power Ethics and the Subject at Work*, London: Sage.

Turner, M. (1995) 'Supervising' in Carter, P., Jeffs, T. and Smith, M. K., *Social Working*, Basingstoke: Macmillan.

Utting, W. (1987) *People Like Us: The Report of the Review of Safeguards for Children Living Away from Home*, London: The Stationery Office.

Utting, W. (1997) *Children in Public Care: A Review of Residential Child Care*, London: HMSO.

Walby, S. (1986) *Patriarchy at Work*, Cambridge: Polity.

Wallis, L. and Frost, N. (1998) *Cause for Complaint*, London: Children's Society.

Walsh, K. (1995) 'Quality through markets: the new public service management', in Wilkinson, A. and Willmott, H. (eds), *Making Quality Critical: New Perspectives on Organizational Change*, London: Routledge.

Warham, J. (1975) *An Introduction to Administration for Social Workers*, London: Routledge and Kegan Paul.

Warner, N. (1992) *Choosing with Care: The Report of the Committee of Inquiry into the Selection, Development and Management of Staff in Children's Homes*, London: HMSO.

Warr, B. and Kelly, D. (1992) 'What is meant by quality in social care', in Kelly, D. and Warr, B. (eds), *Quality Counts: Achieving Quality in Social Care Services*, London: Whiting & Birch.

Weber, M. (1947) *The Theory of Social and Economic Organization*, New York: Free Press.

Weiner, M. E. (1982) *Human Services Management: Analysis and Applications*, Itasca IL: Dorsey.

Westley, F. and Mintzberg, H. (1991) 'Visionary leadership and strategic management', in Henry, J. and Walker, D., *Managing Innovation*, London: Sage.

White, M. (1998) 'Minister launches training body with promise of lessons for managers too', *Community Care*, 26 November–2 December, pp. 4–5.

Williams, G. and McCreadie, J. (1982) *Ty Mawr Community Homes Inquiry*, Cwmbran: Gwent County Council.

Zastrow, C. (1985) *Social Work with Groups*, Chicago, IL: Nelson-Hall.

Index